W9-BNJ-304

Understanding
The Red Badge
of Courage

The Greenwood Press "Literature in Context" Series

Understanding *To Kill a Mockingbird*: A Student Casebook to Issues, Sources, and Historical Documents
Claudia Durst Johnson

Understanding *The Scarlet Letter*: A Student Casebook to Issues, Sources, and Historical Documents
Claudia Durst Johnson

Understanding *Adventures of Huckleberry Finn*: A Student Casebook to Issues, Sources, and Historical Documents
Claudia Durst Johnson

Understanding *Macbeth*: A Student Casebook to Issues, Sources, and Historical Documents
Faith Nostbakken

Understanding *Of Mice and Men*, *The Red Pony*, and *The Pearl*: A Student Casebook to Issues, Sources, and Historical Documents
Claudia Durst Johnson

Understanding Anne Frank's *The Diary of a Young Girl*: A Student Casebook to Issues, Sources, and Historical Documents
Hedda Rosner Kopf

Understanding *Pride and Prejudice*: A Student Casebook to Issues, Sources, and Historical Documents
Debra Teachman

UNDERSTANDING
The Red Badge of Courage

A STUDENT CASEBOOK TO ISSUES, SOURCES, AND HISTORICAL DOCUMENTS

Claudia Durst Johnson

The Greenwood Press
"Literature in Context" Series

GREENWOOD PRESS
Westport, Connecticut • London

Library of Congress Cataloging-in-Publication Data

Johnson, Claudia D.
    Understanding The red badge of courage : a student casebook to
issues, sources, and historical documents / Claudia Durst Johnson.
        p.   cm.—(The Greenwood Press "Literature in context"
series, ISSN 1074–598X)
    Includes bibliographical references and index.
    ISBN 0–313–30122–0 (alk. paper)
    1. Crane, Stephen, 1871–1900. Red badge of courage. 2. United
States—History—Civil War, 1861–1865—Literature and the war.
3. Literature and history—United States—History—19th century.
I. Title. II. Series.
PS1449.C85R395   1998
813'.54—dc21   97–22555

British Library Cataloguing in Publication Data is available.

Copyright © 1998 by Claudia Durst Johnson

Library of Congress Catalog Card Number: 97–22555
ISBN: 0–313–30122–0
ISSN: 1074–598X

First published in 1998

Greenwood Press, 88 Post Road West, Westport, CT 06881
An imprint of Greenwood Publishing Group, Inc.

Printed in the United States of America

The paper used in this book complies with the
Permanent Paper Standard issued by the National
Information Standards Organization (Z39.48–1984).

P

Copyright Acknowledgment

Harold R. Hungerford, " 'That Was at Chancellorsville': The Factual Framework
of *The Red Badge of Courage*," *American Literature* 34:4 (January 1963).
Copyright © 1963, Duke University Press. Reprinted with permission.

Every reasonable effort has been made to trace the owners of copyright
materials in this book, but in some instances this has proven impossible. The
author and publisher will be glad to receive information leading to more
complete acknowledgments in subsequent printings of the book and in the
meantime extend their apologies for any omissions.

Contents

Introduction   ix

1   Literary Analysis of *The Red Badge of Courage*:
    Initiation or Irony?   1

2   The Civil War Setting of the Novel   23

    FROM:

    Harold R. Hungerford, " 'That Was at
    Chancellorsville': The Factual Framework of *The Red
    Badge of Courage*," *American Literature* XXXIV
    (January 1963)   35

    Abner Doubleday, *Chancellorsville and Gettysburg*
    (New York: Charles Scribner's Sons, 1882)   46

    Colonel P. H. Dalbiac, *The American War of
    Secession 1863* (London: Ruskin House, 1911)   48

    Major-General Darius N. Couch, "The
    Chancellorsville Campaign," in *Battles and Leaders
    of the Civil War* (New York: Century Co., 1884)   49

    Major-General Alfred Pleasonton, "The Successes
    and Failures of Chancellorsville," in *Battles and*

Leaders of the Civil War (New York: Century Co.,
1884)   50

Samuel P. Bates, "Hooker's Comments on
Chancellorsville," in *Battles and Leaders of the
Civil War* (New York: Century Co., 1884)   52

Rossiter Johnson, *The Story of a Great Conflict*
(New York: Bryan, Taylor and Co., 1894)   55

General Pennock Huey, "The Charge of the Eighth
Pennsylvania Cavalry," in *Battles and Leaders of the
Civil War* (New York: Century Co., 1884)   55

Captain Andrew B. Wells, "The Charge of the Eighth
Pennsylvania Cavalry," in *Battles and Leaders of the
Civil War* (New York: Century Co., 1884)   56

George Parsons Lathrop, "Keenan's Charge" (1863)   58

3   Desertion in *The Red Badge of Courage*   63

FROM:

Colonel P. H. Dalbiac, "The American War of
Secession 1863," in *The Battles of Chancellorsville
and Gettysburg* (Minneapolis: N.p., 1899)   75

Samuel P. Bates, "Hooker's Comments on
Chancellorsville," in *The Battles and Leaders of the
Civil War* (New York: Century Co., 1884)   77

James Beace, *Chancellorsville* (Philadelphia: N.p.,
1892)   79

John Collins, "When Stonewall Jackson Turned Our
Right," in *Battles and Leaders of the Civil War*
(New York: Century Co., 1884)   83

General Carl Schurz, "The Official Report of General
Carl Schurz, and His Letter to General Hooker," in
Battles and Leaders of the Civil War (New York:
Century Co., 1884)   85

George H. Gordon, "The Guilty Deserter," in *The
Romance of the Civil War* (New York: Macmillan,
1903)   87

Stephen Crane, "The Veteran," *McClure's Magazine*
VII (August 1896)   90

Mark Twain, "The Private History of a Campaign
That Failed," *Century Magazine* (1885)   94

4   The Battlefield and Its Effects   101

    FROM:

    Charles C. Nott, *Sketches of the War* (New York:
    Anson D. F. Randolph, 1865)   108

    *Letters from Two Brothers Serving in the War for
    the Union* (Cambridge, Mass.: Printed for Private
    Circulation, 1871)   113

    George W. Bailey, *A Private Chapter of the War* (St.
    Louis: G. I. Jones and Co., 1880)   115

    William Bircher, *A Drummer-Boy's Diary* (St. Paul,
    Minn.: St. Paul Book and Stationery Co., 1889)   117

    Walt Whitman, "The Wound-Dresser," in *Leaves of
    Grass* (New York: W. E. Chapin and Co., 1867)   119

    John Boudreau, "Wounds That Never Heal," *West
    County Times* (Pinole, Calif.), November 10, 1996 121

    John Boudreau, "Fifty Years of Terror and Loss,"
    West County Times (Pinole, Calif.), November 11,
    1996   128

    John Boudreau, "Night Patrol Never Ends," *West
    County Times* (Pinole, Calif.), November 11, 1996 135

    "In Battle in the Pacific: An Interview with Sam
    Turner," March 20, 1997   137

5   The Soldier's Life in Camp   147

    FROM:

    Charles Carleton Coffin, *My Days and Nights on the
    Battlefield* (Boston: Dana Estes and Company,
    1865)   152

    William Bircher, *A Drummer-Boy's Diary* (St. Paul,
    Minn.: St. Paul Book and Stationery Co., 1889)   155

    James Kendall Hosmer, "Camp Life (1862)," in *The
    Romance of the Civil War*, ed. Albert Bushnell Hart
    (New York: Macmillan, 1903)   157

    James Kendall Hosmer, "On the Way to War," in
    The Romance of the Civil War (New York:
    Macmillan, 1903)   158

William Henry Bisbee, *Through Four American Wars*
(Boston: Meador Publishing Co., 1931)   160

George F. Noyes, "Off for the Front (1862)," in *The
Romance of the Civil War*, ed. Albert Bushnell Hart
(New York: Macmillan, 1903)   161

John D. Billings, "Hardtack and Coffee (1861)," in
The Romance of the Civil War, ed. Albert Bushnell
Hart (New York: Macmillan, 1903)   162

Carlton McCarthy, "On the March (1861)," in *The
Romance of the Civil War*, ed. Albert Bushnell Hart
(New York: Macmillan, 1903)   164

James Kendall Hosmer, "A Turkey for a Bedfellow
(1863)," in *The Romance of the Civil War*, ed.
Albert Bushnell Hart (New York: Macmillan, 1903)   166

Jenkin Lloyd Jones, *An Artilleryman's Diary*
(Madison: Wisconsin History Commission, February
1914)   167

Albert O. Marshall, *Army Life* (Joliet, Ill.: Printed for
the Author, 1883)   169

6 *The Red Badge of Courage* as an Antiwar Novel   175

   FROM:

   Stephen Crane, "XIV," in *The Black Riders and
   Other Lines* (London: William Heinemann, 1896)   182

   Stephen Crane, "XXVII," in *The Black Riders and
   Other Lines* (London: William Heinemann, 1896)   182

   Stephen Crane, "69," in *War Is Kind* (New York:
   F. A. Stokes, 1899)   183

   Samuel Clemens, *The War Prayer* (New York:
   Harper and Row, 1923)   185

   Pledge of the War Resisters International, 1921   189

   "Against War: An Interview with Dick Brown,"
   April 9, 1997   192

Index   205

Introduction

Not long after the publication of *The Red Badge of Courage* in 1895, an old veteran of the American Civil War declared that he had fought with Stephen Crane, the author, at the Battle of Antietam. And Crane himself reported that the British military establishment was convinced that he had fought in the Civil War, believing that only someone with an intense experience of the battlefield could have written the novel. The irony is that *The Red Badge of Courage*, one of the great war novels in the English language and certainly the best novel of the American Civil War, was written by a man who at the time, in his own words, "never smelled even the powder of a sham battle" (from his letter to John Northern Hilliard in 1897). Stephen Crane was not even born until 1871, some six years after the conclusion of the Civil War, one of the most critical, defining events in American history.

Brother fought brother on the farms and in the towns of the country. In a situation that occurred with some frequency, those sympathetic with the Union, like Abraham Lincoln, had close male relatives or in-laws who were fighting for the Confederacy. Some idea of the war's impact is suggested by the sheer numbers of Americans who died in it—some 600,000 men—not to mention those maimed by the war and the lives torn apart by separation, death, and economic loss. Although we have no record from Crane about what drew his interest as a novelist to this war, we know that he grew up in a world deeply scarred by the conflict and still reeling from the five-year national trauma. We know that one of his brothers fought in the war on the Union side and that many other Union veterans lived in his home town of Port Jervis, New York. A story Crane wrote in 1896 entitled "The Veteran" suggests that he had frequently listened to stories of the Civil War told by the town's veterans, many of whom would have still been in their thirties when Crane was a twelve-year-old listener. It stands to reason that almost every adult male he knew in his childhood had fought in the war, that every family in Port Jervis was still suffering from the death or wounds inflicted by that war.

There are numerous war stories in the written literary tradition, notably the Trojan War recorded in Homer's *The Iliad*; the War of the Roses in England, recorded in the plays of William Shakespeare; and Leo Tolstoy's monumental *War and Peace* about Napoleon's invasion of Russia. On a somewhat smaller scale, battle scenes from American history had been depicted in the novels of James Fenimore Cooper and William Gilmore Simms. Crane's was certainly not the only novel about the American Civil War. Writers like Thomas Nelson Page and Charles King romanticized the Civil War as a noble adventure full of dashing heroes, usually officers, involving touching love affairs, intrigues and spy adventures, when the soldiers were not galloping across the battlefield on horseback to defend the honor of their side.

But Crane's treatment of war, especially this war, was a marked departure from the usual novel. It was starkly realistic and was kept within the confines of the battles themselves, without the usual romantic subplots to dilute the realism.

The popularity and high regard for *The Red Badge of Courage* has never waned in its hundred-year history, each generation of readers finding in it a message peculiar to its interests and experiences. At one extreme, the novel has been enjoyed simply as an engaging narrative of war. At the other extreme, it is studied as the universal tale of an "Everyman" or boy, growing toward manhood in a modern, impersonal world where he has little or no control.

Some readers have been primarily drawn to its psychological universality and what it has to say about the fear of death. Others are interested in the sociology of the novel, in what drives an individual to extraordinary action, the social pressures exerted on the individual by the group, and the fear of losing one's good name.

Many readers are drawn to Crane's novel as a historical document: as what the author has to tell us about the life and mind of a regiment in a particular war. Others look at it mainly as a picture of *any* war. In the aftermath of each war since the Civil War, Crane's novel has been taken up by readers who interpret its meaning anew. After World War I, when so many veterans returned, a number forever sickened by mustard gas and having seen the death of many comrades and embittered by the suffering in Europe for a cause they could not grasp, Crane's novel rose in significance. One of those veterans was American writer Ernest Hemingway, who declared that *The Red Badge of Courage* was a masterpiece in portraying a universe that loses all meaning for a generation savaged by war, in a world in which even that grandest of martial attributes—courage—becomes an empty word on the battlefield. This novel may have influenced Hemingway's own war novels.

During the Vietnam War, soldiers and antiwar activists again escalated the popularity of *The Red Badge of Courage*, marveling that the conditions of the battlefield, including its psychological pressures, should have changed so little in sixty years.

And many individuals who have lived in time of war—any war—regard *The Red Badge of Courage* not as America's first great *war* novel but as America's first great *antiwar* novel because of the brutality it portrays.

In the following chapters, Crane's novel will be studied from a variety of perspectives:

• The first chapter, a literary analysis, seeks to examine the more philosophical problems of the novel in the universal framework of a young man approaching manhood. In every culture and many works of literature—from *The Adventures of Huckleberry Finn* to *Catcher in the Rye*—the young, in the course of being tried and tested, suddenly are confronted with stark and unpleasant reality. Such is the case of Henry Fleming, the young soldier in *The Red Badge of Courage*. We follow him as he finds with a shock that not only are those authorities he has been taught to respect actually unworthy of his high regard, but that he himself is of no significance whatsoever in either his society or the great scheme of the universe.

The remainder of this book is a consideration of the novel's context and the issues it raises:

- Chapter Two looks at the novel's setting within the Civil War, more specifically as an event in the Battle of Chancellorsville with its great failures in leadership but also examples of great courage.
- The third chapter considers the problem of cowardice in the novel in the context of the Civil War, with epidemic desertions.
- In the fourth chapter we move from the larger picture of battle tactics to a close-up of the soldier on the battlefield and in the wartime hospital.
- Chapter Five is a consideration of the conditions of everyday life in camp, apart from the battlefield.
- The final chapter is an examination of the issue of pacifism and *The Red Badge of Courage* as an antiwar novel.

The study makes available a variety of pertinent documents:

- Memoirs of Civil War generals at Chancellorsville in marked disagreement with one another over what caused the Union to lose the battle.
- Remembrances of cavalry and foot soldiers and a drummer boy who record incidents of cowardice, carnage, and camp life.
- Poems written by those who experienced the Civil War.
- Short stories about the Civil War by veterans.
- A short story by Stephen Crane.
- A series of newspaper articles on World War II veterans suffering from posttraumatic stress disorder.
- An interview with a World War II veteran of the Pacific theater.
- *The War Prayer* by Mark Twain.
- An interview with an activist in the peace movement and a conscientious objector in World War II.
- Poems on war by Stephen Crane.

Page references are to the Bantam Classic edition of *The Red Badge of Courage* (New York, 1983).

Literary Analysis of *The Red Badge of Courage:* Initiation or Irony?

Stephen Crane's work about a young man's struggles in approaching manhood is in the tradition of novels such as Charles Dickens's *Great Expectations* and *David Copperfield*, and, in America, Herman Melville's *Redburn* and Mark Twain's *The Adventures of Huckleberry Finn*. In these works, the young male protagonist, in his teens or twenties, often with exaggerated and romantic notions of honor and the real world he has never encountered, embarks on a journey of discovery—not only of the world but of himself. His journey is fraught with unexpected dangers, tests, and trials, which, like those in ancient tribal initiations, have the capacity of dispelling his old romantic notions and bringing him to a clearer and more somber view of the world and himself. Crane's novel departs from the traditional story in that in many ways it seems to be a parody of initiation. Crane leaves us with decided doubts about whether Henry Fleming is actually wiser as a result of his experiences. To put it another way, is Henry's assumed manhood at the novel's end as phony as the "red badge of courage" he sports on returning to his regiment after the first day of battle?

The reader is brought closer to an answer to this question after analyzing the literary components of which the book is constructed. Appropriately one can get a sense of the complexity of Crane's work by beginning with the meanings embedded in the ironic title that resonates with multiple meanings. The "red" represents in particular the blood on the head of Henry, the main character, when he gets knocked down by one of his fellow soldiers. We also find the red blood pouring from the gory wounds of soldiers who are shot in the eyes and throats and abdomens during battle. There is red blood on the green grass of the battlefield. Henry, invariably characterizing war itself as red or having a red eye, is impressed with the red flare of artillery and the red campfires of the enemy. The word *badge* has many meanings. It is an identifying emblem, mark, sign, or symbol, originally worn by a knight, but now identifying a vocation or membership in a group. In this setting, a badge is a wound—a kind of certification, phony though it may be, of courage in battle. Henry's badge is the sham battle wound he receives from having been knocked down after the battle. Other soldiers have real badges—like his childhood friend, Jim Conklin, whose side looks as if it has been chewed by wolves. There are other badges: the uniforms of the common soldiers and of the officers of both sides, the banners or flags on either side, the sun itself in one instance, which appears "pasted in the sky like a wafer." Courage is manifested in multiple ways and defined negatively (what courage is *not*) as the reader is invited to ask, "What exactly *is* a courageous act?"

In determining the genuineness of Henry's initiation, it is also constructive to examine the form, unusual for its time, that Crane chose as the vehicle for his story. He departed from the usual form of prevailing fiction, which followed what might be called a unified dramatic structure. A nineteenth-century novel ordinarily began with a setting of time, place, basic circumstances, and relationships between characters, as, for example, the description of a house party in the country among friends. Something happens to begin the action—say, a murder. Actions then begin to build, one leading to another, as a detective tries to solve the crime. Finally, there is a climax and a resolution, as when the murderer is revealed and the case is wrapped up.

The Red Badge of Courage follows no such structure. Instead, it is constructed of episodes and appears on the surface as if it has no conventional plot and certainly no climax or final resolution. The lack of a neat, unified form in the fiction serves to suggest the lack of form—a plan—in the universe. This is underscored in Crane's novel by the constant uncertainty and chaos of battle: soldiers running in all directions, never knowing what is actually going on or what the next move should be, officers issuing contradictory orders. Thus, the form of the novel is provided not by a steady buildup of action toward a neat conclusion but by a series of tensions and conflicts within episodes. Its episodic form can be seen by looking briefly at the major scenes in the novel and the primary action of each.

There are three major sections of the book: (1) Henry's participation in two skirmishes during his first encounter with battle, (2) his long retreat from battle to rejoin his regiment, and (3) his second battle encounter when he proves heroic.

Following are the major episodes, according to chapters:

Chapter 1—The opening encampment before the regiment has seen any action. Rumors of impending battle reach the regiment, and Henry reflects on his past and wonders how he will meet the challenge of conflict.

Chapter 2—The regiment moves toward battle. Henry's anxieties about his own courage continue. He queries Wilson, his friend, about how they will meet the challenge.

Chapter 3—One night later in camp. At dawn they are being moved again toward the battlefield. They pass a dead soldier in the path. As they get closer, Wilson, who believes he will die, gives Henry letters to keep.

Chapter 4—The chaos of battle.

Chapter 5—Henry faces firing for the first time and does not run.

Chapter 6—The regiment rests momentarily after the skirmish, but a second wave begins, and Henry throws down his gun and flees.

Chapter 7—Henry goes into the woods, where he finds a corpse in a "chapel," a clearing in the trees.

Chapter 8—He runs back toward the other soldiers, finding the dead and dying, including the "tattered man" who befriends him and the dying "spectral" soldier.

Chapter 9—He recognizes the spectral soldier as his childhood friend, Jim Conklin. Henry and the tattered man run after him and watch him die.

Chapter 10—Henry deserts the dying tattered man.

Chapter 11—In his continuing retreat, he ponders his cowardice and attempts to rationalize it.

Chapter 12—He receives a blow on the head from an enraged retreating soldier. A "cheery" soldier leads him back to his regiment.

Chapter 13—He is greeted as a hero by his regiment, especially his friend Wilson, who gives him his bed.

Chapter 14—The next morning they discuss the past and future battles.

Chapter 15—Wilson asks for his letters back, and Henry enjoys the power he has over Wilson.

Chapter 16—They listen to officers and approach another battle.

Chapter 17—Henry is fiercer than all the others in battle. The regiment rests briefly.

Chapter 18—On an abortive trek for water, Henry and Wilson hear the officers calling them "mule drivers."

Chapter 19—The fight resumes, and Henry grabs the flag, becoming the standard-bearer.

Chapter 20—They again go into battle, fighting fiercely.

Chapter 21—In a temporary lull in the fighting, Henry and Wilson hear themselves praised by the regimental lieutenant.

Chapter 22—Henry observes another battle.

Chapter 23—Henry leads his fellows into victory and begins to celebrate his success.

Chapter 24—He contemplates his various acts of cowardice and bravery.

The major theme that gives these episodes form is that in them Henry is afforded experiences that could allow him to achieve manhood. The question is whether he actually does begin to see himself and the world with mature eyes. Certainly his war story includes many of the characteristics of the initiation journey: an untested youth steeped in innocent and romantic illusions; the form of a journey that should lead toward adulthood; the encounter with a nightmarish world of harsh realities, which are sometimes replete with monsters, even "dragons"; the blasting away of old respected authorities and romantic ideas; his own rebellion against authority; the appearance of a mystical mentor or guide; the move from being proud to being humbled; and the persistence of tests and trials often conducted in solitude.

In general summary, John E. Hart, writing of the theme of initiation, provides a list of characteristics of the initiation journey and interprets *The Red Badge* in that light:

> Crane's main theme is the discovery of self, that unconscious self. . . . The progressive movement of the hero, as in all myth, is that of separation, initiation, and return. . . . Henry Fleming, a youth, ventures forth from his known environment into a region of naturalistic, if not super-naturalistic wonder; he encounters the monstrous forces of war and death; he is transformed through a series of rites and revelations into a hero; he returns to identify this new self with the deeper communal forces of the group and to bestow the blessings of his findings on his fellow comrades.[1]

Before the war, Henry is decidedly a sheltered, untried boy. He lives in a Garden of Eden, on a little farm with his mother. It is a time of boyhood inexperience, when his romantic views of life flourish. In his retreat from battle after his desertion, Henry reflects on that Edenic boyhood, which he left such a short time before:

> Amid it he began to reflect on various incidents and conditions of the past. He bethought him of certain meals his mother had cooked at home, in which those dishes of which he was particularly fond had occupied prominent positions. He saw the spread table. The pine walls of the kitchen were glowing in the warm light from the stove. Too, he remembered how he and his companions used to go from the schoolhouse to the bank of a shaded pool. He saw his clothes in disorderly array upon the grass of the bank. He felt the swash of the fragrant water upon his body. The leaves of the overhanging maple rustled with melody in the wind of youthful summer. (70, 71)

Even at the moment before his regiment began its march toward battle, Henry still has a romantic view of war as a "glory from the past." He held the quaint delusion that in the present day people didn't wage war as they did in the old days because religion, education, and economic self-interest had kept the passions and the warlike instinct in check. Still, when war breaks out, he is attracted to it as a rich romance of marches, sieges, and conflicts. Back home, with his uniform first put on, he had "strutted." His pride at times—even arrogance—prevails throughout his later ordeal.

His naive attitude is in sharp contrast to his mother's view. She reacts as if she knows how brutal war can be and how empty dreams of glory are. He, on the other hand, is disappointed that she does not reinforce his notion of the grandeur of war and the grandeur of his gesture in volunteering for the fight.

In the course of his journey, events challenge his youthful view of many aspects of life: of war's romance and glory, of tradition and authorities in his life, of nature's kindliness, and of his own goodness and moral strength. These revelations will put his old views to the test, providing him with at least the opportunity to know not only what the world is but who he is. He realizes before the battle begins that he is "an unknown quantity" (8) and that not until he actually faces the enemy in battle will he know the truth about himself. Uneasy about how he will conduct himself in the fight, he asks his friends whether "th' boys'll run" (9). Unsure of how he will act, he is fearful that he will run and so commit a crime against the "gods of tradition" (12). When it is apparent that he has fought well in the first skirmish and has not run, he believes "the supreme trial had been passed" (37).

Even on this first day of battle, Henry has available to him realities that have the potential of hastening his initiation from naiveté into manhood. Even before he enters the battle, his rebellion against the past has begun, for instead of viewing the officers as glorious father figures, he resents them as fools. They rage and curse; in this moment of terror, they have petty concerns like keeping their trousers clean and getting their boxes of cigars.

Rather than his old view of war as glorious, Henry begins to see its unspeakable horror. The first such incidence is his view of a corpse lying in the road, its bare foot protruding from the end of the ragged shoe, its eyes open and staring. While he is in battle, he sees the man next to him get shot in the face, and another in the stomach and another in the leg. As the battle temporarily subsides, he sees the dead everywhere in grotesque positions:

> Under foot there were a few ghastly forms motionless. They lay twisted in fantastic contortions. Arms were bent and heads were turned in incredible ways. It seemed that the dead men must have fallen from some great height to get into such positions. (36)

A short while later he stumbles into a chapel made of trees, only to find a gruesome corpse. Another encounter with the harsh reality of life and war comes when Henry watches the agonizing death of his childhood friend, Jim Conklin, whose side "looked as if it had been chewed by wolves" (56).

In the midst of this horror, nature itself takes on an attitude different from that of his youth. Whether he intellectualizes the sentiment, whether it dawns on him what his observation means, he sees nature not as a beautiful and sympathetic force but as totally impersonal, the sun shining brightly on all the horror:

> As he gazed around him the youth felt a flash of astonishment at the blue, pure sky and the sun gleaming on the trees and fields. It was surprising that Nature had gone tranquilly on with her golden process in the midst of so much devilment. (37)

Nature is not only unfeeling and impersonal; in a later scene, he observes it as absolutely horrific when he sees ants crawling across the face of the corpse in the chapel made by trees.

Henry is presented with a second test during the second skirmish on his first day of battle. This he fails by deserting under fire. In the course of his retreat, the reader becomes aware that although he has had available sad truths about himself, this reality has not sunk in. Instead, he rationalizes his cowardice, at first believing it is justified because his side in the war may have lost, therefore making his own desertion understandable. He also begins to think (when a squirrel runs away after he has thrown something at it) that his running away is natural and therefore not dishonorable. He argues that in running away, he has saved a piece of army property for another later fight. His primary aim throughout his retreat and reunion with his regiment is not to face and learn from his experience but to conceal the truth and make excuses for himself.

A large part of Henry's new knowledge involves his superior officers. Even before his first battle, he has begun to rebel against these gods of tradition. In the general retreat, after his desertion, he sees that the officers are as dangerous as the enemy, for in their horse-drawn artillery wagons, they mow down any man who stands in the way.

In this second major section of the novel, after Henry's desertion from his front-line post, he fails another test in this obstacle course he must complete before his initiation into manhood. The crime is again desertion—this time his abandonment of the tattered man. He will later remember this as his more serious desertion. Despite his own wounds, the tattered man had unselfishly given his support to Henry, a complete stranger, at the time of Jim Conklin's horrible death. And the tattered man was more concerned about the possibility that Henry might have an internal wound than he was about his own seemingly fatal wounds.

Innocents in classic initiation stories usually encounter mentors or guides at some point, as Henry does when he meets the cheery man, who possesses "a wand of a magic kind" (72) and is able to lead him back to his regiment.

In the final section of the novel, the tests of initiation and evidences of the truth of the adult world abound, but upon returning to the regiment—his community—from the deep forests of his trials, Henry begins his new life with a lie. He claims to have been shot, cockily passing himself off as a hero. His fake red badge of courage gives him the optimism to believe again that in this battle landscape, the world is good and nature loved him: "His self-pride was now entirely restored. . . . He had license to be pompous and veteran-like . . . he was an individual of extraordinary virtues . . . chosen by the gods" (84–86).

Ironically, pride and arrogance (an attitude that interferes with Henry's assessment of himself) is now completely lacking in Wilson, who had only shortly before been supremely cocky.

> The youth took note of a remarkable change in his comrade since those days of camp life upon the river bank. He seemed no more to be continually regarding the proportions of his personal prowess. He was not furious at small words that pricked his conceits. He was no more a loud young soldier. (80)

In the magical third period of Henry's trials, he proves himself to be an unquestionably fierce fighter, unthinkingly and violently overcoming the enemy. Whether it should be labeled bravery is open to debate. Visions of war's hideous cruelty surface, even in the regiment's brief victory, with the agony of Jimmie Rogers, a fellow soldier who was "thrashing about in the grass, twisting his shuddering body into many strange postures" (97). Henry considers himself heroic after the initial skirmish, but neither the forces of nature nor the universe, not even the general, seem to care. The enlightenment that he is offered on every side is that he is totally insignificant. Nature especially is as uncaring and indifferent to the regiment's costly victory and Henry's success in fighting as it was to their defeat on the previous day. After the bloody encounter, he again notices that the sun was now "bright and gay in the blue-enameled sky" (96).

In the lull between battles, as Henry and Wilson go for water, Henry's whole attitude is altered by what he sees and hears of his superior officers who, in declaring his regiment to be the most expendable, declare that they "fight like a lot 'a mule drivers" (99). It is as if in his journey toward initiation into manhood he has been allowed to overhear a conversation of the gods about the real meaning of life. Finally, something has shocked him into a harsh revelation.

> New eyes were given to him. And the most startling thing was to learn suddenly that he was very insignificant. The officer spoke of the regiment as if he referred to a broom. (99)

He realizes that he and his regiment are regarded as inept and insignificant as mule drivers and are being sent into a battle as cannon fodder. As he goes into his next battle and begins firing, he feels that "he was now in some new and unknown land" (103).

Rage still drives him, as it had in the earlier battle. His actions are unconscious and irrational, as before, like that of an animal—a sheep being driven to the sacrifice and later "wolflike." Only now it is rage at the officers who considered them to be mule drivers rather than at the enemy who had refused to let them rest. He and his comrades feel that they have been betrayed:

> A dagger-pointed gaze from without his blackened face was held toward the enemy, but his greater hatred was riveted upon the man, who, not knowing him, had called him a mule driver. . . . This cold officer upon a monument, who dropped epithets unconcernedly down, would be finer as a dead man, he thought. (108)

Despite Henry's bitter disillusionment with his leaders, he strongly and instinctively loves their emblem, the flag, as he takes it up and becomes the standard-bearer, leading his fellow soldiers into battle. And as the "mule drivers" fighting against impossible odds win a skirmish they were expected to lose, Henry believes that they at last have become men.

Still, even after their brief victory, the awful feeling of their own insignificance, as evidenced by nature and their leaders, presses down their spirits. Leaving the scene of battle, they dread "to be killed in insignificant ways" (112). And another regiment of older men, lying under the trees, belittles their considerable success, corroborating their fears that they do not amount to anything.

> "Was it warm out there, sonny?"
> "Goin' home now, boys?"
> One shouted in taunting mimicry: "Oh, mother, come quick an' look at th' so'jers!" (112)

Even looking back on what had seemed a large tract of land they had won, he sees that it is really very small.

Just as Henry has recuperated enough to regain some sense of personal pride in his own behavior on the battlefield, the general who had called them mule drivers castigates them for making "an awful mess" by quitting too soon. To add insult to injury, the general now says to their colonel, "What a lot of mud diggers you've got anyway!" (114).

The scene reinforces their sense of their own insignificance— that even doing their best is not good enough: "Presently, however, they began to believe that in truth their efforts had been called light" (115).

These harsh realities delivered by the general melt away in the light of stories that reach Henry and Wilson that they have been praised by the company's lieutenant and colonel: "They speedily forgot many things. The past held no pictures of error and disappointment" (117).

In the heat of the last major confrontation, reality descends again as Henry's bitterness toward the general returns: "Some arrows of scorn that had buried themselves in his heart had generated strange and unspeakable hatred" (121). But although Henry takes a step toward adulthood by rebelling against authority, he still naively clings to the idea that he is important and matters in this universe. This leads him to the ridiculous notion that his own death will be a reproach to the general:

It was clear to him that his final and absolute revenge was to be achieved by his dead body lying, torn and glittering, upon the field. This was to be poignant retaliation upon the officer who had said "mule drivers," and later "mud diggers," for in all the wild graspings of his mind for a unit responsible for his sufferings and commotions he always seized upon the man who had dubbed him wrongly. And it was his idea, vaguely formulated, that his corpse would be for those eyes a great and salt reproach. (121)

The battle that ensues is the fiercest one yet, and Henry emerges as one who has fought well and survived. Moreover, he perceives that he has been changed: "He had dwelt in a land of strange, squalling upheavals and had come forth. He had been where there was red of blood and black of passion, and he was escaped" (128). And Henry, who has always been contemplative, now returns to his thoughtful nature to try to make sense of what has happened. For the first time, he begins to look at himself truly, without rationalizing, without being blind to his errors, without arrogance and an exaggerated sense of his own importance. What he sees is that even though the public performance that his fellow soldiers and the officers have seen has been praiseworthy, his hidden deeds have been miserably despicable and unforgivable—not only his flight from battle the day before but, much more important, his desertion of the tattered soldier:

He who, gored by bullets and faint for blood, had fretted concerning an imagined wound in another; he who had loaned his last of strength and intellect for the tall soldier; he who, blind with weariness and pain, had been deserted in the field. (129)

In the final five paragraphs of the story of Henry Fleming's journey, the reader receives clues about his state of mind. Whether he has come through his experience with clear sight into manhood (as he thinks he has) is ambiguous and has long been a matter of literary debate. A careful consideration of what occurs in these paragraphs may yield some hints to assist the reader in considering a conclusion.

As he thinks of his desertion of the tattered soldier and he acknowledges his failure to himself, he seems intent on keeping it a secret from the others. Then he is able to "put the sin at a distance" because he begins seeing everything differently. Primarily he begins to despise "the brass and bombast of his earlier gospels"

(130). He will no longer be intimidated by the guides of the past, nor will he any longer view death as a horror. He feels that he has distanced himself from the "blood and wrath" and "hot plowshares" of the battlefield. "Scars faded as flowers" (130). He begins to feel that the world belongs to him instead of to those epitomized by "oaths and walking sticks" (131). And he acknowledges that while he had been a raging animal on the battlefield, he has now found some kind of inner peace.

Has Henry passed through his trials into true manhood? Or is he continuing to rationalize and fail to face up to his realities? To come to grips with these questions, it is useful to examine the form of the novel and a literary word that is frequently used in connection with Crane's work: *naturalism*.

Crane's work did not arise from the prevailing literary tradition of his time, which is sometimes labeled "genteel." The subject matter of the genteel tradition was often the domestic scene, its characters either members of polite, upper-class society or innocent, romantic farmers. When unpleasantness and psychological complications arose in the stories, they were treated politely, so as not to bring a blush to the cheeks of innocent girls. Such fiction usually contained a strongly worded moral.

The Red Badge of Courage, rather than being in the genteel mainstream, is positioned between the romantic, genteel tradition of the mid-nineteenth century and the severe naturalistic tradition that would flower at the turn of the twentieth century. There are many naturalistic elements in *The Red Badge of Courage*.

Older romantic fiction was often set in the parlours of polite society; naturalistic literature takes its subject matter from the seamier side of human existence. A notable example is Émile Zola's nineteenth-century novel *Nana*, which has as its setting the violent and sordid night world of the prostitute. In Crane's case, the setting is not the world of polite jousts and fencing matches portrayed by the romantic Sir Walter Scott, but a bloody battlefield of mud and gore.

The setting of the battlefield alone does not make *The Red Badge of Courage* naturalistic. Rather, it is the details that Crane chooses for his fiction. Naturalistic literature is marked by explicit, detailed descriptions of the coarse and most unattractive side of life. Zola, for example, described in unflinching detail the physical degeneration of a prostitute dying of syphilis. Crane's novel is naturalistic in this respect, especially in its description of the corpse Henry stumbles onto in the forest chapel. Crane could have just said that Henry came upon a corpse. Instead he provides a number of gory, "naturalistic" details:

> The eyes, staring at the youth, had changed to the dull hue to be seen on the side of a dead fish. The mouth was open. Its red had changed to an appalling yellow. Over the gray skin of the face ran little ants. One was trundling some sort of a bundle along the upper lip. . . . He remained staring into the liquid-looking eyes. (46)

Naturalism was also marked by a philosophical stance called *determinism*. Determinism is based on the view that the fate of humans is determined by forces beyond their control. A person does not succeed or fail in life because he or she makes an independent decision to take a particular action. Instead, the natural forces of heredity and the power of the person's environment are the determiners. Human beings are somewhat helplessly under the control of natural laws or psychological forces or social pressures. Crane's novel has many naturalistic elements of this kind because Henry and his comrades are so often at the mercy of forces beyond their control: group pressures, their commanding officers, and their own emotions, which overtake them. In such a universe, human beings are helpless and insignificant and, to a large extent, not responsible for their actions.

To help the reader toward an interpretation of the end of the novel, it is useful to get some idea of the stance Crane takes toward the determinism that permeates the work. This can be done by noticing a certain pattern that emerges in the treatment of contrasting attitudes and actions—for example,

- Reflection versus action.
- Individualism or solitariness versus the group and society.
- Idealism versus stark realism.
- Cowardice versus heroism.

Henry moves between these oppositions as the story unfolds, and we see that they form a pattern. For example, when Henry is reflective, he is, of course, most solitary, but also most in control of himself and most human—for good and ill. When he is active, he is most a part of the group, least in charge of his own actions, and most instinctively like an animal—whether he is being led like a sheep, raging forward heroically like a lion, or running away like a rabbit. How a reader measures these oppositions may determine how he or she will judge the outcome of Henry's journey.

The whole regiment swings back and forth between moving and resting, action and inaction, but the more important tension is seen in the person of Henry, by nature a solitary, reflective person. At the novel's opening, as other soldiers shout, argue, play cards, and talk, Henry is off by himself wondering when the fighting will begin and how he will conduct himself under fire. Even as they march toward the battlefield, his intellectual side remains uppermost while he considers himself "separated from the others." Not until he is in the front lines actually firing his rifle does he become primarily a man of action. On the last day of battle, he laments that the enemy is resolved "to give him no rest, to give him no time to sit down and think. . . . For to-day he felt that he had earned opportunities for contemplative repose" (92). But the battlefield is not the place for exercise of the higher faculties like the intellect.

It is in his active moments that he becomes least egocentric and most a person in a group:

> He suddenly lost concern for himself, and forgot to look at a menacing fate. He became not a man but a member. He felt that something of which he was a part—a regiment, an army, a cause, or a country—was in crisis. He was welded into a common personality which was dominated by a single desire. (32)

It is also at this moment that he becomes animalistic, like a cornered and enraged beast. In one paragraph he is compared to "a pestered animal," "a well-meaning cow worried by dogs," and "a driven beast" (33). His actions are not thoughtful but instinctive, like those of an animal. "He fought frantically for respite for his senses, for air, as a babe being smothered attacks the deadly blankets" (33). And he notices that the sounds coming from the other men are animalistic: snarls, growls, unintelligible babbling.

In the second onslaught, when Henry throws down his rifle and runs, he is no less a member of the group and instinctive than he was when he had stayed and fought a few minutes earlier. The horror of the man near him who runs frantically is contagious, and Henry, like him, "ran like a rabbit" (39). He compares himself not only to a rabbit but to a "chicken" who has lost its sense of direction. The dehumanizing effect of battle can also be seen in the comparisons of Henry and his comrades to machines instead of to human beings: "They must be machines of steel" (40) and "Machinelike fools!" (41).

Determinism comes into play in this first section of the novel in that the closer Henry gets to the battlefield, the less in control he is of his own actions. He is swept along in this "blue wave" or "demonstration" of the regiment. The officers seem to be the gods or determining fates of this universe—on their high horses, aloof from Henry and his comrades, who seem less like human beings than like cannon fodder. It is the officers who decide where all the members of the regiment will go and what they will do. It is understandable in time of battle that the officers could not allow the men to decide for themselves about where to go and how to conduct themselves, but the leaders also refuse to give the common soldiers any information whatsoever about the larger picture and the options they are considering, treating them like animals and machines. Henry's helplessness at the hands of other forces is frustrating as he approaches his first trial in battle. He feels boxed in by the regiment moving all around him:

> It inclosed him. And there were iron laws of tradition and law on four sides. He was in a moving box.
> As he perceived this fact it occurred to him that he had never wished to come to the war. He had not enlisted of his free will. He had been dragged by the merciless government. (21)

On the final day of battle, Henry sees that he and his fellow soldiers "stood as men tied to stakes" (91).

It is not only the officers and the government—in short, society—that prevents Henry from choosing his own course as a thinking human being; it is his own animal nature that directs him and takes over his rational human self. This is what happens each time he goes into battle. The intuitive need to fire his rifle to stay alive (like a baby fighting off smothering blankets) takes him over in his first experience with battle, and in the second it is pure animal fear and panic. In the third section, the rational Henry has again given way to the irrational as he plunges into battle. He feels "like a kitten chased by boys." The soldiers "resembled animals tossed for a death struggle into a dark pit" (93). The men feel so cornered they could all develop teeth and claws (92). He compares the regiment and the men to a snake, a dog, wild cats, and a beast. Charles C. Walcott, pointing out the dueling techniques of naturalism and impressionism in the novel, stresses the animalism of the fighting man:

> If *The Red Badge of Courage* were only an exposure of an ignorant farm boy's delusions, it would be a contemptible book. Crane shows that Henry's delusions image only dimly the insanely grotesque and incongruous world of battle into which he is plunged. There the movement is blind or frantic, the leaders are selfish, the goals are inhuman. One farm boy is made into a mad animal to kill another farm boy, while the great guns carry on a "grim pow-wow" or a "Stupendous wrangle" described in terms that suggest a solemn farce or a cosmic and irresponsible game.[2]

The emotion that drives him to fight in the first skirmish of the last day of battle is rage at the enemy that will not let him rest. In his unthinking, almost unconscious state on the battlefield, he continues to fire his rifle in a frenzy even though there is nothing to fire at. Henry's taking up of the flag in these last battles is a compelling ambiguity, though difficult to unravel. In one sense, his pushing ahead of the regiment, unarmed except for the colors, can be seen as an act of courage bordering on the foolhardy—pushing his bravery to the limit.

Still, while there are elements of naturalism and determinism in the novel, the reader should not assume that Crane endorses a deterministic view of the universe in this fiction. Indeed, Henry is often intellectually independent and in charge of his actions. Because he is also most human at such times, Crane seems to recommend resistance to determinism. Stanley B. Greenfield addresses the problem of determinism in the novel, which, because so much happens as a result of biological instincts and traditional conditioning, leads us to ask, " 'Is there care in Heaven?' "[3]

Along with the novel's naturalistic pictures of the pain and death of war, the inherent pattern of these oppositions would seem to be a strong indictment of war, showing that man on the battlefield, although society labels him strong and heroic, is exercising not the *highest* faculties of human character but the *lowest*, except in one regard. That is, man in battle is not choosing, thinking man. However, he is sometimes *unselfish* man, and overcoming the experience of battle leads him to new insights.

Does this tell us anything about Henry's revelation at the novel's end? What are "the brass and bombast of his earlier gospels," which he has come to despise? Is the bombast his earlier view that war is glorious? Is the reader convinced that he really has come to a view of war as despicable? Why does his newfound truth, if we are to believe that is what it is, make him gleeful, assured, tranquil, and at home in the world? How, after the horror of war, can he think that the world is peaceful, golden, and bright? Is he just further deluded, continuing to rationalize his actions? Or has he put his sins behind him and determined to go on with his life? These are questions that thoughtful students of Stephen Crane have quarreled about since the book was published.

Crane's use of two other literary devices in *The Red Badge of Courage* are key to the novel's meaning: his uses of irony and impressionism. Irony can be defined as a figure of speech in which the intended meaning is the opposite of what is expressed and sometimes results in sarcasm as, for example, when the words used may sound like praise but actually imply ridicule.

The final shades of irony are often difficult to determine, but it clearly operates throughout the novel. For example, there is irony in Henry's desertion just after he thinks he has proved himself. There is irony in the fact that his war wound had been delivered not under fire by the enemy but in retreat and by a fellow soldier. The title itself is ironic in that what Henry calls his red badge of courage is the blow from another soldier. It is a red badge, but it is certainly not courageous. Critics use the word *irony* in discussing the final meaning of the novel. Many argue that the ending is ironic in that Henry believes he is a man and believes he sees things as they are when in fact he is still a deluded boy. Marston LaFrance, however, is one of the critics who rejects the notion that the ending is ironic:

I am unable to find much irony in the closing paragraphs of the novel. Henry is exhausted from all his battles and gratefully marching to a rest. Only the most romantically obtuse reader at this point could believe in the actuality of "an existence of soft and eternal peace," but the image aptly describes how inviting the coming rest must seem to a weary young soldier. Certainly Henry is not fooling himself; his quiet confidence that he will "no more quail before his guides wherever they should point" would be meaningless if he really anticipated an existence of soft and eternal peace.[4]

Stark naturalism is opposed in this work to a romantic impressionism. Impressionism is defined in the *Oxford English Dictionary* as expressing "the general impression produced by a scene or object to the exclusion of minute details or elaborate finish" (1391). Impressionism, with its beautiful use of colors and shading to create a natural scene, would seem to be the very opposite of the stark, unstinting reality of the naturalistic scene. But Crane has managed to incorporate both into his novel. The novel tends to move back and forth between the two techniques. In those impressionist portions of the novel, we are seeing how Henry's eyes and brain color what he experiences. In the naturalistic portions of the novel, we are seeing how the world actually is.

The conclusion of one student of the novel serves to enlarge and provoke our own speculations about Crane's meaning. Marston LaFrance sums up what he sees as Crane's view of the human situation in *The Red Badge of Courage:*

> Crane's view of the human situation, set forth more clearly in *The Red Badge* than in his earlier work, is that man is born into an amoral universe which is merely the external setting in which human moral life is lived, and that if moral values are to exist and man's life is to be meaningful, morality must be the creation of man's weak mental machinery alone.[5]

What Crane has done is to allow us to see inside a young man's head as he endures the tests of manhood in wartime and comes to grips with his own fear of death. While Crane has given us reason to find Henry's observations of what is happening to be reliable, he has not told us explicitly which of Henry's judgments and conclusions are on target and which are delusions. As a consequence, Crane has left an inordinate amount of work for his readers to do. On one hand, a student may object, "Why doesn't Crane just *tell* us whether Henry successfully completes his initiation into manhood and save us all this trouble?" On the other hand, Crane, while he gives his reader a lot of work to do, has paid his readers a high compliment in showing that he believes he does not have to tell them what to think. He can present the unadorned facts of Henry's mind and leave us to draw our own conclusions about him, just as we must draw our own conclusions in everyday life. In a real sense, the reader becomes a co-creator of the novel with the author.

NOTES

1. John E. Hart, "*The Red Badge of Courage* as Myth and Symbol," in *Norton Critical Edition of The Red Badge of Courage*, ed. Sculley Bradley, Richmond Croom Beatty, E. Hudson Long, and Donald Pizer (New York: W. W. Norton, 1976), p. 206.

2. Charles C. Walcott, "Stephen Crane: Naturalist and Impressionist," in *Norton Critical Edition*, p. 221.

3. Stanley B. Greenfield, "The Unmistakable Stephen Crane," in *Norton Critical Edition*, p. 232.

4. Marston LaFrance, "Private Fleming: His Various Battles," in *Norton Critical Edition*, p. 349.

5. Ibid., p. 333.

TOPICS FOR ORAL AND WRITTEN EXPLORATION

1. Examine the title closely, and write an essay on the multiple meanings of each of the words *red*, *badge*, and *courage*.

2. Examine the dynamics between Henry and his mother as he leaves for war. What would you tell each of them to help in understanding the other?

3. Research the reference on page 4 to his returning "with his shield or on it." From where does the term come, and how does it have meaning to Henry's situation?

4. Write an essay on or discuss the changes that occur in Wilson and their significance for Henry's story.

5. Define courage using your own examples. What tests would you apply to determine whether an action is courageous? Are there examples of courage in the novel? How does the U.S. government define courageous in awarding medals?

6. If there are significant disagreements about what determines courage, have a debate on the meaning.

7. What is shown in the fact that Henry wants to be so cruel to Wilson? He has not shown this tendency before his first battle. Why now?

8. Write an essay cataloging Crane's references to color. Does any pattern develop that helps us to interpret the meaning of various colors and their significance in the novel?

9. Write an essay on the theme of rumor in the story. Why is rumor so unsettling and divisive?

10. Look at Henry's act of cowardice under fire. Why exactly do you think he runs?

11. Write an essay on the officers, characterizing them generally.

12. What effect is created by the fact that so few characters have names?

13. Some have argued that Henry takes up the banner because he regards it as a magical token that protects him; others say that he is being foolhardy. Why do you think Henry takes up the banner?

14. As a major class project, discuss what constitutes maturity. In bringing your own definition to the class discussion, formulate reasons for your definition. Buttress your definition with interviews or examples from life and literature, as well as negative definitions—that is, what maturity is *not*.

15. As a second class project, discuss manhood, looking closely at your

own neighborhood culture and the use of the word *macho*. How do young women figure in a *macho* culture?

16. Write an essay on how Henry deludes himself.

17. Is Henry deluding himself at the end? If not, what exactly opens his eyes?

18. What exactly is meant at the end by Henry's seeing the world as "prospects of clover"?

19. What does Henry mean by saying that "the world was a world for him"?

20. What accounts for Henry's change from running from battle to being the fiercest fighter?

21. Examine the scene where the veteran soldiers on his own side taunt the young soldiers who have just been through hell. Does this have any bearing on the outcome of the story? What effect do you suppose Crane wanted to have keeping that scene in there?

22. Detail the references to animals throughout the work. How do these references serve the meaning of the story?

23. How would you summarize Crane's view of nature? Is it benevolent or hostile or uncaring?

SUGGESTED READINGS

Bassan, Maurice, ed. *Stephen Crane: A Collection of Critical Essays*. Englewood Cliffs, N.J.: Prentice Hall, 1967.

Benfey, Christopher. *The Double Life of Stephen Crane*. New York: Alfred A. Knopf, 1992.

Berryman, John. *Stephen Crane*. New York: William Sloane Associates, 1950.

Cady, Edwin. *Stephen Crane*. New York: Twayne Publishers, 1962.

Cazemajou, Jean. *Stephen Crane*. Minneapolis: University of Minnesota Press, 1969.

Gibson, Donald B. *The Fiction of Stephen Crane*. Carbondale: Southern Illinois University Press, 1968.

Gullason, Thomas A., ed. *Stephen Crane's Career: Perspectives and Evaluations*. New York: New York University Press, 1972. (Contains twelve essays on Crane and *The Red Badge of Courage*)

Kazin, Alfred. *On Native Grounds*. New York: Reynal and Hitchcock, 1942.

Solomon, Eric. *Stephen Crane: From Parody to Realism*. Cambridge: Harvard University Press, 1966.
Wertheim, Stanley, and Paul Sorrentino. *The Crane Log*. New York: G. K. Hall, 1994.

The Civil War Setting of the Novel

All quiet on the Rappahannock. (87)

SELECTED CHRONOLOGY OF THE CIVIL WAR

1820 Missouri Compromise denoting where slavery could exist
1831 Abolitionist movement begins
1850 Fugitive Slave Law allowing slave holders to track down
      runaways
1852 *Uncle Tom's Cabin* published
1854 Kansas-Nebraska Act which negated Missouri Compromise
      Formation of Republican party
1857 *Dred Scott* decision forcing return of slave to his owner
1859 Raid on Harper's Ferry by abolitionist John Brown
1860 Election of Abraham Lincoln
      December—Secession of South Carolina from the Union
1861 Confederate States of America organized
      April 12—Attack on Fort Sumter and start of Civil War
      Battle of Bull Run (Virginia, July 21)

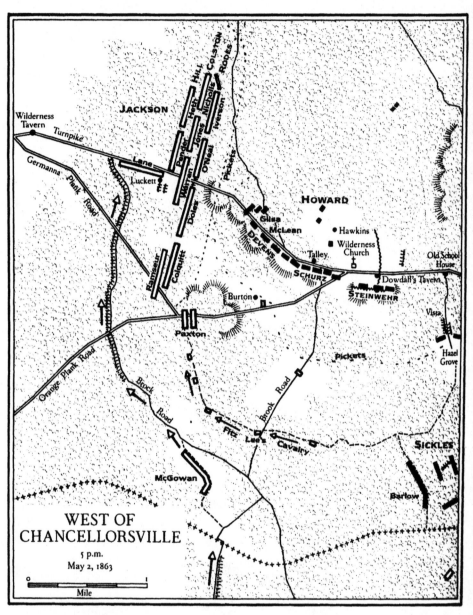

Map showing the position of troops at 5 p.m. on May 2, 1863. From *Chancellorsville,
1863* by Ernest B. Furguson. Copyright © by Ernest B. Furguson. Maps Copyright ©
1992 by William J. Clipson. Reprinted by permission of Alfred A. Knopf, Inc.

George B. McClellan appointed commander of Union army

1862 Battle of Shiloh (Tennessee, April 6–7)

Robert E. Lee appointed commander of Confederates

Second Battle of Bull Run (Virginia, August 29, 30)

Battle of Antietam (Maryland, September 17)

Battle of Fredericksburg (Virginia, December 13)

Battle of Chancellorsville (Virginia, May 1–4)

Battle of Gettysburg (Pennsylvania, July 1–3)

Capture of Vicksburg (Mississippi, June 28)

1864 Battle of the Wilderness (Virginia, May 4–5)

Battle of Cold Harbor (Virginia, June 3)

Capture of Atlanta (Georgia, September 2)

1865 Capture of Columbia, South Carolina (February 17)

Surrender of Lee to Grant at Appomattox (Virginia, April 9)

Nowhere in *The Red Badge of Courage*, as one critic has pointed out, does Stephen Crane make particular reference to the meaning, tactics, politics, or outcome of the war in which Henry Fleming is engaged or the causes that have set the armies against one another. The absence of such particulars tends to universalize the story and make an "Everyman" of Henry: he is any young man of any era facing a trial by fire in any battle. But given Crane's time and place, the mention of the rebels, and descriptions of the countryside and course of the skirmishes, any reader knows that Crane's classic battle takes place in the American Civil War. Scholars have even identified the battle described in the novel: there is little doubt that Henry is engaged in the Battle of Chancellorsville in northern Virginia, one of the pivotal battles of the war.

The causes of the war for which Henry Fleming volunteered were several of varying importance, deriving in no small measure from the very differences in character between the North and the South. The North was rapidly becoming urbanized and industrialized, had attracted many immigrants to work in its factories, argued for stiff tariffs on incoming goods in order to protect its industry, supported a policy of providing free land to western settlers, and in general supported a strong central government. The South, on the other hand, was still rural and agricultural, depending almost solely on the single crop of cotton. It had not only modest family farms, like many in the North, but, unlike the North, a system of large plantations whose owners exercised immense political power in the region. Unlike the North, the South found that protective tariffs were detrimental to the plantation economy. Its politicians and large plantation owners wanted the power of the federal government transferred to the states. There were also major differences over where transcontinental railroads would be located, each region wanting the benefits of such a network to accrue to its own people.

It has often been pointed out that the two regions would probably have been able to work out these disputes and avoid a major conflict if their differences had stopped there. But the presence of slavery, on which the Southern plantation system depended, was the issue that, when added to other fundamental differences, made war inevitable. Before 1850, the Northerners who objected to slavery did so more from political reasons (to keep the spread of slavery from giving the South a political advantage) than from outrage at the system's inhumanity. North and South fought each other for control of the new lands opening up in western territories. If a territory were opened to slaveholding, the South would have additional allies and votes at the federal level. If slaveholding were prohibited, there was more likelihood that the citizens who settled there would be sympathetic to the North. So as settlers applied for statehood or status as a territory, a variety of intricate compromises were hammered out, concessions being made to appease both sides. The most famous was the Missouri Compromise (1820), which allowed slavery in new territories in the southernmost half of the country and outlawed it in territories in the northernmost part. As a result, Southerners and Southern sympathizers tended to settle in Missouri and points south and supported Southern causes in the U.S. legislature.

Although many Northerners either did not object to slavery or believed that the nation should not interfere with the status quo in the South, several events led to the marshaling of sentiment against the existence of slavery within the nation's borders and hastened the day when a divided nation would be at war. One was the passage of the Fugitive Slave Law in 1850, which allowed slaveholders to hunt down runaway slaves in free territory. The law required little proof of ownership and specifically forbade any legal testimony on the part of the fugitive. The second event that marshaled antislavery sentiment was the publication in 1852 of the phenomenally popular *Uncle Tom's Cabin* by Harriet Beecher Stowe, which alerted the general public to the cruelties of slavery. Another event that enraged Northerners was the U.S. Supreme Court decision in 1854 to nullify the Missouri Compromise, specifically denying any rights to former slaves in free territory and declaring that the U.S. Constitution protected the institution of slavery. It followed that slavery could not be barred from any new territory. The violence that ensued on the part of supporters and opponents of slavery, especially that perpetrated by John Brown in Kansas, served to force a breach between Southerners and Northerners that moderates had no hope of bridging.

Southerners were overwhelmingly Democrats, and many Northerners who objected to slavery were Republicans. When Abraham Lincoln won the presidency in 1860, after a campaign in which slavery was an issue, the South's position had already hardened. The talk that had been in the air for some time, about the South's withdrawing from the Union, became a reality as South Carolina declared its secession from the Union on December 20, 1860. Six other cotton states rapidly followed with similar declarations. Many legislators tried desperately to frame compromises that would save the Union but were unsuccessful. Eventually the entire South would join the Confederacy, and its capital would move from Montgomery, Alabama, to Richmond, Virginia.

The formation of the Southern states into a separate country meant that various lands understood to belong to and be controlled by the entire Union now stood in foreign territory. In his first inaugural address, Lincoln emphasized that the federal government would not just turn over such land to the Confederacy. In response, Jefferson Davis, the president of the new nation, ordered one of his generals to take over Fort Sumter, a federal military base in Charleston harbor. Cannons were fired on the fort, and the Union men who were stationed there fled to the North. From this moment, the war was inevitable. Lincoln immediately asked the states still in the Union to provide 75,000 soldiers out of state militia for the federal government to use in its defense. The officers were chosen by the vote of the group or were political appointments, more often than not comprising civilians, often local leaders, with no military training. The training that men in the state militia had received consisted of how to march in military parades. Most had never had any instruction in how to work with units greater than their small-town companies, which explains the general chaos in *The Red Badge of Courage*. And there was little in the way of arms or ammunition to back them up.

The Northern army was at a disadvantage in that it always had to be on the offensive, trying to invade the Confederacy and, for example, take back Richmond, the capital of the Confederacy. Furthermore, Union soldiers were often suffering real pains and discomforts for an abstraction—holding together the Union—while Southern soldiers had great motivation in defending their homeland. The Union advantages were greater manpower, industrial strength, and wealth.

The war was initially waged on two main fronts: in the East, primarily in Virginia and Pennsylvania, and in the near-western states of Tennessee and Kentucky. The rebel capital of Richmond and the federal capital of Washington, D.C., were only a hundred miles apart in the East, and the first strategy for the North was to seize Richmond. Although officers knew full well that their untrained volunteers were not yet ready to make a major move, public sentiment forced them to make a major offensive in the summer of 1861. After two minor victories against the Confederates in western Virginia, General Irvin McDowell was directed to move toward Richmond in July by taking the junction called Manassas, which was now occupied by the enemy. The encounter was called the Battle of Bull Run, named for the river that ran through Manassas separating the troops. The Union force was completely disorganized; the men, most of whom had never fought before, wandered off occasionally to follow their own whims, and the logistics of their leaders fell in complete disarray. Orders, at those rare times when they were issued, were either ignored or misunderstood. A number of men deserted. Although there was confusion within both armies, the Confederates outperformed the Union soldiers, who were forced to withdraw without achieving their objective. The retreat was the height of confusion and chaos, with blocked roads and general panic.

At this point, time had run out for federal use of the state militia, and the Union had to recruit new volunteer soldiers for a three-year term. Henry Fleming obviously joined the army at this stage.

General George B. McClellan continued plans to capture the rebel capital at Richmond, but Lincoln and his cabinet distrusted him because he moved so slowly. McClellan's every effort seemed to meet with disaster because in reaction to political pressure, he began offensives much sooner than he was ready to move. His next move on Richmond was made taking a very circuitous route. Partly because leaders in Washington had no confidence in his plan, he was ordered to leave many of his troops behind to defend Washington, D.C., from attack. In any case, McClellan's army was beaten, and Washington was left vulnerable to Confederate attack. He was relieved of his command in the fall of 1862 and replaced briefly by General Ambrose E. Burnside, who, after the debacle at the Battle of Fredericksburg, was also relieved of command. By January 26, 1863, General Joseph Hooker had taken over command of the Army of the Potomac.

In the spring of 1863, Hooker was in charge of one of the most pivotal and controversial battles of the Civil War, one that scholars agree was the battle Crane had in mind in *The Red Badge of Courage*. This was the Battle of Chancellorsville. The town of Chancellorsville, Virginia, little more than a mansion-turned-tavern with several outbuildings, was situated just south of the Rappahannock River, roughly halfway between Richmond and Washington, D.C., the headquarters of the Union army. An attempt to reach Richmond might well carry the Union army through those areas like Chancellorsville. Confederate General Robert E. Lee already had 60,000 men at Fredericksburg, east of Chancellorsville. The main generals under Hooker's command in this battle were Oliver O. Howard, Henry W. Slocum, George Gordon Meade, John Sedgwick, Daniel E. Sickles, and Alfred Pleasonton. Among their forces were 30,000 men who had never seen action and some 23,000 men whose terms of military service were about to expire.

Chancellorsville was also one of the most controversial battles of the Civil War for a number of reasons, chiefly arising from charges of incompetence made against the Union officers, a theme that reverberates through *The Red Badge of Courage*. The major events that call into question the Union generals' competence are these:

• General Hooker's withdrawal from clear ground to the wooded terrain around Chancellorsville after the first day of battle.

- General Howard's failure to prepare for an attack from "the Wilderness" that resulted in a slaughter and the desertion of hundreds of his men.

- Blame for desertion being entirely and falsely placed on one German division under Howard's command.

- The ordering of a suicide mission to divert the enemy at Hazel's Grove.

- The failure of General Hooker's staff to assume command at a critical moment when he was incapacitated by a wound to the head.

- General Hooker's retreat and withdrawal, putting an end to the Battle of Chancellorsville.

The first part of Hooker's plan went smoothly. In the last days of April, several regiments crossed two hazardous rivers and maneuvered forty-six miles of terrible roads.

April 29, 5:00 A.M.: Forces cross the treacherous Rappahannock River at several locations.

April 30: Hooker establishes his headquarters in the tavern at Chancellorsville and places his troops in areas immediately around the village. The troops had supplies for only a few days, most of the armaments being north of the treacherous river they had just crossed. From this day, everything goes downhill. Hooker, who had decided that it was of utmost importance to concentrate on taking three railroads out of Confederate hands, is unprepared for Lee's concentration of defenses on the roads. Nor is Hooker able to locate the Confederate forces or believe that Lee planned to leave Fredericksburg and move toward Chancellorsville. So Hooker, instead of moving swiftly along to the open country east of Chancellorsville, as he had planned to do and was advised to do by all the intelligence operators, keeps his forces in the area around Chancellorsville. The terrain itself was bound to work to the Union army's disadvantage. Because of impenetrable woods and underbrush, it was impossible to see more than a few feet in any direction to know what the enemy was up to; but Lee, born and reared not far away, knew the area intimately and had the advantage. In 1878, a military man named Captain Willard Glazier, looking back, described the area as "a labyrinth of forests, traversed in every direction by narrow roads and paths, all well known to the enemy, but unknown even to most of [Hooker's] guides" (236).

Hooker's fatal delay at Chancellorsville doomed the whole effort to capture Confederate strongholds south of the Rappahannock River.

May 1: At first Hooker orders an eastward advance, but having been told that a large number of enemy forces are moving westward toward him from Fredericksburg, he stops his offensive thrust, reinforces fortifications around Chancellorsville House, refuses to move his troops from wooded areas, and assumes a defensive posture.

May 2, 8:00 A.M.: A column of Confederates is attacked by General Birney, and by the end of the day the Union forces take 500 prisoners and the road.

May 2, 9:00 A.M.: General Sickles, on the road to Fredericksburg, encounters a company of General Robert E. Lee's Confederate men, who force Sickle's corps and part of another corps to fall back, leaving behind significant numbers of dead and badly wounded. Lee follows them through the woods, attacking with sharpshooters. At the same time cannon are placed above the hills overlooking Hooker's headquarters at Chancellorsville House.

May 2, late afternoon: General Howard, ignoring the danger of a possible Confederate attack, refuses reinforcements from other companies, fails to post pickets around the camp, and has his men stack their rifles to the side (out of easy reach) and begin cooking their supper. His forces are suddenly attacked by the Confederates, under the leadership of Stonewall Jackson. Hooker sends a message to the Graham brigade to move to assist Howard, but the message is either lost or ignored or Howard turns help away. This corps is destroyed. Captain Glazier describes the scene in this way: "Whole divisions were now overwhelmed by the Rebel hordes, that swept forward amid blazing musketry and battle-shouts, which made the wilderness resound" (238). Those who are not killed immediately run in frantic retreat from the Confederates. Hooker's staff sees them running past headquarters in Chancellorsville House. Union artillery is abandoned by the 11th Corps in the road and taken by the Confederates without the Union army's firing a shot. The 3d Corps retreats, leaving 75,000 rounds of ammunition behind.

May 2, sunset: Generals Sickles and Pleasonton order Major

Keenan of the 8th Pennsylvania Cavalry to charge into the woods again on what seems to be a suicide mission: "You must charge into those woods with your regiment, and hold the Rebels until I can get some of these guns into position. You must do it at whatever cost." So Keenan leads 500 of his men against 10,000 Confederates under the leadership of Stonewall Jackson. Captain Glazier reports in 1878:

> The forlorn charge was made, but the martyr-leader, with the majority of his dauntless troopers, soon baptized the earth upon which he fell, with his life blood. But the precious sacrifice was not in vain. The Rebel advance was greatly checked, as when a trembling lamb is thrown into the jaws of a pursuing pack of ravenous wolves. (239)

Three successive Confederate charges are made against the Union lines, now reinforced with cannon. Each charge was mowed down, as Captain Glazier describes it: "Three successive and desperate charges were made, one of them to within a few yards of the guns, but each was repulsed with terrible slaughter. In many places the dead were literally in heaps" (240).

May 2, midnight: General Sickles regains some of the territory once occupied by the 11th Corps, which had lost to the Confederates, but Confederates have gotten to within a mile of Hooker's headquarters.

May 3, daybreak: Confederate General Stuart attacks Union forces, which give way. Union ammunition is running out. General Sickles sends Hooker an insistent message for immediate help or he will have to yield ground. As the message reaches Hooker's headquarters, a Confederate cannonball has collapsed a wall of Chancellorsville House, and Hooker is knocked unconscious. For a few minutes, he is thought to be dead. When he finally regains consciousness, he is seriously stunned and dizzy, not recovering until noon. In the confusion, no one acts on Sickles's request for reinforcements. Sickles must retreat, hotly pursued by Confederate forces.

Union General Sedgwick begins moving south from the Rappahannock River in the early morning hours with reinforcements.

The Union army suffers its greatest casualties on this day.

May 4: In the wee hours of the morning, heavy Confederate offensives force a general retreat of all Union forces from Chancellorsville toward the Rappahannock. For two days Sedgwick's forces are engaged in a horrific battle at Salem Church, between Fredericksburg and Chancellorsville.

May 5: Sedgwick is surrounded and driven back across the Rappahannock River at night, leaving 5,000 Union soldiers killed, wounded, or taken prisoner. An afternoon storm makes roads and terrain almost impassable and visibility impossible as Union troops move north. The weather turns brutally cold.

May 5, midnight: Hooker orders all forces to recross the Rappahannock, now swollen and furious by the storm.

The Battle of Chancellorsville ended with a defeat of the Union forces and a loss of about 18,000 men on both sides, making it the bloodiest battle of the Civil War. The battle was a major setback for Union plans to capture Richmond and made possible a Confederate invasion of the North.

A number of characteristics of the Battle of Chancellorsville can be seen in Crane's novel:

- The large number of completely inexperienced men facing battle for the first time.
- The confusion and incompetence even among the upper ranks, caused by Hooker's indecision and the many failures in communication.
- The massive desertions in every corps, but particularly the 11th.
- The terrain of heavy woods and underbrush.
- The muddy, impassable roads.
- The chaos of retreats through woods and roads and the danger to the men on foot posed by retreating wagons.
- The sacrifice of a small group of men to draw attention away from the Union army's effort to set up cannon.

The following excerpts enlarge on the Battle of Chancellorsville as a setting of *The Red Badge of Courage*. The first details the parallels between Henry Fleming's war and the Battle of Chancellorsville. The second includes figures on losses in the battle. The next three selections are charges of incompetence on the part of General Hooker, followed by Hooker's defense of himself. Four accounts of the sacrifice at Hazel Grove follow; the last is a poem memorializing Keenan.

HAROLD R. HUNGERFORD, " 'THAT WAS AT CHANCELLORSVILLE': THE FACTUAL FRAMEWORK OF *THE RED BADGE OF COURAGE"*

Harold Hungerford made the definitive argument for the Battle of Chancellorsville as the model for Henry Fleming's war experience in *The Red Badge of Courage.* Note the major evidence he presents: Crane's story entitled "The Veteran"; the place names in the story; the time; the nature of the terrain; the chaos of the retreat; the man with a German dialect; the suicidal charge on the morning of May 3; and the general confusion and ignorance about where they were and what was going on.

Largely as a result of Hungerford's work, no one now seems to question that Henry Fleming's first experience with war took place near Chancellorsville.

FROM HAROLD R. HUNGERFORD, " 'THAT WAS AT CHANCELLORSVILLE': THE FACTUAL FRAMEWORK OF *THE RED BADGE OF COURAGE"*
(*American Literature* XXXIV [January 1963], 520–31)

The name of the battle in which Henry Fleming achieved his manhood is never given in *The Red Badge of Courage.* Scholars have not agreed that the battle even ought to have a name; some have implied that it is a potpourri of episodes from a number of battles.[1] Yet an examination of the evidence leads to the conclusion that the battle does have a name—Chancellorsville. Throughout the book, it can be demonstrated, Crane consistently used the time, the place, and the actions of Chancellorsville as a factual framework within which to represent the perplexities of his young hero.[2]

I

Evidence of two sorts makes the initial hypothesis that Crane used Chancellorsville probable. In the first place, Crane said so in his short story "The Veteran," which was published less than a year after *The Red Badge.* In this story he represented an elderly Henry Fleming as telling about his fear and flight in his first battle. "That was at Chancellorsville,"

Henry said. His brief account is consistent in every respect with the more extended account in *The Red Badge*; old Henry's motives for flight were those of the young Henry, and he referred to Jim Conklin in a way which made it clear that Jim was long since dead.

This brief reference in "The Veteran" is, so far as I know, the only direct indication Crane ever gave that the battle in *The Red Badge* was Chancellorsville. He appears never to have mentioned the matter in his letters, and his biographers recount no references to it. Such evidence as that cited above must be used with discretion; Crane might conceivably have changed his mind. But there is no good reason why he should have done so; and in any case, the clue given us by "The Veteran" can be thoroughly corroborated by a second kind of evidence, that of time and place.

No one questions that *The Red Badge* is about the Civil War; the references to Yanks and Johnnies, to blue uniforms on one side and to gray and butternut on the other, clearly establish this fact. If we turn now to military history, we find that the evidence of place and time points directly to Chancellorsville.

Only three actual place-names are used in the book: Washington, Richmond, and the Rappahannock River.[3] Henry Fleming and his fellow-soldiers had come through Washington to their winter quarters near the Rappahannock River, and their army was close enough to Richmond that cavalry could move against that city. Such a combination points to northern Virginia, through which the Rappahannock flows, to which Union soldiers would come through Washington, and from which Richmond would be readily accessible. Chancellorsville was fought in northern Virginia.

Furthermore, the battle was the first major engagement of the year, occurring when the spring rains were nearly over. The year cannot be 1861; the war began in April, and soldiers would not have spent the winter in camp. Nor can it be 1862; the first eastern battle of 1862, part of McClellan's Peninsular Campaign, in no way resembled that in the book and was far removed from the Rappahannock. It cannot be 1864; the Battle of the Wilderness was fought near the Rappahannock but did not end in a Union defeat. Its strategy was in any case significantly different from that of the battle in *The Red Badge*. Finally, 1865 is ruled out; Lee had surrendered by the time the spring rains ended.

If we are to select any actual conflict at all, a *reductio ad absurdum* indicates the first eastern battle of 1863, and that battle was Chancellorsville. Moreover, 1863 marked the turning-point in the Union fortunes; before Gettysburg the South had, as Wilson remarked in *The Red Badge*, licked the North "about every clip." After Gettysburg no Union soldier would have been likely to make such a statement; and Gettysburg was the next major battle after Chancellorsville.

Like the evidence of "The Veteran," the evidence of time and place points to Chancellorsville, and it is therefore at least a tenable hypothesis that Chancellorsville and *The Red Badge* are closely connected. In the next three sections I shall present independent proof of that hypothesis by showing that the battle in Crane's novel is closely and continuously parallel to the historical Chancellorsville.[4]

II

The events preceding the battle occupy the first two chapters and part of the third (pp. 5–21). The opening chapter establishes the situation of the Union army. As winter passed into spring, that army was resting in winter camp across a river from a Confederate army. It had been there for some time—long enough for soldiers to build huts with chimneys, long enough for a new recruit to have been encamped for some months without seeing action. ". . . [T]here had come months of monotonous life in a camp . . . [S]ince his regiment had come to the field the army had done little but sit still and try to keep warm" (p. 10). Such was the situation of the Army of the Potomac in April, 1863; it had spent a cold, wet winter encamped at Falmouth, Virginia, on the north bank of the Rappahannock River opposite the Confederate army. The army had been inactive since mid-December; its men had dug themselves into just such huts, covered with folded tents and furnished with clay chimneys, as Crane describes (pp. 6–7). Furthermore, the arrival of a new Union commander, General Joseph Hooker, had meant hour after hour of drill and review for the soldiers; and Henry was "drilled and drilled and reviewed, and drilled and drilled and reviewed" (p. 10).

To this monotony the "tall soldier"—Jim Conklin—brought the news, "The cavalry started this morning. . . . They say there ain't hardly any cavalry left in camp. They're going to Richmond, or some place, while we fight all the Johnnies. It's some dodge like that" (p. 12). He had earlier announced, "We're goin' t' move t'-morrah—sure. . . . We're goin' 'way up th' river, cut across, an' come around in behint 'em" (p. 5). Of course Jim was "the fast-flying messenger of a mistake," but the mistake was solely one of dates; the infantry did not move at once. Many soldiers at Falmouth jumped to Jim's conclusion when eleven thousand cavalrymen left camp April 13 for a raid on the Confederate railroad lines near Richmond. No one in the book denied that the cavalry had left; and Jim's analysis of the flank movement was to be confirmed at the end of the book when another soldier said, "Didn't I tell yeh we'd come aroun' in behint 'em? Didn't I tell yeh so?" (p. 108). The strategy Jim had predicted was precisely that of Chancellorsville.

The Union army at Falmouth did not leave camp for two weeks after the departure of the cavalry, and such a period accords with the time represented in the book; "for days" after the cavalry left, Henry fretted about whether or not he would run (pp. 13–14).

Finally Henry's regiment, the 304th New York, was assembled, and it began to march before dawn. When the sun rose, "the river was not in view" (p. 16). Since the rising sun was at the backs of the marching men, they were going west. The eager soldiers "expressed commiseration for that part of the army which had been left upon the river bank" (p. 16). That night the regiment encamped; tents were pitched and fires lighted. "When another night came" (p. 20), the men crossed a river on *two* pontoon bridges and continued unmolested to a camping place.

This description fits aptly the march of the Second Corps. Many of its regiments were mustered before dawn on April 28, and then marched west and away from the Rappahannock. The Second, unlike the other corps marching to Chancellorsville, was ordered not to make any special secret of its whereabouts and was allowed fires when it camped. The Second crossed the Rappahannock on *two* pontoon bridges the evening of April 30 and camped safely near Chancellorsville that night; all the other corps had to ford at least one river, without the convenience of bridges. Furthermore, by no means all of the army moved at once; two full corps and one division of the Second Corps were left behind at Falmouth to conduct a holding action against Lee.

It is clear from the text that at least one day intervened between the evening on which Henry's regiment crossed the bridges and the morning of its first day of fighting (pp. 20–21). If Crane was following the chronology of Chancellorsville, this intervening day of pensive rest was May 1, on which only the Fifth and Twelfth Corps saw fighting.

III

Action began early for Henry's regiment the next day, the events of which parallel those at Chancellorsville on May 2. The statements (pp. 21–37) about what Henry and his regiment did are clear enough. He was rudely awakened at dawn, ran down a wood road, and crossed a little stream. His regiment was moved three times before the noon meal, and then moved again; one of these movements took Henry and his companions back, for in the afternoon they proceeded over the same ground they had taken that morning and then into new territory. By early afternoon, then, Henry had seen no fighting. At least a brigade ahead of them went into action; it was routed and fled, leaving the reserves, of which Henry's regiment was a part, to withstand the enemy. The regiment successfully resisted the first charge, but when the enemy re-attacked, Henry fled.

It might seem that tracing the path of Henry and his regiment before his flight would not be impossible, but it has proved to be so. The regimental movements which Crane describes loosely parallel the movements of many regiments at Chancellorsville; they directly parallel the movements of none.[5] Nevertheless, broad parallels do exist. Many regiments of the Second Corps moved southeast from Chancellorsville on May 2; many of them first encountered the enemy in mid afternoon.

Furthermore, it can be demonstrated that the 304th, like the regiments of the Second Corps, was near the center of the Union line. In the first place, the "cheery man" tells Henry, and us, so (p. 62). His testimony deserves some credence; anyone who can so unerringly find a regiment in the dark should know what he is talking about. Moreover, the conversation of the soldiers before the assault (pp. 26–27) makes it clear that they were not facing the rebel right, which would have been opposite the Union left. Nor were they far to the Union right, as I shall show later.

The evidence given us by the terrain Henry crossed also points to a position at about the center of the Union line. During the morning and early afternoon he crossed several streams and passed into and out of cleared fields and dense woods. The land was gently rolling; there were occasional fences and now and then a house. Such topographical features, in 1863, characterized the area south and east of Chancellorsville itself. Further east, in the area held by the Union left, the terrain opened up and the dense second-growth forest thinned out; further west the forest was very thick indeed, with few fields or other open areas. But southeast of Chancellorsville, where the Union center was located, the land was cultivated to a degree; fields had been cleared and cut off from the forest by fences. Topography so conditioned action at Chancellorsville that every historian of the battle perforce described the terrain; if Crane knew the battle as well as I suggest he did, he must have known its topography.

Topography also gives us our only clue to the untraceable path of Henry's flight. At one point he "found himself almost into a swamp. He was obliged to walk upon bog tufts, and watch his feet to keep from the oily mire" (p. 41). A man fleeing from the center of the Union line would have encountered swamps after a few miles of flight. The detail is perhaps minor, but it corroborates the path Henry had to follow to reach the place where he received his "red badge of courage." He went west, toward the Union right held by the Eleventh Corps.

Henry's flight led him to the path of the retreating wounded soldiers, among them Jim Conklin. The scene of Jim's death (pp. 47–51) contains no localizing evidence, for Crane was concentrating upon the men, not their surroundings. Nevertheless, it is appropriate to Chancellorsville; the roads leading to the river were clogged with retreating Union wounded in the late afternoon of May 2. There were no ambulances near the battle lines, and many wounded men died as they walked.

By contrast, the scene of Henry's wound can be readily fixed. He received it in the middle of the most-discussed single action of the battle, an action which cost Stonewall Jackson his life and a major general his command, almost surely won the battle for Lee, and generated thirty-five years of acrimonious debate. Even today, to mention Chancellorsville is inevitably to bring up the rout of the Eleventh Corps.

About sunset on May 2, 1863, Stonewall's crack troops attacked the predominantly German Eleventh Corps. The Eleventh, which was on the extreme right of the Union line and far from the fighting, was taken wholly by surprise, and many soldiers turned and ran in terrified disorder. The result was near-catastrophe for the Union; now that Jackson's men had turned the flank, the path lay open for an assault on the entire unprotected rear of the Union army.

Appropriately enough for such a battle, Jackson's men were halted by one of history's more extraordinary military maneuvers. For in a battle in which hardly any cavalry were used, a small detachment of cavalrymen held Jackson's corps off long enough to enable artillery to be dragged into place and charged with canister. The cavalrymen could do so because the dense woods confined Jackson's men to the road. The small detachment was the Eighth Pennsylvania Cavalry; the time was between 6:30 and 7:00 P.M. Theirs was the only cavalry charge at Chancellorsville, and it became famous not only because it had saved the Union army—perhaps even the Union—but also because no two observers could agree on its details; any historian is therefore obliged to give the charge considerable attention.

All these elements fit the time and place of Henry's wounding. Night was falling fast after his long afternoon of flight; "landmarks had vanished into the gathered gloom" (p. 59). All about Henry "very burly men" were fleeing from the enemy. "They sometimes gabbled insanely. One huge man was asking of the sky, 'Say, where de plank road?' " A popular stereotype holds that all Germans are burly, and an unsympathetic listener could regard rapidly-spoken German as "gabbling." Certainly the replacement of the *th* by *d* fits the pattern of Germans; Crane's Swede in "The Veteran" also lacks *th*. These might be vulgar errors, but they identified a German pretty readily in the heyday of dialect stories. Furthermore, plank roads were rare in northern Virginia; but a plank road ran through the Union lines toward the Rappahannock.

One of these fleeing Germans hit Henry on the head; and after he received his wound, while he was still dazed, Henry saw the arrival of the cavalry and of the artillery:

Around him he could hear the grumble of jolted cannon as the scurrying horses were lashed toward the front. . . . He turned and watched the mass of guns, men, and horses sweeping in a wide curve toward a gap in a fence. . . . Into the unspeakable jumble in the roadway rode a squadron of cavalry. The faded yellow of their facings shone bravely. There was a mighty altercation. (p. 60)

As Henry fled the scene, he could hear the guns fire and the opposing infantry fire back. "There seemed to be a great ruck of men and munitions spread about in the forest and in the fields" (p. 61).

Every element of the scene is consistent with contemporary descriptions of the rout of the Eleventh Corps. The time is appropriate; May 2 was the first real day of battle at Chancellorsville as it was the first day for Henry. The place is appropriate; if Henry had begun the day in the Union center and then had fled west through the swamps, he would have come toward the right of the Union line, where the men of the Eleventh Corps were fleeing in rout. The conclusion is unavoidable: Crane's use of the factual framework of Chancellorsville led him to place his hero in the middle of that battle's most important single action.

The first day of battle in *The Red Badge* ended at last when the cheery man found Henry, dazed and wandering, and led him back to his regiment by complicated and untraceable paths.

IV

The second day of battle, like the first, began early. Henry's regiment was sent out "to relieve a command that had lain long in some damp trenches" (p. 74). From these trenches could be heard the noise of skirmishers in the woods to the front and left, and the din of battle to the right was tremendous. Again such a location fits well enough the notion of a center regiment; the din on the right, in the small hours of May 3, would have come from Jackson's men trying to re-establish their connection with the main body of Lee's army.

Soon, however, Henry's regiment was withdrawn and began to retreat from an exultant enemy; Hooker began such a withdrawal about 7:30 A.M. on May 3. Finally the retreat stopped and almost immediately thereafter Henry's regiment was sent on a suicidal charge designed to prevent the enemy from breaking the Union lines. This charge significantly resembles that of the 124th New York, a regiment raised principally in the county which contains Port Jervis, Crane's hometown; and the time of this charge of the 124th—about 8:30—fits the time-scheme of *The Red Badge* perfectly.[6]

The next episode (pp. 98–101) can be very precisely located; Crane's description is almost photographically accurate. Henry was about a quarter of a mile south of Fairview, the "slope on the left" from which the "long row of guns, gruff and maddened, denounc[ed] the enemy" (p. 99). Moreover, "in the rear of this row of guns stood a house, calm and white, amid bursting shells. A congregation of horses, tied to a railing, were tugging frenziedly at their bridles. Men were running hither and thither" (p. 99). This is a good impression of the Chancellor House, which was used as the commanding general's headquarters and which alone, in a battle at which almost no cavalry were present, had many horses belonging to the officers and orderlies tied near it.

The second charge of the 304th, just before the general retreat was ordered, is as untraceable as the first. It has, however, its parallel at Chancellorsville: several regiments of the Second Corps were ordered to charge the enemy about 10 A.M. on May 3, to give the main body of the army time to withdraw the artillery and to begin its retreat.

The last two days of battle came to an end for Henry Fleming when his regiment was ordered to "retrace its way" and rejoined first its brigade and then its division on the way back toward the river. Such a retreat, in good order and relatively free from harassment by an exhausted enemy, began at Chancellorsville about 10 A.M. on May 3. Heavy rains again were beginning to make the roads into bogs; these rains prevented the Union soldiers from actually recrossing the river for two days, for the water was up to the level of several of the bridges. "It rained" in the penultimate paragraph of *The Red Badge*; and the battle was over for Henry Fleming as for thousands of Union soldiers at Chancellorsville.

V

This long recitation of parallels, I believe, demonstrates that Crane used Chancellorsville as a factual framework for his novel.[7] We have reliable external evidence that Crane studied *Battles and Leaders of the Civil War* in preparation for *The Red Badge* because he was concerned with the accuracy of his novel. He could have found in the ninety pages *Battles and Leaders* devotes to Chancellorsville all the information he needed on strategy, tactics, and topography. A substantial part of these ninety pages is devoted to the rout of the Eleventh Corps and the charge of the Eighth Pennsylvania Cavalry. These pages also contain what someone so visually minded as Crane could have hardly overlooked: numerous illustrations, many from battlefield sketches. The illustrations depict, among other subjects, the huts at Falmouth; men marching in two parallel columns;[8] pontoon bridges; the Chancellor House during and after the battle; and the rout of the Eleventh. With these Crane could have buttressed the unemotional but authoritative reports of Union and Confederate officers which he found in *Battles and Leaders*.

VI

Two questions remain unanswered. First, why did Crane not identify the battle in *The Red Badge* as he did in "The Veteran"? One answer is fairly simple: no one called the battle Chancellorsville in the book because no one would have known it was Chancellorsville. No impression is more powerful to the reader of Civil War reports and memoirs than that officers and men seldom knew where they were. They did not know the names of hills, of streams, or even of villages. Probably not more than a few hundred of the 130,000 Union men at Chancellorsville knew until long afterwards the name of the four corners around which the battle raged. A private soldier knew his own experiences, but not names of strategy; we have been able to reconstruct the strategy and the name because Crane used a factual framework for his novel; and the anonymity of the battle is the result of that framework.

Of course the anonymity is part of Crane's artistic technique as well. We do not learn Henry Fleming's full name until Chapter 11; we never learn Wilson's first name. Crane sought to give only so much detail as was necessary to the integrity of the book. He was not, like Zola or Tolstoi, concerned with the panorama of history and the fate of nations, but with the mind and actions of a youth unaccustomed to war. For such purposes, the name of the battle, like the names of men, did not matter; in fact, if Crane had named the battle he might have evoked in the minds of his readers reactions irrelevant to his purpose, reactions which might have set the battle in its larger social and historical framework. It would have been a loss of control.

Why, with the whole Civil War available, should Crane have chosen Chancellorsville? Surely, in the first place, because he knew a good deal about it. Perhaps he learned it from his brother, "an expert in the strategy of Gettysburg and Chancellorsville." (Thomas Beer, *Stephen Crane*, p. 47) More probably he had heard old soldiers talk about their war experiences while he was growing up. Many middle-aged men in Port Jervis had served in the 124th New York; Chancellorsville had been their first battle, and first impressions are likely to be the most vivid. It is hard to believe that men in an isolated small town could have resisted telling a hero-worshipping small boy about a great adventure in their lives.

Moreover, Chancellorsville surely appealed to Crane's sense of the ironic and the colorful. The battle's great charges, its moments of heroism, went only to salvage a losing cause; the South lost the war and gained only time from Chancellorsville; the North, through an incredible series of blunders, lost a battle it had no business losing. The dead, as always, lost the most. And when the battle ended, North and South were just where they had been when it began. There is a tragic futility about Chancellorsville just as there is a tragic futility to *The Red Badge*.

Finally, Chancellorsville served Crane's artistic purposes. It was the first battle of the year and the first battle for many regiments. It was therefore an appropriate introduction to war for a green soldier in an untried regiment.

The evidence of this study surely indicates that Crane was not merely a dreamer spinning fantasies out of his imagination; on the contrary, he was capable of using real events for his own fictional purposes with controlled sureness. Knowledge of the ways in which he did so is, I should think, useful to criticism. For various cogent reasons, Crane chose Chancellorsville as a factual framework within which to represent the dilemma of young Henry Fleming. Many details of the novel are clearly drawn from that battle; none are inconsistent with it. Old Henry Fleming was a truthful man: "that was at Chancellorsville."

NOTES

1. Lyndon Upson Pratt in "A Possible Source for The Red Badge of Courage," *American Literature*, XL, 1–10 (March, 1939), suggests that the battle is partially based upon Antietam. Lars Ahnebrink denies his arguments and favors elements from Tolstoi and Zola in *The Beginnings of Naturalism in American Fiction*, "Upsala Essays and Studies in American Language and Literature," IX (Upsala, 1950). Both argue from a handful of parallel incidents of the sort which seem to me the common property of any war; neither makes any pretense of accounting for all the realistic framework of the novel.

2. This study developed from a class project in English 208 at the University of California (Berkeley) in the spring of 1958 and 1959. I am grateful to those who worked with Crane in these courses, and I am particularly grateful to George R. Stewart, who was unfailingly helpful to me in many ways and to whose scholarly acumen and knowledge of the Civil War I am deeply indebted.

3. For Washington, see p. 10; for Richmond, p. 12; for the Rappahannock, p. 75. Henry's reference to the Rappahannock may be an ironic twist on a journalist's cliché, but the twist itself—the original was Potomac—seems to me to be the result of conscious intent on Crane's part.

4. The literature on Chancellorsville is substantial. The most useful short study is Edward J. Stackpole, *Chancellorsville: Lee's Greatest Battle* (Harrisburg, Pa., 1958). The definitive analysis is John Bigelow, Jr.'s, *The Campaign of Chancellorsville: A Strategic and Tactical Study* (New Haven, 1910). Orders, correspondence, and reports are available in *The War of the Rebellion: A Compilation of the Official Records of the Union and*

Confederate Armies, ser. 1, vol. XXV, parts 1 and 2 (Washington, D.C., 1880). See also *Battles and Leaders of the Civil War* (New York, 1884), III, 152–243. The parallels presented below are drawn from these; all are in substantial agreement.

5. So flat a statement deserves explanation. I have read with great care all of the 307 reports of unit commanders in the *Official Records*. I have also studied more than a dozen histories of regiments which first saw action at Chancellorsville. Many show general parallels; none show parallels with the novel which I consider close enough to be satisfactory.

6. See Cornelius Weygandt, *History of the 124th New York* (Newburgh, N.Y., 1877).

7. Thomas Beer, *Stephen Crane* (New York, 1923), pp. 97–98. Corwin Knapp Linson, *My Stephen Crane*, ed. Edwin H. Cady (Syracuse, 1959), pp. 37–38, corroborates Beer's account.

8. Here the illustration seems to explain the otherwise inexplicable description in the novel (p. 16); Civil War soldiers rarely marched thus.

LOSSES AT CHANCELLORSVILLE:
ABNER DOUBLEDAY

Abner Doubleday, a general in the Union army (and often credited with being the inventor of the game of baseball), compiled statistics on the Battle of Chancellorsville in his history published in 1882. Doubleday indicates that his numbers are from official reports but warns readers that he has reason to believe the Confederate losses are "far from being accurate." The general assumption is that the Confederate losses were equal to those of the Union. In any case, his figures give an idea of the magnitude of the battle's destruction. Note that in the 11th Corps, where desertion was widespread, the "missing" far exceeds the dead and wounded, unlike the usual pattern.

FROM ABNER DOUBLEDAY, *CHANCELLORSVILLE AND GETTYSBURG*
(New York: Charles Scribner's Sons, 1882, p. 71)

Losses at Chancellorsville

	Union		
	Killed & Wounded	Missing	Total
First Corps (Reynolds)	192	100	292
Second Corps (Couch)	1,525	500	2,025
Third Corps (Sickle)	3,439	600	4,039
Fifth Corps (Meade)	399	300	699
Sixth Corps (Sedgwick)	3,601	1,000	4,601
Eleventh Corps (Howard)	508	2,000	2,508
Twelfth Corps (Slocum)	2,383	500	2,883
Cavalry	150		150
Total	12,197	5,000	17,197
	Confederate		
	10,266	2,753	13,019

CHARGES OF HOOKER'S INCOMPETENCE

In his great anxiety his heart was continually clamoring at what he considered the intolerable slowness of the generals. (12)

They were marched from place to place with apparent aimlessness. . . . He considered that there was denoted a lack of purpose on the part of the generals. . . . When, however, they began to pass into a new region, his old fears of stupidity and incompetence reassailed him. (24, 25)

Tales of hesitation and uncertainty on the part of those high in place and responsibility came to their ears. (87)

COLONEL P. H. DALBIAC

From the time of their encampment, the men in Henry's outfit are convinced that their officers do not know what they are doing and that they will lose the battle because the soldiers are kept sitting around without engaging the enemy. They are eager, they say, to get underway, to begin fighting. The historical record suggests that their complaints may have been founded on substance rather than solely on their naive boredom with camp life and bravado. Hooker, the general in command of the Army of the Potomac, was accused of dooming the Union army from the outset by withdrawing to Chancellorsville and refusing to move eastward on the offensive. Colonel P. H. Dalbiac, a soldier and military historian, was convinced of widespread incompetence on the part of officers in the Civil War and especially on the part of General Hooker, who oversaw operations in the Battle of Chancellorsville. In his words:

In the study of no other war, probably, can we find so many extremes of military capacity and incapacity, so many examples of strategic possibilities and impossibilities, or such a catalogue of tactical blunders as in the war which devastated the Eastern States of North America for a period of four years. (71)

FROM COLONEL P. H. DALBIAC, *THE AMERICAN WAR OF
SECESSION 1863: CHANCELLORSVILLE AND GETTYSBURG*
(London: Ruskin House, 1911, pp. 53–66)

It seems almost incomprehensible that any general with such over-
whelming numerical superiority, and with everything in his favour up to
a certain point, could have eventually so signally failed. And yet it
was so.

The halt at Chancellorsville was the first step in his [Hooker's] down-
ward course. Had the march been continued for even one hour, or at
worst resumed at daylight, his army would have got well clear of the
tangled vastness of the Wilderness without meeting any formidable opposition; and once clear would have been in a position where its great
superiority of numbers must have told. No doubt the scantiness of his
information went far towards compelling a halt—his initial error coming
home to roost for the first time—but, whether this were so or not, it is
hard to imagine the frame of mind which would preclude a commander
from hastening on to get clear of such a place as the Wilderness, where
maneuvering was well-nigh impossible, when excellent ground for the
development of his full strength lay within two miles of him. Had his
troops been tired some valid excuse might be urged; but this was not so,
and his decision is, therefore, the more inexplicable.

One of the most prominent features which must strike the student was
the absolute failure of Hooker to bring about any co-operation between
the two wings of his army, separated as they were by not more than a
day's march. Staff work was never the strong point in either of the armies
during the war; but the arrangements made by Hooker's staff must have
been even more execrable than usual, in this history of indifferent staff
work, to have produced such an absolute want to co-operation as occurred on this occasion.

There have been other Hookers, and many a campaign has been frit-
tered away by generals who have allowed themselves to be led away from
their original purpose by minor events; and whose power of decision,
like Hooker's has been inadequate to meet at once a change of plans
necessitated by unexpected developments on the part of the enemy.

MAJOR-GENERAL DARIUS N. COUCH

One charge against Hooker came from one of the generals serving under him at Chancellorsville. Major-General Couch remembers the confusion and disbelief of the officers under Hooker when they are told to withdraw back to Chancellorsville. He also expresses his belief that Hooker, despite his superior forces, had been "out-generaled" by Robert E. Lee, the commander of the Confederate forces.

The accounts of Couch and other military men are contained in *Battles and Leaders of the Civil War*, which Hungerford believes Stephen Crane read before writing *The Red Badge of Courage*.

FROM MAJOR-GENERAL DARIUS N. COUCH, "THE
CHANCELLORSVILLE CAMPAIGN," IN *BATTLES AND LEADERS OF
THE CIVIL WAR*
(New York: Century Co., 1884, pp. 154–171)

Shortly after Hancock's troops had got into a line in front, an order was received from the commanding general "to withdraw both divisions to Chancellorsville." Turning to the officers around me, Hancock, Sykes, Warren, and others, I told them what the order was, upon which they all agreed with me that the ground should not be abandoned, because of the open country in front and the commanding position. An aide, Major J. B. Burt, dispatched to General Hooker to this effect, came back in half an hour with positive orders to return. Nothing was to be done but carry out the command, though Warren suggested that I should disobey, and then he rode back to see the general. In the meantime Slocum, on the Plank road to my right, had been ordered in, and the enemy's advance was between that road and my right flank. Sykes was first to move back, then followed by Hancock's regiments over the same road. When all but two of the latter had withdrawn, a third order came to me, brought by one of the general's staff: "Hold on until 5 o'clock." It was then perhaps 2 P.M. Disgusted at the general's vacillation and vexed at receiving an order of such tenor, I replied with warmth unbecoming in a subordinate: "Tell General Hooker he is too late, the enemy are already on my right and rear. I am in full retreat."

• • •

Proceeding to the Chancellor House, I narrated my operations in front to Hooker, which were seemingly satisfactory, as he said: "It is all right,

Couch, I have got Lee just where I want him; he must fight me on my own ground." The retrograde movement had prepared me for something of the kind, but to hear from his own lips that the advantages gained by the successful marches of his lieutenants were to culminate in fighting a defensive battle in that nest of thickets was too much, and I retired from his presence with the belief that my commanding general was a whipped man.

• • •

In looking for the causes of the loss of Chancellorsville, the primary ones were that Hooker expected Lee to fall back without risking battle. Finding himself mistaken he assumed the defensive, and was outgeneraled and became demoralized by the superior tactical boldness of the enemy.

MAJOR-GENERAL ALFRED PLEASONTON

General Pleasonton was one of the primary figures in the Battle of Chancellorsville. In criticizing his commander, General Hooker, Pleasonton tells of stumbling on important intelligence about the Confederates' plan when the diary of a Confederate engineer and officer, whom he had taken prisoner, fell into his hands. The diary made clear that the Confederates knew and had prepared for the fact that the first battle in May would be at Chancellorsville. Pleasonton rushes to get this information to Hooker, expecting that the general will move the forces eastward, out of the terrible wooded terrain in which it would be disastrous for the Union army to try to do battle. Always, he, like the soldiers in *The Red Badge of Courage*, seems to be aware that he is operating in utter confusion.

FROM MAJOR-GENERAL ALFRED PLEASONTON, "THE
SUCCESSES AND FAILURES OF CHANCELLORSVILLE," IN
BATTLES AND LEADERS OF THE CIVIL WAR
(New York: Century Co., 1884, pp. 172–182)

At 2 o'clock P.M. . . . I reported to General Hooker at Chancellorsville, and submitted to him the diary and General Lee's dispatch, both of which he retained, and I suggested that we had evidently surprised General Lee by our rapid movements across the river, and, as Lee had prepared for a battle at Chancellorsville, we had better anticipate him by moving on toward Fredericksburg. A march of three or four miles would take us out of the woods into a more open country, where we could form our line of battle, and where our artillery could be used to advantage; we would then be prepared to move on Fredericksburg in the morning.

• • •

I was much surprised to find that General Hooker, who up to that time had been all vigor, energy, and activity, received the suggestion as a matter of secondary importance, and that he considered the next morning sufficiently early to move on Fredericksburg. Up to that time General Hooker's strategy had been all that could have been desired. He had outflanked the enemy and had surprised him by the rapidity of his movements. At 2 o'clock P.M., on the 30th of April, General Hooker had ninety chances in his favor to ten against him. . . . General Hooker had it in his power at that time to have crushed Lee's army and wound up the war. The Army of the Potomac never had a better opportunity, for more than half its work had been done before a blow had been struck, by the brilliancy of its strategy in moving upon Chancellorsville.

I camped my command about a mile from General Hooker's headquarters, which were at the Chancellor House, and such were my misgivings as regarded the situation of the army that about dusk I called upon the general again and stated to him our perilous position.

To the east, toward Fredericksburg, the woods were thick for three or four miles; to the south, toward Spotsylvania Court House, the woods extended about the same distance; to the west, from Hazel Grove, the same condition of things existed; while the country between Chancellorsville and the Rappahannock River, in our rear, was rough, broken, and not at all suitable for the operations required of an army. The position of the army at Chancellorsville extended about three miles from east and west in the narrow clearings, which did not afford sufficient ground to maneuver an army of the size of the Army of the Potomac. Besides this, we were ignorant of what might be going on outside of this cordon of woods, and were giving the enemy every opportunity to take us at a disadvantage. Every instinct induced me to suggest to General Hooker, to relieve ourselves from our embarrassments, to send the Eleventh Corps, which was in a miserable position in the woods, down to Spotsylvania Court House by the Jack Shop road.

HOOKER'S DEFENSE AGAINST CHARGES OF INCOMPETENCE

In October 1876, Samuel P. Bates, General Hooker's literary executor, took a trip with Hooker to the area where the Battle of

Chancellorsville had taken place. Bates, who recorded Hooker's comments about the battle, quotes Hooker's defense of failing to move rapidly against the enemy on the first day of the battle when it would have been to his advantage to do so, and his defense of ordering the entire army to retreat across the Rappahannock on May 5. Hooker contends that much of the criticism he received may have come from professional jealousy on the part of General Burnside, the military man he replaced as commander of the Army of the Potomac.

FROM SAMUEL P. BATES, "HOOKER'S COMMENTS ON CHANCELLORSVILLE," IN *BATTLES AND LEADERS OF THE CIVIL WAR*
(New York: Century Co., 1884, pp. 215–223)

Upon our arrival at the broad, open, rolling fields opposite Bank's Ford, some three or four miles up the stream, General Hooker exclaimed, waving his hand significantly: "Here, on this open ground, I intended to fight my battle. . . . But at midnight General Lee had moved out with his whole army, and by sunrise was in firm possession of Bank's Ford, had thrown up this line of breastwork which you can still follow with the eye, and it was bristling with cannon from one end to the other. Before I had proceeded two miles the heads of my columns, while still upon the narrow roads in these interminable forests, where it was impossible to maneuver my forces, were met by Jackson with a full two-thirds of the entire Confederate army. I had no alternative but to turn back, as I had only a fragment of my command in hand, and take up the position about Chancellorsville which I had occupied during the night, as I was being rapidly outflanked upon my right, the enemy having open ground on which to operate.

"And here again my reputation has been attacked because I did not undertake to accomplish an impossibility, but turned back at this point; and every history of the war that has been written has soundly berated me because I did not fight here in the forest with my hands tied behind me, and allow my army to be sacrificed. I have always believed that impartial history would vindicate my conduct in this emergency."

• • •

[On his retreat on May 5, ending the battle] I ventured to ask him why he did not attack when he found that the enemy had weakened his forces in the immediate front and sent them away to meet Sedgwick. "That," said he, "would seem to have been the reasonable thing to do. But we were in this impenetrable thicket. All the roads and openings leading through it the enemy immediately fortified strongly, and planted thickly his artillery commanding all the avenues, so that with reduced numbers he could easily hold his lines, shutting me in, and it became utterly impossible to maneuver my forces. My army was not beaten. Only a part of it had been engaged. The First Corps, Reynolds, whom I regarded as the ablest officer under me, was fresh and ready and eager to be brought into action, as was my whole army. But I had been fully convinced of the futility of attacking fortified positions, and I was determined not to sacrifice my men needlessly, though it should be at the expense of my reputation as a fighting officer. . . . Accordingly, when the eight days' rations with which my army started out were exhausted, I retired across the river.

SACRIFICE AT HAZEL GROVE: JOHNSON, HUEY, AND WELLS

"What troops can you spare?" . . .
   "But there's th' 304th. They fight like a lot 'a mule drivers.
I can spare them best of any." . . .
   "Get 'em ready, then. . . . It'll happen in five minutes. . . . I
don't believe any of you mule drivers will get back."
   The other shouted something in reply. He smiled. (99)

When Henry Fleming and his friend go into the woods to fill
some canteens, they see and hear an encounter between a general
and another officer under his command. They are shocked to hear
themselves referred to derisively as mule drivers and to learn that,
because they are expendable, they are, in five minutes, going to
be sacrificed in a mission to give the general some time. It is un-
likely, he says, that any of them will come back alive. The circumstances surrounding the battle that Henry Fleming and his
comrades go into subsequently bear some resemblance to the battle led by Major Keenan following the disastrous skirmish at the
Plank Road led by General Howard. When this is over, the army
needed time to put cannon and other armaments in place at key
points in the Chancellorsville area. To do this, the attention of
General Stonewall Jackson's Confederates needed to be diverted
before another enemy attack, so General Sickle asked General Pleasonton, under his command, to order Major Peter Keenan of the
8th Pennsylvania Cavalry to charge into the woods, on what all
concerned knew to be a suicide mission. According to most accounts, Major Keenan readily and willingly agreed, and he was
mowed down with most of his men, one historian saying it was
like throwing an innocent lamb to a pack of wolves. A folklore grew
up about the meeting when General Pleasonton ordered Keenan
and his 400 men immediately to charge 10,000 Confederates.
Keenan reportedly responded cheerfully, "It is the same as saying
we must be killed, but we'll do it." As an abuse of humanity, it
was detestable; as a military maneuver, it was successful. The army
at large was given time to prepare, and the Confederates withdrew,
believing from the heroic fighting of the sacrificed outfit that

thousands more Union men were charging them. Three accounts of the event follow: one by a historian, one by a general, one by a captain.

FROM ROSSITER JOHNSON, *THE STORY OF A GREAT CONFLICT*
(New York: Bryan, Taylor and Co., 1894, p. 245)

Howard's corps was doubled up, thrown into confusion, and completely routed. The enemy was coming on exultingly, when General Sickles sent General Alfred Pleasonton with two regiments of cavalry and a battery to occupy an advantageous position at Hazel Grove, which was the key-point of this part of the battlefield. Pleasonton arrived just in time to see that the Confederates were making toward the same point and were likely to secure it. There was but one way to save the army, and Pleasonton quickly comprehended it. He ordered Major Peter Keenan, with the 8th Pennsylvania cavalry regiment, about four hundred strong, to charge immediately upon the ten thousand Confederate infantry. "It is the same as saying we must be killed," said Keenan, "but we'll do it." This charge, in which Keenan and most of his command were slain, astonished the enemy and stopped their onset, for they believed there must be some more formidable force behind it. In the precious minutes thus gained, Pleasonton brought together twenty-two guns, loaded them with double charges of canister, and had them depressed enough to make the shot strike the ground half-way between his own line and the edge of the woods where the enemy must emerge.

FROM GENERAL PENNOCK HUEY, "THE CHARGE OF THE EIGHTH PENNSYLVANIA CAVALRY," IN *BATTLES AND LEADERS OF THE CIVIL WAR*
(New York: Century Co., 1884, p. 186)

From the information I had received from General Pleasonton, and from hearing the aide make his report before I started, I had no idea that we would meet the enemy till after I had reported to General Howard. Therefore the surprise was as great to us as to the enemy, as we were entirely unprepared, our sabers being in their scabbards. When we arrived almost at the Plank road, we discovered that we had ridden right into the enemy, them in great force, and that we were completely surrounded, the woods at that point being filled with flankers of Jackson's column, who were thoroughly hidden from our view by the thick undergrowth. It was here that I gave the command to "draw sabers and charge," which order was repeated by Major Keenan and other officers. The charge was led by the five officers already named, who were riding at the head of the regiment when we left Hazel Grove. On reaching the Plank road it appeared to be packed about as closely with the enemy as it possibly could be. . . . Three . . . officers fel at the same time and from the same volley, Major Keenan falling against me and lighting on the ground under my horse. A few days afterward his body was found near the spot where he had fallen.

FROM CAPTAIN ANDREW B. WELLS, "THE CHARGE OF THE EIGHTH PENNSYLVANIA CAVALRY," IN *BATTLES AND LEADERS OF THE CIVIL WAR*
(New York: Century Co., 1884, pp. 187–188)

Our regiment on the second day of May, 1863, was waiting orders in a clearing of wooded country called Hazel Grove. We had been there some little time. Everything was quiet on the front. The men were gathered in groups, chatting and smoking, and the officers were occupied in much the same manner, wondering what would turn up next.

About 4 o'clock I suggested a game of draw poker. An empty cracker-box with a blanket thrown over it, served as a card-table. The party playing, if I mistake not, was composed of Major Keenan, Adjutant Haddock, Captain Goddard, Lieutenant W. A. Daily, and myself. We had been playing about two hours—the game was a big one and we were all absorbed in it—when, about 6 P.M., it was brought to an abrupt end by the appearance of a mounted officer. Riding up to where we were playing, he asked in an excited manner; "Who is in command of this regiment?" Major Keenan, who was seated beside me, turned his head and said, in a joking way: "I am; what's the trouble?" Our visitor replied: "General Howard wants a cavalry regiment." And before we had time to ask further questions, he was off, and the next moment we were all on our feet, and our game was ended. I remember it perfectly well, for I was out of pocket on the play. The regiment was mounted, I mounting at the same time and alongside of Major Keenan. We then moved out of Hazel Grove by twos.

• • •

We or the second squadron knew that our time was at hand, and Captain Corrie gave the order to draw sabers and charge. Taking a trot, we found that the road took a bend as we proceeded. When we turned the corner of the wood-road a sight met our eyes that it is impossible for me to describe. After charging over the dead men and horses of the first squadron we charged into Jackson's column, and, as luck would have it, found them with empty guns—thanks to our poor comrades ahead. The enemy were as thick as bees, and we appeared to be among thousands of them in an instant.

After we reached the Plank road we were in columns of fours and on the dead run, and when we struck the enemy there occurred a "jam" of living and dead men, friends and enemies, and horses, and the weight of the rear of our squadron broke us into utter confusion, so that at the moment every man was for himself.

Can any man who was a soldier for one moment imagine an officer deliberately planning a charge by a regiment of cavalry, strung out by twos in a column half a mile long in a thick wood?

GEORGE PARSONS LATHROP, "KEENAN'S CHARGE"

In 1863, one year after the Union defeat at the Battle of Chancellorsville, George Parsons Lathrop wrote a poem honoring Major Peter Keenan, the commanding officer of the regiment, who was killed in the battle and became a martyr in the eyes of those who supported the Union. "You must charge into those woods with your regiment, and hold the Rebels until I can get some of these guns into position. You must do it at whatever cost." Supposedly Keenan replied simply, "I will," and charged 10,000 Confederates with a mere 400 men. They were what has come to be known as "cannon fodder," sent out with the acknowledged purpose of being killed. Keenan and almost all of his men were slaughtered. One soldier and historian of the battle, Captain Willard Glazier, in reinforcing the martyrdom of Keenan, uses a horrible image: he compares Keenan and his company to "a trembling lamb" who is thrown to a pack of wolves to divert them. Note other words that have religious overtones: *martyr, baptized, blood, precious sacrifice, lamb:*

> The forlorn charge was made, but the martyr-leader, with the majority of his dauntless troopers, soon baptized the earth upon which he fell, with his life blood. But the precious sacrifice was not in vain. The Rebel advance was greatly checked, as when a trembling lamb is thrown into the jaws of a pursuing pack of ravenous wolves. (*Battles for the Union*, 239)

GEORGE PARSONS LATHROP, "KEENAN'S CHARGE" (1863)

> By the shrouded gleam of the western skies,
> Brave Keenan looked in Pleasonton's eyes
> For an instant—clear, and cool, and still;
> Then, with a smile, he said: "I will."
>
> "Cavalry, charge!" Not a man of them shrank.
> Their sharp, full cheer, from rank on rank,

Rose joyously, with a willing breath—
Rose like a greeting hail to death.
Then forward they sprang, and spurred and clashed;
Shouted the officers, crimson-sashed;
Rode well the men, each brave as his fellow,
In their faded coats of the blue and yellow;
And above in the air, with an instinct true,
Like a bird of war their pennon flew.

With clank of scabbards and thunder of steeds,
And blades that shine like sunlit reeds,
And strong brown faces bravely pale
For fear their proud attempt shall fail,
Three hundred Pennsylvanians close
On twice ten thousand gallant foes.

Line after line the troopers came
To the edge of the wood that was ringed with flame;
Rode in and sabred and shot—and fell;
Nor came one back his wounds to tell.
And full in the midst rose Keenan, tall
In the gloom, like a martyr awaiting his fall,
While the circle-stroke of his sabre, swung
'Round his head, like a halo there, luminous hung.

Line after line; ay, whole platoons,
Struck dead in their saddles, of brave dragoons
By the maddened horses were onward borne
And into the vortex flung, trampled and torn;
As Keenan fought with his men, side by side.

So they rode, till there were no more to ride.

But over them, lying there, shattered and mute,
What deep echo rolls?—It's a death-salute
From the cannon in place; for heroes, you braved
Your fate not in vain: the army was saved!

Over them now—year following year—
Over the graves the pine-cones fall,
And the whip-poor-will chants his spectre-call;
And they stir not again: they raise no cheer;

They have ceased. But their glory shall never cease,
Nor their light be quenched in the light of peace.
The rush of their charge is resounding still
That saved the army at Chancellorsville.

TOPICS FOR ORAL AND WRITTEN EXPLORATION

1. Carefully note the features of the landscape that Henry encounters. Compare it with what is written of the landscape here in this chapter. Be more exact, with hypothetical examples, about the disadvantages of fighting in such a landscape. Find out about the terrain in which most of the Vietnam War was fought, and do a comparison.

2. Note carefully every reference to and description of officers in the novel. Can you discern Crane's attitude from this? When the men are being critical of officers, is Crane agreeing with their opinions or satirizing them? Explain your answer.

3. Note the similarities between the words exchanged between the officers in the novel when men are being ordered on the suicide mission and the words exchanged between Pleasonton and Keenan.

4. After studying the Battle of Chancellorsville further, hold a mock investigation into General Hooker's conduct of the battle. Did he deserve to be censured, or was he the victim of professional jealousy?

5. Conduct a similar investigation into the conduct of General Howard.

6. In the Battle of Chancellorsville, both officers and men were often left in a state of confusion about what other regiments were doing and what they would be doing next and where they were physically. Follow the theme of confusion in *The Red Badge of Courage*.

7. The real suicide mission at Chancellorsville was conducted on horseback, by cavalry. The one in the novel was conducted by men on foot. How does this change things?

8. Define myth. How has Lathrop turned the war into myth? Hasn't Crane done the same thing? Show how.

9. Note the religious overtones in Lathrop's poem and in the description of Jim Conklin's death. Why has war assumed religious meaning for Crane?

SUGGESTED READINGS

Catton, Bruce. *The Civil War*. Boston: Houghton Mifflin, 1960.
———. *This Hallowed Ground*. Garden City, N.Y.: Doubleday, 1956.
Furguson, Ernest B. *Chancellorsville 1983*. New York: Alfred A. Knopf, 1992.
Griffith, Paddy. *Battle Tactics of the Civil War*. New Haven: Yale University Press, 1989.
Luvaas, Jay, and Harold W. Nelson, eds. *The U.S. Army War College Guide*

to the Battles of Chancellorsville and Fredericksburg. Carlisle, Penn.: South Mountain Press, 1988.

McPherson, James M. *Battle Cry of Freedom: The Civil War Era*. New York: Oxford University Press, 1988.

Nelson, H. A. *The Battles of Chancellorsville and Gettysburg*. Minneapolis: n.p., 1909.

Webb, Willard, ed. *Crucial Moments of the Civil War*. New York: Bonanza, 1961.

Williams, T. H. *Lincoln and His Generals*. New York: Alfred A. Knopf, 1952.

Desertion in *The Red Badge of Courage*

He ran like a rabbit. (37)

The major theme of *The Red Badge of Courage* is Henry Fleming's fear and desertion and his way of dealing with his actions. The terms *cowardice* and *desertion* are used unambiguously in connection with the battlefield, cowardice being the lack of courage in the face of danger and desertion being the abandonment of a duty or a person to which one has a moral obligation. Although the terms are not synonymous (a parent, for example, can desert a child without experiencing the fear usually associated with cowardice), cowardice and desertion are frequently related, as in Henry Fleming's case, when his cowardice results in desertion.

After agonizing about how he will react, Henry remains steadfast at his post in his first experience under fire. However, only a few minutes afterward, flush with self-congratulation and relaxing and chatting with other soldiers, he hears someone yell, "Here they come a'gin! Here they come a'gin!" (38), and at the same time he hears someone else yell, "Why can't somebody send us supports?" (38). The enemy has attacked again. He picks up his rifle and fires into what seems a mob of insane imps rushing toward him. Then the man next to him "suddenly dropped [his rifle] and ran with howls." Instantaneously, Henry also throws down his gun and runs. "There was no shame in his face. He ran like a rabbit" (35). And so Henry commits his first act of cowardice by deserting his post at the front lines under fire.

The idea of cowardice and desertion in the face of fire connects *The Red Badge of Courage* decisively with the Battle of Chancellorsville. The following discussion moves from the specific to the general, beginning with a particular skirmish during the battle at Chancellorsville, analogous to one in *The Red Badge of Courage*, then to the subject of desertion throughout the Civil War, and ending with a discussion of desertion and cowardice in general.

DESERTION AT THE PLANK ROAD, BATTLE OF CHANCELLORSVILLE

At no other time in the Civil War was the threat of desertion so widespread in the Army of the Potomac as it was in the winter before the Battle of Chancellorsville. The temper of the men and the threat of desertion from camp (from rebellion rather than cowardice) was the chief topic of concern in and around the Union capital in December and January. The low morale and the unruly and insurgent spirit of the men were attributable to a number of conditions, notably the losses at Fredericksburg, Virginia, and the loss of all confidence in their military leadership, especially that of General Ambrose Burnside. The fact that the men had not been paid and lacked any real discipline, much less direction, or knowledge of what was happening with the war added to the despondency.

The army at this time was described as being ravaged by desertion. Every day hundreds of soldiers left and went back home. Theoretically the army that General Joseph Hooker took over in late January had 256,545 soldiers, but more than 85,000 officers and enlisted men had been away without leave, many of them never intending to return. To drive home the point of the seriousness of desertions, one has only to consider that four days after Hooker assumed command from Burnside, the army's morning report showed only 147,184 men present (out of 256,545). Among the force that Hooker had to invade Confederate territory across the Rappahannock were 30,000 short-timers (men who had enlisted for two years' time, and some for only three months) whose time would be up in May and who would be able to go home, and they were understandably interested in staying alive on the eve of their exit from the army.

One soldier, James Coburn, speculated in his diary at the end of January that if something were not done soon, all the soldiers would leave and go home. Their temper, he notes, is shown in the frequency of drunkenness. So many were drunk all the time that one could scarcely find enough for picket duty, both enlisted men and high-ranking officers often so drunk that they fell in the mud.

Captain A. H. Nelson of the 57th Pennsylvania Volunteers, in 1863 a young uncommissioned soldier, gives his version of the mood of the men on the Potomac who soon would be ordered toward Chancellorsville:

> When General Hooker took command, I repeat, the outlook for ever putting down the rebellion was indeed gloomy. This feeling was pretty general throughout the whole army. It was no uncommon thing to hear, as you were passing the camps, soldiers using the most insurrectionary language. One day as I was passing through a strange camp, about Feb. 16, 1863, I heard men cursing the President and the commanding generals, and boasted that they intended to desert the first opportunity. The officers standing by did not attempt to rebuke them. This, in view of the fact that we were soon to meet the enemy again in battle, I must confess, made me feel very serious. (*The Battles of Chancellorsville and Gettysburg* [Minneapolis: n.p., 1909])

In spite of or because of the large numbers of desertions, the punishment for desertion was random but extremely severe. In one case (quoted by Ernest B. Furguson from an unknown soldier's account in January 1863), a deserter's public punishment was especially severe: his head was shaven and his trousers pulled down so that he could be branded with a red-hot iron on the buttocks. A group of men with drawn bayonets were ordered to follow him to the tune of the "Rogue's March."

Desertion was so serious that Hooker instituted many new policies for dealing with the problem—some positive, as, for example, the awarding of furloughs. But some of his measures were severe, as in his orders for more diligence in arresting deserters and even execution by firing squad of several deserters (even though they were at the time not in combat situations) as lessons to the other men. Hooker also ordered the interception of packages from home, which often contained letters urging desertion.

This was the mood and the attitude regarding desertion as General Hooker took his army across the Rappahannock in late April to engage the Confederate army in what would come to be known as the Battle of Chancellorsville. The skirmish that, because of questionable military decisions and mass desertions, became so controversial in the annals of the Civil War began late in the evening on May 2, one day after the actual fighting had begun. Late in the day, in an area west of the Chancellors House where Hooker had his headquarters, General Oliver Howard was in charge of a two-mile line going from east to west, along what was known as the Plank Road. Stretched along the road were the forces of Generals von Gilza, McLean, Devens, Schurz, and Steinwehr, all subordinate to Howard. It was reported later that General Howard in various ways had ignored every ominous sign of impending attack, including a directive from General Hooker, so his generals had ordered the men under them to stack their rifles and prepare for a relaxed evening of supper, song, and sleep. Meanwhile, to the west, in a one-mile line running north to south on either side of the turnpike, Confederate General Stonewall Jackson was planning an attack. The first indication that something out of the ordinary was afoot came when into the Union camp of soldiers singing and preparing their meals came one and then another and then another wild animal. Before the men could figure out that the animals were being driven ahead of an attacking Confederate army, shells began bursting over the encampment, and the men heard the frightening sounds of Confederate soldiers charging them in unrelenting fury. Union soldiers could not even get to their rifles, and general chaos and confusion reigned in every part of the camps. When the Union officers were able to analyze their positions, they found that the Confederates were approaching not just on one flank but on two, making any sort of maneuvering almost impossible. Under these difficult circumstances, officers and enlisted men in both front and support lines began to flee in mass. For example, men in the 17th Connecticut began fleeing from their position even before Major Allen G. Brady gave the orders to retreat through the woods. Brady said later that no man in his command even once fired his gun. General von Gilza later said that his own men in the front lines fought as long as was humanly possible before falling back to what they thought would be support farther behind them, only to find that both men and officers in those less exposed positions had fled. He wrote:

> Retreating, I expected surely to rally my brigade behind our second line, formed by [General Schurz's] Division, but I did not find the second line; it was abandoned before we reached it.
>
> I am obliged to express my thanks to the men of my brigade, with very few exceptions, for the bravery and coolness which they have shown in repulsing three attacks, and they retreated only after being attacked in front and from the rear at the same time; but I am also compelled to blame most of my line officers that they did not or could not rally their companies half a mile or a mile more back, no matter if it could be done under the protection of a second line, and I hope that in the next engagement every officer and man of my brigade will try to redeem this unsoldierlike conduct. (*War of the Rebellion*, Official Records, 25 pt. 1, 636)

Some, including Generals Howard and MacClean, described a rush of fugitives—a mass of men furiously running for their lives. Howard, on his horse, and a few other officers tried to stop the masses of his men from retreating by yelling at them and threatening to shoot them, but that proved to be like whistling in the wind. When an officer suggested to Howard that orders be issued to shoot them, Howard drew the line, saying that he would never fire on his own men.

After the assault began, General Hooker and his staff, totally ignorant of what was going on and hearing nothing of the fierce battle being waged just beyond the group of trees they saw, were chatting outside headquarters when they heard what seemed to be earthshaking thunder coming their way. Alarmed, they rode a little distance toward the sound to investigate. What they encountered was a solid wall of men—it seemed like the entire Union army—rushing in frantic retreat across the field. One of Hooker's staff described it as, "for all the world like a stampede of cattle, a multitude of yelling, struggling men who had thrown away their muskets, panting for breath, their faces distorted by fear, filled the road as far as the eye could reach" (Washington Roebling in *Battles and Leaders of the Civil War*. N.Y.: Century Co., 1887).

Hooker and his men were soon engulfed by this sea of fleeing men with no other goal than to put the Rappahannock River between themselves and the Confederates. Adding to the chaos were the packhorses, dragging their loads in the dirt. Some of the officers noticed that a number of those fleeing were German. Hooker himself and members of his staff tried to keep them from running farther by hitting at them with the flat side of their swords. Hooker's men actually shot some of those fleeing, but it was like trying to stop an avalanche. No one knows exactly how many returned to their posts to continue in subsequent fighting and how many kept on going until they reached their homes. One estimate indicates that of the 2,508 men of the 11th Corps under General Howard, 2,000 ended up missing.

Like many others, Captain Willard Glazier, providing a firsthand account of the event, placed the blame on the incompetency of the generals rather than the cowardice of the men:

> Just before dark Stonewall Jackson, with about twenty-five thousand veterans, fell like a whirlwind upon the Eleventh Corps, which he had flanked so cautiously and yet so rapidly that our German comrades were taken by surprise while preparing their suppers, with arms stacked, and no time to recover. It is not at all wonderful that men surprised under these circumstances should become panic stricken and flee. Let not the censure rest upon the rout, but upon the carelessness that led to the surprise.
>
> Whole divisions were now overwhelmed by the Rebel hordes, that swept forward amid blazing musketry and battle-shouts, which made the wilderness resound; and a frantic stampede commenced which not all the courage and effort of commanding generals, or the intrepidity of some regiments could check, and which threatened to rout the entire army. This unforeseen disaster changed the whole programme of the battle, and greatly disheartened our men. (*Battles for the Union* [Hartford, Conn.: Dustin, Gilman and Co., 1878])

But while some officers might have regarded the retreat, even at the time, as necessary and the contemporary historian might look back on the impossibility of unprepared soldiers fighting at the Plank Road, many of those looking back on the situation and even some on the scene at the time were afraid that significant numbers of men would desert and labeled what they saw at Chancellorsville as little more than mass desertion of duty. It is also true that General Hooker and others believed that from this desertion the battle was lost.

DESERTION THROUGHOUT THE CIVIL WAR

Desertion among troops of both sides during the Civil War—not just of the Union's 11th Corps at the Plank Road in Chancellorsville—was a widespread, incessant, and devastating problem for military leaders. The deserters on the Union side between 1863 and 1865 were estimated at a whopping 278,644. Desertions on the Southern side were comparable.

Men began to desert their posts as soon as the armies were formed in 1861. These early desertions appeared to be of two kinds: desertion by volunteers and desertion in the border states from the Union to Confederate side. By 1862 desertions or extended unauthorized furloughs had reached monumental proportions. Lincoln explained to one civilian group that while General McClellan had 180,000 men on the Army of the Potomac's official roles, 70,000 of those were "absent" when he had to fight the Battle of Antietam. Furthermore, within two hours after the battle had begun, 30,000 others had deserted. The problem of desertion that existed on the Potomac also plagued the army in the West. In 1862 General Buell reported that 14,000 enlisted men, volunteers, and officers were missing from his Tennessee troops. The number escalated in 1863, reaching what the newspapers called "fearful proportions." In 1864 General Ewing reported that nearly half of his militia in Missouri had deserted. The severity of the problem of desertions in the East in 1864 can be seen in the fact that executions of deserters were occurring daily.

Desertion of officers was an especially troublesome reality. The *New York Tribune* reported in 1863 that more than 350 commissioned officers were absent from one division, and some 1,200 were absent from the entire Army of the Potomac. Aside from desertions, reports indicated that from 100 to 200 officers a month were away without official leave (AWOL).

The reasons for the enormous number of desertions from both Confederate and Union armies during the Civil War were numerous and complex, and only a minuscule number arose from the kind of cowardice of which Henry Fleming was guilty. The chief reason for the desertion under fire for men like Henry Fleming was that very young men were thrown into horrendous situations without even a modicum of training or warning about what they would face in battle. Many complained that they had not even been instructed in the operation of the particular rifles issued them. Without any information or guidance, they had no defenses with which to confront the horrors of battle. As in *The Red Badge of Courage*, no one told the men—all of them ignorant and untested—what they might see or feel; nor was there any advice on how to get through the experience without disgracing themselves. Furthermore, there seemed to be a custom of keeping men with the same inexperience together, without veteran soldiers to serve as mentors. Henry's group, for example, is not mixed with veteran fighting men.

Another reason for desertions of a more calculated sort was the remoteness of the cause for which they were fighting. It is extremely significant and telling that nowhere in *The Red Badge of Courage* are the reasons for the fighting ever given. As in reality, the causes for which the Civil War was fought had little personal meaning for most simple, uneducated, ordinary soldiers on both sides. In the North, the cause to many soldiers was the rather vague notion of preserving the Union and forcing the South, which was like a foreign country to them anyway, to rejoin the Union. In the minds of many unsophisticated Northern boys, slavery was either scarcely distinguishable from the servitude of the laboring force of Northern factories or was so unknown as to be nonexistent. In the line of fire, they might well ask, "For what reason am I risking my life?"

While Confederates might have had more of a sense of immediate purpose in that their homeland was being invaded, the desertions on the Confederate side were also phenomenally high. Indeed, what profound reason to fight had most Confederate soldiers? The same system and the same few plantation-owning families that had exploited the black man in the South had exploited poor whites as well. To go to war under the leadership of young Southern gentry to defend a system that kept both blacks and whites ignorant and miserable seemed the height of stupidity. Added to this was the practice whereby wealthy Southerners bought their way out of military service, leaving some flamboyant members of their class to strut as officers and the poor to serve as cannon fodder. It became a cliché in the South that this was a "rich man's war and a poor man's fight."

When Nathaniel Hawthorne, author of *The Scarlet Letter* and a lifelong New Englander, toured a Union prison to observe the Confederate soldiers held there, he was struck by their confusion and ignorance of their situations and the reasons for the war. Lacking a strong commitment to a cause, a young rebel facing a barrage of bullets might well decide to flee with his life.

There were other reasons for the more calculated kind of desertions. First were the harsh physical conditions of filth, hard marches, mud and rain and cold, diseases, and inadequate supplies. Many soldiers on both sides were barefooted for most of the war. Some complained of having had no food for twenty-four-hour periods. Many faced forced marches through mud up to their knees.

Another reason for desertions was the failure of the army to pay them on time. Some reported going for eight months without pay.

Another reason for desertions in the Civil War (as it had been in the American Revolution) was the dire need of the families of the men back home. Soldiers received letters from their families who were starving to death, pleading with the absent men to do something or their children and parents would die. This got to be so severe that the Confederate army censored soldiers' mail. Officials refused to deliver thousands of letters, storing them in warehouses, where they remained for almost a century.

Desertion may have been high because men on both sides of the war had extremely independent pioneer spirits, and were ignorant of what war and the military were all about. They had no knowledge at all of military expectations and were by background and inclination resistant to the conformity required by those going into battle.

Another reason for desertions was the character of the officers in the Civil War—men whom General Meade described as ignorant, inefficient, and worthless for the most part. They had no military training and were unable to discipline the men or command their respect; not only did they desert themselves, they were often the reason for desertion on the part of the men subordinate to them.

Men unaccustomed to the requirements of the military often refused to leave their states. If ordered to proceed with the rest of their divisions to faraway places where they were needed, they would refuse and desert.

A substantial number of desertions could be attributed to bounty seekers. These men would join the army for a substantial bounty (money), desert, and then join another outfit for another bounty, repeating this process over and over again.

Desertion is always a problem to some degree in any war, but the closest parallel for Americans to the situation in the Civil War is probably the Battle of the Bulge in Germany in 1944–1945. Here as in Chancellorsville, the attack was unexpected; the territory was heavily wooded and more familiar to the enemy than to the Americans fighting in the war; there was general confusion about what was occurring; and the fighting was especially bloody. Soldiers found themselves responsible to nobody: lost, separated from their units, in heavy fog and snow, and bitter cold, with communications ruptured or destroyed, their commanding generals unable to keep up with rapidly shifting positions in a chaos of retreats and unplanned movements, and individual soldiers often finding themselves stranded somewhere alone and in the dark and snow in a truck, a jeep, or on foot. British historian Peter Elstob (*Hitler's Last Offensive*. N.Y.: Macmillan, 1971), estimated that as many as 18,000 men deserted or were AWOL in the Battle of the Bulge. In this situation, many soldiers found themselves in positions similar to Henry Fleming: lost from their units in the heavy fog, and, since men were temporarily assigned to units other than their own, often unsure of what unit they were assigned to or where it was. As a consequence, a fairly significant number of soldiers went AWOL until the battle was over.

DESERTION AND INDIVIDUAL RELATIONSHIPS

Desertion is a rather specific and technical military term, but it also has a broader meaning, similar to the word *abandon*, which explains a deliberate refusal to carry out one's duty to another person. In this sense, the term is often applied to failures within the family, the usual one having to do with a man who deserts his wife or a mother who deserts her children, for example. While desertion from the military might have a profound effect on general morale or, if magnified many times, on the outcome of a battle and the success of a national cause, desertion of a single person who depends on us seems to be more reprehensible morally because we are acting independently as individuals rather than following expectations as one member of a larger group. In the military, it may be fear of punishment that keeps an individual from deserting, but on a personal level, it is strength of character.

Relevant to this more personal kind of individual desertion is the second, more important act of cowardice and desertion that Henry commits. In this second instance, he is not under fire nor does he fear for his life. Rather, he deserts the tattered man from fear for his reputation, believing that the tattered man will discover and reveal Henry's cowardice. The tattered man has attached himself to Henry in the general retreat, believing that Henry is badly wounded and needs help. Taking the role of an older brother, the tattered man stays by Henry's side in the woods where they have followed his fatally wounded friend, Jim Conklin, and continues to accompany him after Jim dies a horrible death and they rejoin the retreat. Seriously wounded himself, the tattered man's only concern is to "take keer" of Henry, whom he sees in his delirium as his boyhood friend. Henry, fearful that the tattered man's persistent, solicitous questions will reveal his earlier cowardice, deserts him, leaving him "wandering about helplessly in the field" (60). At the end of the book, it is this second act of desertion that haunts Henry, who describes the tattered soldier as a saint:

> There loomed the dogging memory of the tattered soldier—he who, gored by bullets and faint for blood, had fretted concerning an imagined wound in another; he who had loaned his last of strength and intellect for the tall soldier; he who, blind with weariness and pain, had been deserted in the field. (129)

Perhaps one reason this second act of desertion bothers Henry more than the first is that the object of his desertion is tangible: not just a nebulous cause he never thinks about but a living human being. And perhaps it is worse in his mind because he has a harder time justifying it as a deed he was caused to commit as a mindless, will-less part of the group driven by group dynamics and nature, even though in the end he justifies it to himself in just that way.

The following selections address the problem of desertion during the Civil War. The first group of memoirs places the blame for desertion not as much on the men as on General Howard. The next is from an 1892 book on Chancellorsville written by James Beace, a member of the 12th Massachusetts Volunteer Infantry, who tries to sort out just what the truth of the situation was. John L. Collins describes the general frantic character of the mass retreat at the Plank Road in *Battles and Leaders of the Civil War*. This is followed by General Carl Schurz's defense of the 11th Corps against charges of cowardice and desertion.

General George H. Gordon's "The Guilty Deserter" follows these accounts of desertion at Chancellorsville.

The last two accounts are by two American fiction writers. The first of these, by Stephen Crane, is presented as fiction and is called "The Veteran." The second, by Mark Twain, is about his own true experience in the Civil War.

CHARGES OF HOWARD'S INCOMPETENCE

"B'jiminey, we're generaled by a lot 'a lunkheads."

"More than one feller has said that t-day," observed a man. . . .

"Well, then, if we fight like the devil an' don't ever whip, it must be the general's fault," said the youth grandly and decisively. "And I don't see any sense in fighting and fighting and fighting, yet always losing through some derned old lunkhead of a general." (88–89)

COLONEL P. H. DALBIAC

The encounter around the Plank Road on May 2 was one of the more controversial in the Battle of Chancellorsville. The men had stacked their rifles out of easy reach, and Howard had not thought it necessary to place sentries all around the camp. Everyone had relaxed and was preparing for supper when they were the object of a surprise Confederate attack. There were comparatively few casualties but reports of wholesale desertion from the lines. In any case, the Union soldiers under General Howard's command lost miserably to the Confederates. Howard blamed the loss on his failure to receive adequate intelligence and warning and blamed it on the cowardice of his men. Others insisted that Howard, warned more than once, arrogantly ignored the warnings and refused assistance from other officers. Military historian Dalbiac has no sympathy for Howard's defense.

The "Jackson" referred to in the excerpt is the Confederate General "Stonewall" Jackson, who died by "friendly fire" on this same night.

FROM COLONEL P. H. DALBIAC, "THE AMERICAN WAR OF SECESSION 1863," IN *THE BATTLES OF CHANCELLORSVILLE AND GETTYSBURG*
(Minneapolis: N.p., 1899, pp. 57–64)

That [Hooker] was sensible of the weakness of this flank is clearly shown by his ordering Graham's brigade of Sickles' Corps to reinforce

Howard on the evening of the 1st May; and again, after Jackson's Corps had been discovered making their flank movement on the following morning, he despatched a message telling Howard of what had been seen and warning him to secure his position.

• • •

For Howard, himself, excuse of any sort is impossible. The rout of his corps was possible only through the grossest neglect of the most elementary of military precautions. He had refused reinforcements the previous evening, and he neglected Hooker's orders on the 2nd of May, then, to crown all, when Jackson halted, after his toilsome march, for upwards of two hours in open ground within two miles of his lines, he was in total ignorance of the fact. A single patrol sent a mile up the road would have discovered the whole movement, and given him ample time to have strengthened his position, or at least form up in line of battle; as it was many of his troops, when the enemy was actually upon them, were engaged in the ordinary routine of camp life—cooking, killing cattle and drawing rations.

Howard in his report endeavored to excuse himself by saying; "*Though constantly threatened and apprised of the moving of the enemy, yet the woods were so dense that he was able to mass a large force, whose exact whereabouts neither patrols, reconnaissances nor scouts ascertained.*" . . . He here admits that he was constantly apprised of the moving of the enemy, yet he neglected the precaution of even a single picket on his unprotected right flank, the presence of which would have been sufficient to prevent the disaster. Did he suppose that Jackson would run such a risk, and spend the whole day on a laborious march, merely to fritter away his men in a frontal attack on a line of entrenchments?

• • •

What might have happened had Howard possessed any of the natural instincts of a soldier needs no explanation. Lee and Jackson were separated at 4 P.M. by some eight miles, with no means of communication, and with the whole of Hooker's force between them; but the determination of Jackson, aided by the apathetic imbecility of Howard, prevailed.

SAMUEL P. BATES

In Samuel Bates's interview with General Hooker at Chancellorsville in 1876, Hooker tells him that General Howard had ignored his orders to prepare for a Confederate onslaught, even though Howard consistently claimed he had never received any communication from Hooker and so remained ignorant of the danger he faced. But Hooker's claim was proved by a dispatch he sent to Howard and by a letter from one of Howard's officers, General Carl Schurz, who claimed that he had put the dispatch into Howard's hands himself and seen him read it.

FROM SAMUEL P. BATES, "HOOKER'S COMMENTS ON CHANCELLORSVILLE," IN *THE BATTLES AND LEADERS OF THE CIVIL WAR*
(New York: Century Co., 1884, pp. 215–223)

"Upon my return to headquarters I was informed that a continuous column of the enemy had been marching past my front since early in the morning, as of a corps with all its *impedimenta*. This put an entirely new phase upon the problem, and filled me with apprehension for the safety of my right wing, which was posted to meet a front attack from the south, but was in no condition for a flank attack from the west. . . . I immediately dictated a dispatch to 'Generals Slocum and Howard,' the latter commanding the Eleventh Corps."

[The dispatch sent to General Howard is included as evidence in the investigation that followed the battle.]

H'DQ'RS, Army of the Potomac, Chancellorsville, VA., May 2nd, 1863, 9:30 A.M. *Circular*. **Major-Generals Slocum and Howard:** I am directed by the Major-General commanding to say that the disposition you have made of your corps has been with a view to a front attack by the enemy. If he should throw himself upon your flank, he wishes you to examine the ground and determine upon the position you will take in that event, in order that you may be prepared for him in whatever direction he advances. He suggests that you have heavy reserves well in hand to meet this contingency. The right of your line does not appear to be strong enough. No artificial defenses worth naming have been thrown up, and there appears to be a scarcity of troops at that point, and not, in the general's opinion, as favorably posted as might be. We have good reason to suppose that the enemy is moving to our right. Please advance your pickets for purposes of observation as far as may be safe, in order to obtain timely information of their approach. J. H. Van Alen, Brigadier-General and Aide-de-camp.

[General Carl Schurz verifies that General Howard actually received not only one but two warnings from General Hooker.]

"About noon or a little after on the day of the attack on the Eleventh Corps I was at General Howard's headquarters, a house on the Chancellorsville road near the center of our position. General Howard, being very tired, wanted to rest a little, and asked me as next in rank to open dispatches that might arrive and to wake him in case they were of immediate importance. Shortly after a courier arrived with a dispatch from you [Hooker] calling General Howard's attention to the movement of the enemy toward our right flank, and instructing him to take precautionary measures against an attack from that quarter. I went into General Howard at once, and read it to him, and, if I remember rightly, while we were speaking about it another courier, or one of your young staff-officers, arrived with a second dispatch of virtually the same purport. We went out and discussed the matter on the porch of the house."

[Hooker continues:]

"This failure of Howard to hold his ground cost us our position, and I was forced, in the presence of the enemy to take up a new one. Upon investigation I found that Howard had failed properly to obey my instructions to prepare to meet the enemy from the west."

WHAT IS THE TRUTH?

JAMES BEACE

In an attempt to unravel the controversies about desertion and officer incompetence at Chancellorsville, James Beace, who had served in the 12th Massachusetts Volunteer Infantry during the Civil War and had been, as he states, a member of the Army of the Potomac, delivered a paper in 1888 to the United Service Club of Philadelphia, indicating a number of contradictions, showing the questionable statements of some of the officers who had tried to justify their actions or those of their companies. In the course of his treatise, he speaks of the wholesale desertion of men before the battle began and after the assault by the rebels near the Plank Road. But although he acknowledges desertion, especially on the part of the 11th Corps (which their leader, General Schurz, denied), he finds no grounds for the veracity of General Howard, who had been first among the officers to blame the men's cowardice rather than his own incompetence for the failure at the Plank Road in the late afternoon of May 2.

Two slang words referred to deserters: they were called "stragglers" and were said (the Union borrowing a term from the confederates) to have "skedaddled."

FROM JAMES BEACE, *CHANCELLORSVILLE*
(Philadelphia: N.p., 1892, pp. 1–10)

Those of us who then served in the Potomac army will recollect the feeling of discontent which had arisen, and certainly none can withhold from General Hooker all praise for the transformation that followed his assumption of command. He himself impulsively declared it "the finest army on the planet," but it contained elements of discord. The service of twenty-three thousand short-term men was about to expire, and with much unanimity these declined further duty. I well recollect one regiment which on April 28 flatly refused to break camp. De Peyster, a general, alludes to thirty-eight regiments which left the line on the morning of May 4, and speaks of others as having to be forced up at the point of the bayonet. Have we all forgotten the rumors of a "stragglers' brigade"?

• • •

Early that morning Hooker had ordered the First Corps to his right, but the messenger lost his way and did not reach General Reynolds till nearly five o'clock that evening. Hooker also personally visited General Howard's position, and at half-past nine o'clock A.M. wrote an order to Howard in which he avers, "The right of your line does not appear strong enough; please advance your pickets."

Howard denies having received this order, and is backed by his adjutant general. The order appears in Howard's letter-book among some June memoranda, which shows it eventually reached him. Did he get it on May 2?

General Schurz avers that he received it and read it to Howard on May 2. The Eleventh Corps chief-of-staff is quoted as saying that Howard read the order and pocketed it. Which statement shall we believe?

• • •

On its face it certainly looks as though Hooker had taken all possible precaution. It was not his fault that the despatch to the First Corps miscarried; he had notified Howard to be careful; and Professor Bates claims a message from Howard, dated eleven o'clock, A.M., in which Howard refers to this moving column of the enemy as visible from the extreme right, and says he is "taking measure to resist an attack from the west." ... While he was busy with his dispositions let us see what "measures" Howard had taken to "resist an attack from the west."

A section of artillery facing westwardly, two regiments, the men standing three feet apart, and thirty-five cavalrymen as patrol. The rest of the corps facing south. General Devens says, "These dispositions were ordered by Major-General Howard, and examined by him after they were made." Having in this fashion made his line secure, Howard accompanied Barlow's brigade in its journey in quest of Sickles. Meanwhile the Eleventh Corps was formally notified to get its supper, make itself comfortable, and—go to bed!

General Sickles says "I was about to open my attack in full force; had got all ready for that purpose." Thus we have a corps commander about to open an attack with a division that is preparing to bivouac.

This is not the only strange thing about this forward movement to the furnace. If the Third Corps reports are to be believed the wearers of the diamond badge displayed some backwardness in going forward.

Colonel Blaisdell—styled by his corps general "a circumspect and intrepid commander"—says of the Berdan sharpshooters sent out with him, "It was impossible to keep them to the front." His lieutenant-colonel adds, "They shamefully ran from the enemy's fire."

The chief-of-artillery Third Division Third Corps complains that one of his batteries received a volley from its infantry support. One of General

Birney's regimental commanders speaks of "rallying fragments of regiments" of his own division "even at the point of the bayonet." General Birney himself reports two colonels and two lieutenant colonels of his division as "behaving badly." There are frank admissions, and one cannot help inferring that all was not what fond fancy could wish.

• • •

Jackson found the Eleventh Corps with its right in air and a gap of nearly two miles on its left. He formed on either side of and perpendicular to the turnpike—Rodes in advance, followed by Coston, and A. P. Hill in support. The orders were of the most positive nature,—"stop for nothing," "push right on," "under no circumstances pause." An hour was spent in preparation, and soon after five P.M. the signal was given, and Jackson swiftly moved forward.

The Eleventh Corps reports are unanimous in declaring that the section of artillery posted in the road promptly departed without firing a shot. One officer adds, "Neither did they undertake to fire a gun." And the brigade on the extreme right not only abandoned its position with much haste, but in its flight stampeded McLean's brigade. This practically put an end to General Devens' division. General Schimmelfennig, who was on the left of McLean, avers that Von Gilsa fired one round, McLean none, and neither could be rallied again. General Schurz's division appears to have made some effort at resistance, for the Confederates admit some fighting in this vicinity; but by the time they had eliminated Schurz and reached the solitary brigade representing Steinwehr's division they acknowledge "stubborn resistance," "heavy fire of artillery and musketry."

By dark the Confederates were within a mile of Hooker's headquarters [and] the Eleventh Corps had vanished. . . . This sudden onslaught of Jackson and consequent withdrawal of the Eleventh Corps found the Third Corps general "about to open an attack on Jackson's forces." He promptly abandoned this purpose and managed to regain the Union lines. In this movement his ordnance officer left as a souvenir seventy thousand rounds of ammunition snugly cased on the packs of thirty-five mules.

• • •

Very early in the morning of May 3 Stuart [Jeb Stuart, Confederate general] pushed his troops forward. That there was some heavy fighting is attested by the Union losses, and the fact that it took hours to force Hooker's line. Yet the student is puzzled, for the reports cheerfully testify to much of running away.

A Second Corps officer says "The regiments in the rifle-pits on the right gave way, and passed us in disorder. About 11:30 o'clock the 66th New

York broke and fled in dismay." General Sickles alludes to the "prema-
ture and hasty retirement of the 3rd of Maryland." A Third Corps colonel
reports "the front lines having broken and fallen back in some confusion." Another complains that "men from other regiments of the corps
came rushing through my line in great confusion." Still another found
"a great stream of men belonging to the Third Corps going to the rear."
Yet another, "While retiring the regiment was divided and separated by
other troops." Another officer took nearly a brigade to the rear, and at
noon reports having one thousand seven hundred and fifteen men, representing nine regiments, which he had recruited from "a constant
stream of stragglers." It is wearisome to cite, yet to show that the picture
is not overdrawn, I quote a few phrases from Third Corps official reports
all having reference to Third Corps troops on May 3.

A brigadier of the Twelfth Corps says "I ordered the regiments of the
Third Corps which were lying down in my front to move forward and
assist our men at the barricade. I failed, for a regiment of red-legged
zouaves came pell-mell from our left with less than half their number of
the enemy close at their heels. They could not be rallied, and were the
cause of giving way of General Berry's line and our own, as they carried
with them the troops intended as reenforcements. These never came up
nor fired a shot." Another says "The Third Corps troops on my right
yielded to the enemy;" while a colonel formally rebukes a regiment of
his own division for firing into him.

JOHN COLLINS

> He saw dark waves of men come sweeping out of the woods
> and down through the field. . . . They charged down upon him
> like terrified buffaloes. (67)

John L. Collins, a member of the 8th Pennsylvania horse cavalry,
was called in with his regiment to the Plank Road. Collins's horse
is killed in the battle, and he is pitched off. He writes: "Here I
parted company with the regiment. When I jumped to my feet I
had time to take only one glance at my surroundings. My sole
thought was to escape capture or death." Collins captures the horror of the chaos and desperation in the mass flight of soldiers
under General Howard's command.

FROM JOHN COLLINS, "WHEN STONEWALL JACKSON TURNED
OUR RIGHT," IN *BATTLES AND LEADERS OF THE CIVIL WAR*
(New York: Century Co., 1884, pp. 183–185)

The Plank road, and the woods that bordered it, presented a scene of
terror and confusion such as I had never seen before. Men and animals
were dashing against one another in wild dismay before the line of fire
that came crackling and crashing after them. The constantly approaching
rattle of musketry, the crash of the shells through the trees, seemed to
come from three sides upon the broken fragments of the Eleventh Corps
that crowded each other on the road. The horses of the men of my regiment who had been shot, mingled with the pack-mules that carried the
ammunition of the Eleventh Corps, tore like wild beasts through the
woods. I tried in vain to catch one.

• • •

I now gave up hope of a mount, and seeing the Confederate lines
coming near me, tried to save myself on foot. Once, when throwing myself down to escape the fury of the fire, I saw a member of my own
regiment, whose horse also had been shot, hiding in a pine top that had
been cut down by a shell. He had thrown his arms away that he might
run the faster, and he begged me to do the same. This I refused to do,
and I got in safely with my arms, while he was never seen again. I turned
into the Plank road to join the very bad company that came pouring in
by that route. More than half of the runaways had thrown their arms
away, and all of them were talking in a language that I did not understand, but, by their tones, evidently blaming some one for the disgrace
and disaster that had befallen their corps. They appeared to share the
prevailing confusion on that part of the field, where the front and the
rear seemed reversed. Yet, as misery loves company, I cast my lot with
them and continued my flight.

I doubt if any of us knew where we were going, further than that we
were fleeing before the pursuing lines of the enemy. . . .

In the very height of the flight, we came upon General Howard, who
seemed to be the only man in his own command that was not running
at that moment. He was in the middle of the road and mounted, his
maimed arm embracing a stand of colors that some regiment had deserted, while with his sound arm he was gesticulating to the men to make
a stand by their flag. With bared head he was pleading with his soldiers,
literally weeping as he entreated the unheeding horde. . . . As the front
became clear, we fired a few shots at the advance line of the Confederates, but a fresh mass of fugitives in blue soon filled the road, and we

had to stop firing. The general now ordered us to cover the whole line of retreat so as to let none pass, and the officers, inspired by his devotion, ran in front of their men, drew their swords, and attempted to stop them. As the number constantly increased, the pressure became greater upon the line that blocked the way; but this line was constantly reinforced by officers and others, and offered some resistance to the pressure. At last the seething, surging sea of humanity broke over the feeble barrier, and General Howard and his officers were carried away by main force with the tide. Pharaoh and his chariots could have held back the walls of the Red Sea as easily as those officers could resist this retreat. I started again on my race for life, this time alone. . . .

A DEFENSE FROM THE OFFICIAL REPORT OF GENERAL CARL SCHURZ

Many reports of the mass desertion at the Plank Road in Chancellorsville indicated that most of the deserters were German forces fighting for the Union. Indeed, most of the commanders of the 11th Corps, under General Howard, were German-Americans, and more than two-thirds of the corps troops were in regiments completely German or with mixed nationality. It had the name of "the foreign contingent." The troops themselves were composed primarily of recent immigrants to the country who had little investment in the causes they were fighting for. Predictably, desertion among emigrants was very high. The German officers who led them were men far superior in their European military training to the ordinary officers in the Union army. But, for the most part, the German officers as well as their men were derided and belittled by the rest of the Union soldiers.

After the war, General Schurz testified in defense of his men and bitterly criticized General Howard, whom he regarded as having lied about not having received Hooker's warning to prepare himself for an assault and who had, according to Schurz, justified his own incompetence by blaming the disaster at the Plank Road on the cowardice of the German troops. In the report addressed to Howard, Schurz, for example, reminds Howard that he (Schurz) had reported what he knew of the danger of an attack, asked for Howard's orders to prepare, and had received none, a failure of action that finally placed the men in an impossible situation, giving them no choice but to retreat. He also reports that many Germans were wounded and killed in this horrible battle but that his troops have been maligned with charges of desertion. The letter addressed to General Hooker on 1876 is in response to Hooker's request for more information on the battle. Here Schurz reports that, contrary to Howard's claim, Hooker's letter warning him to prepare his troops for an assault had reached Howard because Schurz had read it to him. He repeats his objection to his German troops having been labeled as cowards.

FROM "THE OFFICIAL REPORT OF GENERAL CARL SCHURZ,
AND HIS LETTER TO GENERAL HOOKER," IN *BATTLES AND
LEADERS OF THE CIVIL WAR*
(New York: Century Co., 1884, pp. 119, 220, 221)

From the Report to General Howard

In the course of the forenoon I was informed that large columns of the enemy could be seen from General Devens' headquarters, moving from east to west. . . . I observed them plainly as they moved on. I rode back to your headquarters, and on the way ordered Captain Dilger to look for good artillery positions on the field fronting west, as the troops would in all probability have to execute a change of front. The matter was largely discussed at your headquarters, and I entertained and expressed in our informal conversations the opinion that we should form upon the open ground we then occupied, with our front at right angles with the Plank Road, lining the church grove and the border of the woods east of the open plain with infantry, placing strong echelons behind both wings, and distributing the artillery along the front on ground most favorable for its action, especially on the eminence on the right and left of Dowdall's Tavern. . . . In the absence of orders, but becoming more and more convinced that the enemy's attack would come from the west and fall upon our right and rear, I took it upon my own responsibility to detach two regiments from the second line of my Second Brigade and to place them in a good position on the right and left of Ely's Ford road, west of Hawkins's farm, so as to check the enemy if he should attack our extreme right and penetrate through the woods at that point. This was subsequently approved by you. . . . With these exceptions, no change was made in the position occupied by the corps. The losses suffered by my division in the action of May 2d were very severe in proportion to my whole effective force. I had 15 officers killed, 23 wounded, and 15 missing, and 102 men killed, 365 wounded, and 441 missing,—total 953 [later revised to 9 officers and 120 men killed, 32 officers and 461 men wounded, and 8 officers and 290 men captured or missing]. My whole loss amounted to about 23 per cent. . . . In closing this report I beg leave to make one additional remark. The Eleventh Corps, and by error or malice, especially the Third Division, has been held up to the whole country as a band of cowards. My division has been made responsible for the defeat of the Eleventh Corps, and the Eleventh Corps for the failure of the campaign. Preposterous as this is, yet we have been overwhelmed by the army and the press with abuse and insult beyond measure. We have borne as much as human nature can endure. I am far from saying that on May 2d everybody did his duty to the best of his power.

But one thing I will say, because I know it: these men are no cowards. . . . I have seen, with my own eyes, troops who now affect to look down upon the Eleventh Corps with sovereign contempt behave much worse under circumstances far less trying. . . .

From the Letter to General Hooker

. . . About noon or a little after one the day of the attack on the Eleventh Corps I was at General Howard's headquarters, a house on the Chancellorsville road near the center of our position. General Howard, being very tired, wanted to rest a little, and asked me as next in rank to open dispatches that might arrive and to wake him in case they were of immediate importance. Shortly after a courier arrived with a dispatch from you calling General Howard's attention to the movement of the enemy toward our right flank, and instructing him to take precautionary measures against an attack from that quarter. I went into General Howard at once and read it to him. . . .

I have seen it stated that my troops were already gone when General Devens' division in its hurried retreat reached my position. This is utterly untrue. Some of my regiments, which had remained in their old position, succeeded in wheeling round under the fire of the enemy; others were swept away, but those whose front I had changed during the afternoon in anticipation of the attack held their ground a considerable time after the debris of General Devens's division had swept through our line. I saw General Devens, wounded, carried by, and he had long been . . . in the rear when we were overpowered and fell back upon Colonel Buschbeck's position, where General Howard in the meantime had been trying to rally the routed troops. . . . My loss in killed and wounded was quite heavy: if I remember rightly, about twenty percent.

GEORGE H. GORDON

George H. Gordon was a general from Massachusetts serving in the Union army. His article about the execution of a deserter shows the gravity of the crime and suggests the prevalence of desertion at the time. The public humiliation and horror of the execution suggest the opprobrium with which desertion was regarded, explaining the apprehensiveness that Henry Fleming feels about having anyone find out about his own desertion under fire.

It is also apparent that not all of the thousands of deserters could be executed, but that the officers used selected deserters as scapegoats to execute publicly and horribly as a deterrent. That a civilian brought along his children (the youngest is six) to attend the execution not only shows the shocking insensitivity of the age, when children were frequently present at public executions, but also underscores the heinousness of the crime despite its frequency.

FROM GEORGE H. GORDON, "THE GUILTY DESERTER," IN *THE ROMANCE OF THE CIVIL WAR*
(New York: Macmillan, 1903, pp. 156–159)

I had received six soldiers who had been tried and sentenced to be shot for the crime of desertion. At Warrenton Junction [Conn.] the sentences were to have been carried into execution. The field had been selected, coffins made, and doom announced; but a sudden movement ordered for the day had caused a week's suspension, during which five of the fated ones were recommended to the President for pardon. For the sixth, however, a ringleader, the sentence was unchanged; and again my division was ordered to form on the morrow to witness his execution. The hopelessness of his reprieve had been communicated, the chaplain had performed his last office, the firing party had been detailed, when again an order to march at five o'clock in the morning threatened another inhuman interruption,—which, however, did not happen, as will appear.

With the stoutest of the troops this convict had marched sturdily and manfully to Greenwich, following his coffin fifteen weary miles. Here, at the end of his last march, his last hour on earth had come. A field near the camp had been selected, and preparations made for a fitting termination of the ghastly ceremony, when the planter, who had heard that his own field was to be devoted to this novel use, bustled up to ask with puffy earnestness, "Is it true, General, that you are going to shoot one of your men today?" Then, without awaiting a reply, he continued, "Now, my dear sir, you must not think any worst of me if I say this executing is a dreadful thing! And yet it is an incident of the war; why, sir, it is historical, and—bless my soul, sir!—I want to see it; and, if you do not think it improper, I should like to take my little boys with me."

"If you are so inclined, you may," I replied. And indeed he did so incline, for he took a position as near to the scene as he could with safety. With umbrella under his arm, a linen coat over his shoulders, a little dog in front of him, and three small children (aged six, eight, and ten) by his side, he was the first on the field and the last to leave it.

Many years ago, hanging on the wall of an accustomed haunt, I remember finding a strange fascination in a coarse print of a military execution. Often have I stood spellbound before the picture. The condemned kneeling by the side of his grave, the coffin, the blindfolded victim, the platoon of soldiers with levelled muskets, the coming word, and in the distance a horseman galloping towards the spot, waving in his hand a pardon. Could he but fly? and did he reach there in time? I could never forget the dreadful reality, even with the consciousness that it was after all but a painting, a creation perhaps of the imagination. But this execution at Greenwich was not a dream. Here there was no coloring. A sad, stern duty was before me, and there was no reprieve. The hour had come; and the division was formed on three sides of a hollow square, leaving the fourth with an open grave and fresh earth on its edge, when a mournful procession approached.

Advancing slowly, silently, a firing party of six soldiers preceded an ambulance in which a soldier was seated upon his coffin, his arms pinioned and his eyes cast down. The provost guard followed. The ranks were motionless; all eyes were fixed upon the condemned. He was assisted to the ground, the soldiers placed the coffin by the side of the grave, and then the poor, unhappy victim knelt upon his coffin. Not a sound was heard save the mournful prayer and solemn tones of the death sentence. Not a man moved, as the bandage which shut out forever the last ray of God's sunlight was placed over the eyes of one poor fellow-being. There was no pity and no hope. The sharp "Ready! aim!" and then came the awful choking suspense, relieved by the ringing volley that drowned that word of dread. For an instant the form remained erect, still on its knees; the next, a corpse rolled over its last receptacle to the brink of a yawning grave.

On their way back to their encampments the troops moved in column by the corpse. Death, so real, had set its seal upon this human face; death, so solemn, so earnest, had driven a soul so completely from its human tenement that I could hardly realize that this rigid form had ever felt a human passion, or given way to human weakness. When the last look

had been taken and the field cleared of troops, a small burial party low-
ered the body, filled the grave with earth, covered the slight mound with
a green sod, and left the scene of this tragedy alone with the dead. Of
the six guns in the hands of the firing party but five were loaded; no one,
therefore, could tell who held the blank. But four guns were discharged;
and from these but two bullets struck the condemned man,—one passing
through his arm, another through his breast, near his heart. He died
without a struggle. He died, and left no word, save that, as at last he
realized the awful truth, he begged that he might have an interview with
myself or General Meade. But this was humanely denied, for I was only
carrying out the will of General Meade, and he had passed relentlessly
upon his case. The law had been defied; and so, at last, the law was
vindicated.

STEPHEN CRANE AND MARK TWAIN

STEPHEN CRANE, "THE VETERAN"

Stephen Crane's story "The Veteran" appeared in *McClure's Magazine* in August 1896, one year after the novel's publication. The veteran designated in the story is an adult Henry Fleming, old enough now to have a grandson. Looking back, he openly admits his fear in battle in the hearing of his grandson, who, like the young Henry in *The Red Badge of Courage*, is appalled by the idea of his grandfather's cowardice.

But the subsequent physical actions of the old man, in a crisis fraught with danger, are in every way opposite of cowardice. Unlike those early days of cowardice and courage in wartime, the cause is personal and clear. Nor is his purpose, as it had been in his youth, a concern with his image or to prove himself. The endangered animals in the story become more important than his own ego.

Although Chancellorsville is never mentioned by name in *The Red Badge of Courage* (Henry would not have known the name of the battle he was fighting in then), here Henry Fleming, in his old age, identifies the first battle of his youth as Chancellorsville.

STEPHEN CRANE, "THE VETERAN"
(McClure's Magazine VII [August 1896], 222–224)

Out of the low window could be seen three hickory trees placed irregularly in a meadow that was resplendent in springtime green. Farther away, the old dismal belfry of the village church loomed over the pines. A horse meditating in the shade of one of the hickories lazily swished his tail. The warm sunshine made an oblong of vivid yellow on the floor of the grocery.

"Could you see the whites of their eyes?" said the man who was seated on a soap-box.

"Nothing of the kind," replied old Henry warmly. "Just a lot of flitting figures, and I let go at where they 'peared to be the thickest. Bang!"

"Mr. Fleming," said the grocer—his deferential voice expressed somehow the old man's exact social weight—"Mr. Fleming, you never was frightened much in them battles, was you?"

The veteran looked down and grinned. Observing his manner, the entire group tittered. "Well, I guess I was," he answered finally. "Pretty well scared, sometimes. Why, in my first battle I thought the sky was falling down. I thought the world was coming to an end. You bet I was scared."

Every one laughed. Perhaps it seemed strange and rather wonderful to them that a man should admit the thing, and in the tone of their laughter there was probably more admiration than if old Fleming had declared that he had always been a lion. Moreover, they knew that he had ranked as an orderly sergeant, and so their opinion of his heroism was fixed. None, to be sure, knew how an orderly sergeant ranked, but then it was understood to be somewhere just shy of a major-general's stars. So when old Henry admitted that he had been frightened, there was a laugh.

"The trouble was," said the old man, "I thought they were all shooting at me. Yes, sir, I thought every man in the other army was aiming at me in particular, and only me. And it seemed so darned unreasonable, you know. I wanted to explain to 'em what an almighty good fellow I was, because I thought then they might quit all trying to hit me. But I couldn't explain, and they kept on being unreasonable—blim!—blam!—bang! So I run!"

Two little triangles of wrinkles appeared at the corners of his eyes. Evidently he appreciated some comedy in this recital. Down near his feet, however, little Jim, his grandson, was visibly horror-stricken. His hands were clasped nervously, and his eyes were wide with astonishment at this terrible scandal, his most magnificent grandfather telling such a thing.

"That was at Chancellorsville. Of course, afterward I got kind of used to it. A man does. Lots of men, though, seem to feel all right from the start. I did, as soon as I "got on to it," as they say now; but at first I was pretty flustered. Now, there was young Jim Conklin, old Si Conklin's son—that used to keep the tannery—you none of you recollect him— well, he went into it from the start just as if he was born to it. But with me it was different. I had to get used to it."

When little Jim walked with his grandfather he was in the habit of skipping along on the stone pavement in front of the three stores and the hotel of the town and betting that he could avoid the cracks. But upon this day he walked soberly, with his hand gripping two of his grandfather's fingers. Sometimes he kicked abstractedly at dandelions that curved over the walk. Any one could see that he was much troubled.

"There's Sickles's colt over in the medder, Jimmie," said the old man. "Don't you wish you owned one like him?"

"Um," said the boy, with a strange lack of interest. He continued his reflections. Then finally he ventured: "Grandpa—now—was that true what you was telling those men?"

"What?" asked the grandfather. "What was I telling them?"

"Oh, about your running."

"Why, yes, that was true enough, Jimmie. It was my first fight, and there was an awful lot of noise, you know."

Jimmie seemed dazed that this idol, of its own will, should so totter. His stout boyish idealism was injured.

Presently the grandfather said, "Sickles's colt is going for a drink. Don't you wish you owned Sickles's colt, Jimmie?"

The boy merely answered: "He ain't as nice as our'n." He lapsed then into another moody silence.

One of the hired men, a Swede, desired to drive to the county-seat for purposes of his own. The old man loaned a horse and an unwashed buggy. It appeared later that one of the purposes of the Swede was to get drunk.

After quelling some boisterous frolic of the farm-hands and boys in the garret, the old man had that night gone peacefully to sleep, when he was aroused by clamoring at the kitchen door. He grabbed his trousers, and they waved out behind as he dashed forward. He could hear the voice of the Swede, screaming and blubbering. He pushed the wooden button, and, as the door flew open, the Swede, a maniac, stumbled inward, chattering, weeping, still screaming. "De barn fire! Fire! Fire! De barn fire! Fire! Fire! Fire!"

There was a swift and indescribable change in the old man. His face ceased instantly to be a face; it became a mask, a gray thing, with horror written about the mouth and eyes. He hoarsely shouted at the foot of the little rickety stairs, and immediately, it seemed there came down an avalanche of men. No one knew that during this time the old lady had been standing in her night-clothes at the bed-room door, yelling: "What's th' matter? What's th' matter? What's th' matter?"

When they dashed toward the barn it presented to their eyes its usual appearance, solemn rather mystic in the black night. The Swede's lantern was overturned at a point some yards in front of the barn doors. It contained a wild little conflagration of its own, and even in their excitement some of those who ran fell, a gentle secondary vibration of the thrifty part of their minds at sight of this overturned lantern. Under ordinary circumstances it would have been a calamity.

But the cattle in the barn were trampling, trampling, trampling, and above this noise could be heard a humming like the song of innumerable bees. The old man hurled aside the great doors, and a yellow flame leaped out at one corner and sped and wavered frantically up the old gray wall. It was glad, terrible, this single flame, like the wild banner of deadly and triumphant foes.

The motley crowd from the garret had come with all the pails of the farm. They flung themselves upon the well. It was a leisurely old machine, long dwelling in indolence. It was in the habit of giving out water with a sort of reluctance. The men stormed at it, cursed it; but it continued to allow the buckets to be filled only after the wheezy windlass had howled many protests at the mad-handed men.

With his opened knife in his hand old Fleming himself had gone headlong into the barn, where the stifling smoke swirled with the air-currents, and where could be heard in its fullness the terrible chorus of the flames, laden with tones of hate and death, a hymn of wonderful ferocity.

He flung a blanket over an old mare's head, cut the halter close to the manger, led the mare to the door, and fairly kicked her out to safety. He returned with the same blanket, and rescued one of the workhorses. He took five horses out, and then came out himself with his clothes bravely on fire. He had no whiskers, and very little hair on his head. They soused five pailfuls of water on him. His eldest son made a clean miss with the sixth pailful, because the old man had turned and was running down the decline and around to the basement of the barn, where were the stanchions of the cows. Some one noticed at the time that he ran very lamely, as if one of the frenzied horses had smashed his hip.

The cows, with their heads held in the heavy stanchions, had thrown themselves, strangled themselves, tangled themselves, done everything which the ingenuity of their exuberant fear could suggest to them.

Here, as at the well, the same thing happened to every man save one. Their hands went mad. They became incapable of everything save the power to rush into dangerous situations.

The old man released the cow nearest the door, and she, blind drunk with terror crashed into the Swede. The Swede had been running to and fro babbling. He carried an empty milk-pail, rolling across the floor, made a flash of silver in the gloom.

Old Fleming took a fork, beat off the cow, and dragged the paralyzed Swede to the open air. When they had rescued all the cows save one, which had so fastened herself that she could not be moved an inch, they returned to the front of the barn and stood sadly, breathing like men who had reached the final point of human effort.

Many people had come running. Someone had even gone to the church, and now, from the distance, rang the tocsin note of the old bell. There was a long flare of crimson on the sky, which made remote people speculate as to the whereabouts of the fire.

The long flames sang their drumming chorus in the voices of the heaviest bass. The wind whirled clouds of smoke and cinders into the faces of the spectators. The form of the old barn was outlined in black amid these masses of orange-hued flames.

And then came the Swede again, crying as one who is the weapon of the sinister fates. "De colts! De colts! You have forgot de colts!"

Old Fleming staggered. It was true; they had forgotten the two colts in the box-stalls at the back of the barn. "Boys," he said, "I must try to get 'em out." They clamored about him then afraid for him, afraid of what they should see. Then they talked wildly each to each. "Why, it's sure death!" "He would never get out!" "Why, it's suicide for a man to go in there!" Old Fleming stared absentmindedly at the open doors. "The poor little things," he said. He rushed into the barn.

When the roof fell in, a great funnel of smoke swarmed toward the sky, as if the old man's mighty spirit, released from its body—a little bottle—had swelled like the genie of fable. The smoke was tinted rose-hue from the flames, and perhaps the unutterable midnights of the universe will have no power to daunt the color of this soul.

MARK TWAIN, "THE PRIVATE HISTORY OF A CAMPAIGN THAT FAILED"

Mark Twain's account of his early days as a Confederate soldier is diametrically opposed in tone and attitude to the story of Henry Fleming. There are similarities: both take place in the Civil War, and both soldiers are young, inexperienced boys who know nothing of battle. Neither soldier seems committed to a cause. And both, in different degrees, are guilty of desertion. To Mark Twain, however, even one death strikes him as too many, and for a variety of reasons, including this one, he leaves his post, never to return.

The attitude toward desertion is radically different as well. While Henry Fleming's desertion haunts him and makes him feel excruciating guilt, perhaps even drives him to risk his life heroically afterward, Twain openly and comically admits his desertion and "retreats," ending by bragging, "I knew more about retreating than the man who invented retreating."

FROM MARK TWAIN, "THE PRIVATE HISTORY OF A CAMPAIGN
THAT FAILED"
(*Century Magazine* [1885], 1–15)

The only foes he had seen were some pickets along the river bank. (7)

You have heard from a great many people who did something in the war; is it not fair and right that you listen a little moment to one who started out to do something in it, but didn't? Thousands entered the war, got just a taste of it, and then stepped out again permanently. These, by their very numbers, are respectable, and are therefore entitled to a sort of voice—not a loud one, but a modest one; not a boastful one, but an apologetic one. They ought not to be allowed much space among better people—people who did something. I grant that; but they ought at least to be allowed to state why they didn't do anything, and also to explain the process by which they didn't do anything. Surely this kind of light must have sort of value.

Out West there was a good deal of confusion in men's minds during the first months of the great trouble—a good deal of unsettledness, of leaning first this way, then that, then the other way. It was hard for us to get our bearings. . . . A month later the secession atmosphere had considerably thickened on the Lower Mississippi, and I became a rebel.

Several of us got together in a secret place by night and formed ourselves into a military company. One Tom Lyman, a young fellow of a good deal of spirit but of no military experience, was made captain; I was made second lieutenant. We had no first lieutenant; I do not know why; it was long ago.

For a time life was idly delicious, it was perfect; there was nothing to mar it. Then came some farmers with an alarm one day. They said it was rumored that enemy were advancing in our direction from over Hyde's prairie. The result was a sharp stir among us, and general consternation. It was a rude awakening from our pleasant trance. . . . The question was, which way to retreat. But all were so flurried that nobody seemed to have even a guess to offer. . . . It was now decided that we should fall back on Mason's farm.

• • •

Captain Lyman . . . now gave orders that our camp should be guarded against surprise by the posting of pickets. Some excused themselves on account of the weather; but the rest were frank enough to say they wouldn't go in any kind of weather. This kind of thing sounds odd now, and impossible, but there was no surprise in it at the time. On the contrary, it seemed a perfectly natural thing to do. There were scores of little camps scattered over Missouri where the same thing was happening. These camps were composed of young men who had been born and reared to a sturdy independence, and who did not know what it meant to be ordered all their lives. . . . It is quite within the probabilities that this same thing was happening all over the South.

• • •

Our scares were frequent. Every few days rumors would come that the enemy were approaching. In these cases we always fell back on some other camp of ours; we never stayed where we were. . . . One night a man was sent to our corn crib with the same old warning: The enemy was hovering in our neighborhood. We all said let him hover. We resolved to stay still and be comfortable. . . . We had said we would stay, and we were committed. We could have been persuaded to go, but there was nobody brave enough to suggest it. . . . Presently a muffled sound caught our ears, and we recognized it as the hoof-beats of a horse or horses. And right away a figure appeared in the forest path; it could have been made of smoke, its mass had too little sharpness of outline. It was a man on horseback, and it seemed to me that there were others behind him. I got hold of a gun in the dark, and pushed it through a crack between the logs, hardly knowing what I was doing, I was so dazed with fright. Somebody said "Fire!" I pulled the trigger. I seemed to see a hundred flashes and hear a hundred reports; then I saw the man fall down out of the saddle. My first feeling was of surprised gratification; my first impulse was an apprentice-sportsman's impulse to run and pick up his game. Somebody said, hardly audibly, "Good—we've got him!—wait for the rest." But the rest did not come. We waited—listened—still no more came. There was not a sound, not a whisper of a leaf; just perfect stillness; an uncanny kind of stillness, which was all the more uncanny on account of the damp, earthy, late-night smells now rising and pervading it. Then, wondering, we crept stealthily out, and approached the man. When we got to him the moon revealed him distinctly. He was lying on his back, with his arms abroad; his mouth was open and his chest heaving with long gasps, and his white shirt-front was all splashed with blood. The thought shot through me that I was a murderer; that I had killed a man—a man who had never done me any harm. That was the coldest sensation that ever went through my marrow. I was down by him in a moment, helplessly stroking his forehead; and I would have given anything then—my own life freely—to make him again what he had been five minutes before. And all the boys seemed to be feeling in the same way; they hung over him, full of pitying interest, and tried all they could to help him, and said all sorts of regretful things. They had forgotten all about the enemy; they thought only of this one forlorn unit of the foe. Once my imagination persuaded me that the dying man gave me a reproachful look out of his shadowy eyes, and it seemed to me that I would rather he had stabbed me than done that. He muttered and mumbled like a dreamer in his sleep about his wife and his child; and I thought with a new despair, "This thing that I have done does not end with him; it fall upon *them* too, and they never did me any harm, anymore than he."

In a little while the man was dead. He was killed in war; killed in fair and legitimate war; killed in battle, as you may say.

• • •

The man was not in uniform, and was not armed. He was a stranger in the country; that was all we ever found out about him. . . . My campaign was spoiled. It seemed to me that I was not rightly equipped for this awful business; that war was intended for men, and I for a child's nurse. I resolved to retire from this avocation of sham soldiership while I could save some remnant of my self-respect.

• • •

The rest of my war experience was of a piece with what I have already told of it. We kept monotonously falling back upon one camp or another, and eating up the country.

• • •

The last camp which we fell back upon was in a hollow near the village of Florida, where I was born—in Monroe county. Here we were warned one day that a Union colonel was sweeping down on us with a whole regiment at his heel. This looked decidedly serious. Our boys went apart and consulted; then we went back and told the other companies present that the war was a disappointment to us, and we were going to disband.

• • •

An hour later we met General Harris on the road, with two or three people in his company—his staff, probably, but we could not tell; none of them were in uniform; uniforms had not come into vogue among us yet. Harris ordered us back; but we told him there was a Union colonel coming with a whole regiment in his wake, and it looked as if there was going to be a disturbance; so we had concluded to go home. He raged a little, but it was of no use; our minds were made up. We had done our share; had killed one man, exterminated one army, such as it was; let him go and kill the rest, and that would end the war.

• • •

The thoughtful will not throw this war paper of mine lightly aside as being valueless. It has this value: it is a not unfair picture of what went on in many and many a militia camp in the first months of the rebellion, when the green recruits were without discipline, without all the steadying and heartening influence of trained leaders; when all their circumstances were new and strange, and charged with exaggerated terrors, and before the invaluable experience of actual collision in the field had turned them from rabbits into soldiers. If this side of the picture of that early day has not before been put into history, then history has been to that degree incomplete, for it had and has its rightful place there. There was more Bull Run material scattered through the early camps of this country than exhibited itself at Bull Run. And yet it learned its trade presently, and helped to fight the great battles later. I could have become a soldier myself if I had waited. I had got part of it learned; I knew more about retreating than the man that invented retreating.

TOPICS FOR ORAL AND WRITTEN DISCUSSION

1. Army reports of World War II and Vietnam usually ignore the existence of deserters, yet Civil War officers spoke of them freely. Speculate on the reasons for these differences.

2. Why would General Howard's charge that his troops were deserters absolve him from some of the blame?

3. Stage a class debate about whether Henry Fleming's actions or those of the 11th Corps should rightly be labeled desertion.

4. Make a careful comparison between the firsthand descriptions of the mass retreat from the front lines at the Plank Road with similar scenes in *The Red Badge of Courage*. Explain how such scenes reinforce the idea that people are largely at the mercy of forces outside themselves.

5. Why does hearing that the Union side has won (in this second encounter under fire) make Henry feel bad?

6. How has Henry Fleming's outlook changed from the novel to the later short story? What may have caused the change?

7. Compare Henry's acts of bravery in the Civil War with that at the end of his life. How are they different? Why does the narrator seem to admire the actions at the end of his life more than the one in battle?

8. Are Fleming's actions at the end of his life caused at all by his grandson's reaction to the story of his cowardice?

9. Compare and contrast the young Henry Fleming with the young Mark Twain. What accounts for their difference in attitude toward desertion?

10. Stage a debate on the question of whether desertion under fire is more or less morally important than desertion of individuals.

11. How much of Henry's regret about his desertion under fire comes from his view of it as wrong and how much from his fear of what people will think of him? Look at the theme of concern for self-image throughout the novel.

SUGGESTED READINGS

Bigelow, John, Jr. *Chancellorsville*. New Haven: Yale University Press, 1910.

Catton, Bruce. *The Army of the Potomac*. Garden City, N.Y.: Doubleday, 1952.

Davis, Kenneth C. *Don't Know Much About the Civil War*. New York: Morrow, 1996.

Gallagher, Gary W., ed. *Chancellorsville: The Battle and Its Aftermath*. Chapel Hill: University of North Carolina Press, 1996.

Linderman, Gerald F. *Embattled Courage: The Experience of Combat in the American Civil War*. New York: Free Press, 1987.

Stackpole, Edward J. *Chancellorsville: Lee's Greatest Battle*. Harrisburg, Penn.: Stackpole, 1958.

4

The Battlefield and Its Effects

We have seen in Chapters 2 and 3 the larger canvas of the Civil War—the movements of the armies and the decisions of the generals. Now we zero in for a close-up of the individual soldier on the battlefield. The story of Henry Fleming's first experiences under fire in wartime is a universal one, lived by many soldiers throughout the ages. In *The Red Badge of Courage*, we see a young man's boyhood illusions about himself and his world shattered in the face of battlefield realities. We have seen that before he is tested under fire, Henry thinks of war as a glorious and honorable experience. Nor is he the only soldier in the novel with a ridiculously romantic view of the battlefield. On Henry's first day of battle, as some of the soldiers begin building individual protective barriers to lie behind, others who have not yet seen battle question the propriety of such a strategy, believing that it takes the romance from fighting: "This procedure caused a discussion like duelists, believing it to be correct to stand erect and be, from their feet to their foreheads, a mark" (24). Later, it will seem that in the pursuit of honor and romance, they have ended up in hell, their five senses bombarded with gory scenes that excite fear, horror, disgust, panic, grief, hate, and shame—all in the extreme.

The realities of the army under fire—what Henry calls the "war monster"—have not changed significantly since the Civil War, despite changes in armaments and technology. From the Civil War to the Vietnam War, there is always the graphic and brutal confrontation with dead and mutilated people, always the panic and helplessness in the general chaos. Proof of this exists not only in the records of the wars but especially in the undocumented memories of thousands of war veterans.

Universally the battlefield brings with it utter chaos. Despite the close-drill training, despite the attempt to submerge individuality in a group machine, despite the presence of officers who are charged with directing every action of the men under them, chaos reigns. This was especially true of the Civil War because of the inexperience and lack of training of both men and officers. Chaos ushers in the day of Henry's first battle as conflicting rumors fly and the troops are told nothing about where they are, where they are going, or why. They suspect that they are being marched aimlessly in a circle, from place to place, and that the officers are as confused as they are. Chaos reaches a hellish climax of deafening noise after Henry has deserted the tattered soldier, men running "hither and thither in all directions" (68), yelling desperate questions about their location, as horses and cannon and carts threaten to run them down. To make matters worse, Henry can identify no landmarks. It is this chaos that panics Henry and makes him feel utterly helpless.

Crane biographer Christopher Benfrey argues that although Henry is never initiated into manhood (as he thinks at the end of the novel and as students have traditionally believed), he *is* initiated into a world where death and destructive change are inevitable—a world of mortality. And the horrors of the battlefield are the irrefutable evidence that the body is both real and subject to mutilation and death. To this inevitable result of battlefield fighting Henry is introduced as his regiment encounters a dead soldier with his foot protruding from his shoe. In the course of a few hours, he will see a lieutenant who has been shot in the hand, a field of the "ghastly" bodies of the dead, a hideous corpse in a leafy chapel, a dead soldier lying across a fence in front of him, then battalions of wounded men, including a hysterical soldier with a boot full of blood, and, finally, the grotesque death of his friend Jim Conklin. The horrors he encounters on the next day of battle are even bloodier and more nightmarish.

In civilian life, a single glimpse of violent and unnatural death,

A Harvest of Death, Gettysburg, Pennsylvania. Reprinted by permission of the Houghton Library, Harvard University.

like the foot of a corpse protruding through a shoe, is almost un-thinkable. Even a sensational newspaper today would be loathe to print a picture of something like the corpse in the leafy chapel. Yet on the battlefield, soldiers are bombarded with scene after scene of mass and horrific death, which, in addition to the horror they contain in themselves, are warnings of what could happen to them at any time. Each corpse is a graphic reminder that the body too is mortal.

The death Henry finds on the battlefield is both repugnant and fascinating. Notice how he wants to circle the first battle casualty he sees to ask "the Question": Is there life after death? Is there a heaven or hell? Can the dead observe the living? He peers into the eyes of the corpse in the chapel, searching for some elusive knowl-edge, even perversely tempted to touch it.

Henry is personally affected by the mortality of the battlefield when Jim Conklin is mortally wounded. Before this, he could ob-serve the dead from a certain distance, having never known them as living bodies. But now the reality of death comes home to him graphically in the suffering and death of someone he knows well. Henry becomes hysterical: "the sobs scorched him" (54), and "he saw something in [Jim's eyes] that made him sink wailing to the ground" (56). And, as Benfrey points out, Jim's death becomes a rehearsal for his own death as his actions mirror those of the dying man.

These realistic details of life and death under fire are part of what led many soldiers with front-line experience to believe that Crane himself had to have been a soldier in the Civil War, for we see the same details in personal memoirs of the battlefield. Private Jenkin Lloyd Jones of the 6th Wisconsin Battery writes in *An Ar-tilleryman's Diary* (Madison: Wisconsin History Commission, 1914) of seeing a man with the top of his head blown off after the Battle of Fort Gibson in Mississippi and dead Confederates scat-tered on the ground for four miles after a battle around Clinton, Mississippi (59).

It was not until 1897 that Stephen Crane saw real combat taking place—in the war between Greece and Turkey, which he covered as a war correspondent for William Randolph Hearst's *New York Journal*. What held Crane's attention was not so much the effect that the battle was having on the political situation that provoked the war but, as in *The Red Badge of Courage*, the stark cruelties of the battlefield. For Crane, the real result of war, according to Christopher Benfry, was not that countries were realigned but that bodies were mutilated. This is apparent in one of the early dispatches he sent back to his newspaper:

> On the lonely road from Velestino there appeared the figure of a man. Crane came slowly, and with a certain patient steadiness. A great piece of white linen was wound around under his jaw, and finally tied at the top of his head. . . .
> Under other circumstances one could have sworn that the man had great smears of red paint on his face. It was blood. (*The Works of Stephen Crane*, ed. Fredson Bowers [Charlottesville: University Press of Virginia, 1969–1976], 9: 21–22)

The May 23 issue of the *New York Journal* contains Crane's piece entitled "War's Horrors," his observation of the result of battle as seen aboard an ambulance ship:

> The ship is not large enough for its dreadful freight. But the men must be moved, and so 800 bleeding soldiers are jammed together in an insufferably hot hole, the light in which is so faint that we cannot distinguish the living from the dead.
> . . . Those who died, and there were not a few, could not be removed, and the corpses lay among the living men, shot through arm, chest, leg or jaw. The soldiers endured it with composure, I thought. . . .
> Near the hatch where I can see them is a man shot through the mouth. The bullet passed through both cheeks. He is asleep with his head pillowed on the bosom of a dead comrade. (*Works*, 9: 53–54)

In 1898, Crane covered the battlefields of the Spanish-American War in Cuba, writing for both Hearst's paper again and then for Joseph Pulitzer's *New York World*. There as well, his concern with the stark realities of the battlefield caused one of his reporter comrades, Richard Harding Davis, to write that Crane was the best of the reporters assigned to Cuba.

The shattering effects of the battlefield and its results in the wartime hospital are universal. In the Civil War, what are now recognized as psychological problems as a result of war were attributed to cowardice and poor discipline. Its long-lasting aftermath was

Home of a Rebel Sharpshooter, Gettysburg, Pennsylvania. Reprinted by permission of the Houghton Library, Harvard University.

chronic fear and anxiety. The nightmares and fearfulness of the World War I soldier was called shell shock and was thought to be caused by ruptured blood vessels. In World War II, shell shock came to be called combat fatigue and combat exhaustion. Symptoms, long after the war was over, included depression, nightmares, anxiety, and violent aggression. Breakdown on the battlefield was surprisingly rare in the Vietnam War, but the long-lasting effects of battlefield experience—nightmares, depression, and violent behavior—have been widespread. Only in 1970 did the American Psychiatric Association recognize an official diagnosis and treatment for what has come to be called posttraumatic stress disorder.

The following documents show that the slaughter on the battlefield is universal. The first four are written by men who saw combat during the Civil War. Also included are articles on World War II veterans and an interview with a World War II veteran.

SLAUGHTER ON THE BATTLEFIELD

CHARLES C. NOTT

> He was thrashing about in the grass, twisting his shuddering
> body into many strange postures. (97)

Like Henry Fleming, Charles C. Nott goes into battle for the first
time. Unlike Henry, Nott was a Union captain in the 5th Iowa Cavalry. He had not seen battle at the time he engages the Confederates at the Battle of Shiloh. His accounts were written only days
after his experiences and sent to a school in New York State. He
records the horrible sight of men being killed and wounded on
the hill the two sides were fighting over. He also tries to recreate
the sounds made by various artillery as the enemy "rushed" at him.
The worst sight was the suffering of the wounded, many of them
whose legs and arms had been shot off—much more horrible than
the dead, who seem to lie peacefully on the field. He also writes
of his own reaction under fire for the first time. His assumption of
a matter-of-fact air, which he thinks will calm the men he is leading,
is just the stance that Henry Fleming found despicable in the officers in his regiment.

FROM CHARLES C. NOTT, *SKETCHES OF THE WAR: A SERIES OF
LETTERS TO THE NORTH MOORE STREET SCHOOL OF NEW YORK*
(New York: Anson D. F. Randolph, 1865, pp. 31–37)

At a glance, the real object of the movement was apparent. It came upon
us in an instant, like the lifting of a curtain. The Fourteenth were hurrying
down through the field. The Second, in a long line, were struggling up the
opposite hill, where two glens met and formed a ridge. It was high and
steep, slippery with mud and melted snow. At the top, the breastworks of
the rebels flashed and smoked, whilst to the right and left, up either glen,
cannon were thundering. The attempt seemed desperate. Down through
the field we went, and began to climb the hill. At the very foot I found we
were in the line of fire. Rifle balls hissed over us, and bleeding men lay
upon the ground, or were dragging themselves down the hill. From the
foot to the breastworks the Second Iowa left a long line of dead and

wounded upon the ground. The sight of these was the most appalling part of the scene, and, for a moment, completely diverted my attention from the firing. A third of the way up we came under the fire of the batteries. The shot, and more especially the shell, came with the rushing, clashing of a locomotive on a railroad. You heard the boom of the cannon up the ravine— then the sound of the shell—and then *felt* it rushing at you. At the top of the hill the firearms sounded like bundles of immense powder crackers. They would go r-r-r-r-rap; then came the scattered shots, rap, rap—rap-rap-rap; then some more fire together, rrrrrrap. This resemblance was so striking that it impressed me at the moment.

The bursting of the shells produced much less effect—apparent effect, I mean—than I anticipated. Their explosion, too, was much like a large powder cracker thrown in the air. There was a loud bang—fragments flew about, and all was over. It was so quickly done, that you had no time to anticipate or think—you were killed or you were safe, and it was over. But the most dispiriting thing was that we saw no enemy. The batteries were out of sight, and at the breastworks nothing could be seen but fire and smoke. It seemed as though we were attacking some invisible power, and that it was a simple question of time whether we could climb that slippery steep before we were all shot or not. But suddenly the firing at the summit ceased. The Second Iowa had charged the works, and driven out the regiments which held them. Then came the fire of the Second upon our flying foes, and then loud shouts along the line, "Hurrah, hurrah, the Second are in—hurry up, boys, and support them—close up—forward—forward." We reached the top and scrambled over the breastwork. I saw a second hill rising gradually before us, and on the top of it a second breastwork—between us and it about four hundred yards of broken ground. A second fire opened upon us from these inner works. We were ordered back, and, recrossing those we had taken, lay down upon the outer side of the embankment.

The breastwork that had sheltered the enemy now sheltered us. It was about six feet high on our side, and the men laid close against it. Occasionally a hat was pushed up above it, and then a rifle ball would come whistling over us from the second intrenchment. The batteries also continued to fire, but the shot passed lower down the hill, and did little execution. Having no specific duty to discharge, I turned, as soon as our troops reached the breastworks, and gave my aid to the wounded.

A singular fact for which I could not account was, that those near the foot of the hill were struck in the legs; higher up, the shots had gone through the body, and near the breastworks, through the head. Indeed, at the top of the hill I noticed no wounded; all who lay upon the ground there were dead. A little house in the field was used as a hospital. I tore my handkerchief into strips, and tied them round the wounds which were bleeding badly, and made the men hold snow upon them. I then took a poor fellow in my arms to carry to the little house. "Throw down your gun," I said, "you are too weak to carry it." "No, no," he replied, "I will hold on to it as long as I am alive." The house happened to be in the exact line of one of the batteries, and as we approached it, the shot flew over our path. Fortunately, the house was below the range, but one came so low as to knock off a shingle from the gable end. For a few minutes we thought they were firing on the wounded. We had no red flag to display; but I found a man with a red handkerchief, and tied it to a stick, and sent him on the roof with it. Within the house there were but three surgeons at this time. One of them asked me to take his horse and ride for the instruments, ambulances, and assistants; for no preparation had been made. It was then I passed Major Chipman carried by his soldiers.

When I returned, the ambulances were busy at their work; numerous couples of soldiers were supporting off wounded friends, and occasionally came four, carrying one in a blanket. The wounded men generally showed the greatest heroism. They hardly ever alluded to themselves, but shouted to the artillery that we met to hurry forward, and told stragglers that we had carried the day. One poor boy, carried in the arms of two soldiers, had his foot knocked off by a piece of shell; it dangled horribly from his limb by a piece of skin, and the bleeding stump was uncovered. I stopped to tell the men to tie his stocking round the limb, and to put snow upon the wound. "Never mind the foot, captain," said he, "we drove the rebels out, and have got their trench, that's the most I care about." Yet I confess the sights and sounds were not as distressing as I anticipated. The small round bullet holes, though they might be mortal, looked no larger than a surgeon's lancet might have made. Only once did I hear distressing groans. A poor wretch in an ambulance shrieked whenever the wheels struck a stump. There was no help for it. The road was through the wood, the driver could only avoid the trees, and drive on regardless of his agony.

You will perhaps ask how I felt in the fight. There was nothing upon which I had had so much curiosity as to what my feelings would be. Much to my surprise I found myself unpleasantly cool. I did not get excited, and felt a great want of something to do. I thought if I only had something—my own company to lead on, or somebody to order, I should have much less to think about. There seemed such a certainty of being hit that I felt certain I should be, and after a few minutes had a vague sort of wish that it would come if it were coming, and be over with. The alarming effect of the bullets and shells was less than I supposed it would be, and my strongest sensation of danger was produced by the sight of the dead and wounded. The thing I was most afraid of was a panic among our men, and when the Seventh Illinois was ordered to fall back down the hill, I so much feared that the men might deem it a retreat that I entirely forgot the firing, and walked down in front of them talking to their major, so that any frightened man in the ranks might be reassured by our "matter of course" air. Take it altogether, I think I felt and acted pretty much as I do in an unusual and exciting affair. I know I found myself looking for an illustration of the effect of the shells, and wondering if there was no greater and grander illustration of the musketry than a bunch of powder crackers. I remember that I did little things from habit, as usual; when I threw off my overcoat, for example, I took a pipe which a friend had given me from the pocket, lest it should be lost; and I remember that I once corrected my grammar when I inadvertently adopted the western style of telling the men to *lay* down, and as I did so, I thought that one or two people at North Moore Street would have been very apt to laugh if they had heard it. Yet for all this, I was by no means unconscious of danger. Some officers seemed utterly indifferent to it. Thus, in the fight of Thursday, Colonel Shaw, of the Fourteenth, after ordering his men to lie down, not only remained on horseback, but crossed his legs over the pommel of the saddle, sitting sidewise to be more comfortable. The sharpshooters of the enemy concentrated their fire on him, he being the only person visible. As the bullets thickened about him, the colonel said indignantly, "those rascals are firing at me, I shall have to move," and he threw his leg back, and walked his horse down to the other end of the line.

Our men lay in the trench all night, exposed to the western wind, which blew keenly round the summit of the hill—a large force of the enemy within a few yards, able to rush upon them at any moment.

I had gone back just after dark, with the adjutant, who had been hurt by the explosion of a shell, and my return with him saved me this. When morning came, we went back. As we reached the foot of the hill, we were told that a white flag had been displayed, and an officer had gone into the fort, but that the time was nearly up, and the attack was now to be renewed. We hurried on, expecting in a few moments to be in a second assault. We had nearly reached the trenches when the men sprang from the ditch to the top of the breastwork, waving the colors and giving wild hurrahs. The fort had surrendered.

There was a load lifted off my mind, and I stopped to look around. The first glance fell on the blue coats scattered through the felled trees and stumps. The march of our troops up the hill had been somewhat in the form of a broom. Until near the top they had been in column, leaving a long, narrow line like the handle, and as they rushed at the breastwork, they had spread out like the broom. This ground was plainly marked by the dead. Now that my attention was given, I was surprised to find how many were strewn upon the narrow strip. Here was one close to me;

about the width of a class-room beyond was another; a little further on
two had fallen, side by side. In a little triangle I counted eighteen bodies,
and many I knew had been carried off during the night. Still the scene
was not so painful as the dead-room of the hospital at St. Louis. The
attitudes were peaceful. The arms were in all but one case thrown naturally over the breast, as in sleep; and no face gave any indication of a
painful death. I passed on and entered the breastwork. It was about the
height of a man. On top was a large log, and between the log and the
earthwork a narrow slit. Through this they had fired on us. The log had
hidden their heads, so that, while we were in plain view, they were to
us an invisible foe. Immediately within were six more bodies of the Second Iowa, and one in simple homespun. He was the only one of the
enemy upon the ground. The soldiers, gathering around him, looked, as
I did myself, with some curiosity upon one who had thus met the punishment of his treason. He had been shot through the back of the head
while running, and his face expressed only wonderment and fright. It
showed him a country-bred youth, illiterate, uncultivated—a contrast to
the still intelligent faces that lay around him.

LETTERS FROM TWO BROTHERS FROM THE FRONT

> So it came to pass that as he trudged from the place of blood
> and wrath his soul changed. (130)

The letters of two brothers, Warren and Eugene, serving in different battles of the Civil War in the Union army, corroborate the
picture of battlefield slaughter painted by Stephen Crane. Warren's
first battle was at Antietam, one of the bloodiest of the war. He
also for a time was a prisoner of the Confederates.

Although Warren is somewhat more reserved than his brother
about the cruelties of the battlefield (he only mentions the death
and wounding of those he knew after his father asked him), he
writes of the death of a comrade he had come to know who was
also from Cambridge—a student at Harvard College. Note that he
describes a comrade's being shot in front of him and falling against
him. He also speaks of the looting and great mounds of dead bodies on the field after the battle. A month after the battle, he speaks
of "my baptism in blood," which has left him a changed—hardened—man.

His brother, Eugene, whose illness has kept him working on the
Potomac River, writes graphically of the dead and wounded he sees

lying in the streets of Washington and in the hospitals of the capital, in one of which Louisa May Alcott, author of *Little Women*, served as a nurse.

FROM *LETTERS FROM TWO BROTHERS SERVING IN THE WAR FOR
THE UNION: TO THEIR FAMILY AT HOME*
(Cambridge, Mass.: Printed for Private Circulation, 1871)

[Antietam]
Sept, 1862
Dear Father,
   . . . We went into the fight with 301 men: of this number 136 were killed or wounded, leaving us, at the close of the day but 165 men fit for duty. I fired between fifty and sixty rounds, and had a good mark to aim at every time. I did not waste any ammunition, I can assure you.

I suppose the battle of "An-tee-tam" must be set down as the greatest ever fought on this continent. Each army numbered about 100,000 men, their lines extending between four and five miles. Our loss in killed and wounded will exceed 10,000 men. That of the rebels will never be known, but it exceeds ours by thousands. They spent the whole day after the battle in burying their dead and removing the wounded; and after their retreat the ground for miles was strewn with their dead, and houses and barns filled with their wounded. . . .

Warren

Near Sharpsburg, MD. October 3, 1862
Dear Father,— . . .

You ask if I could not send home some trophies of the Antietam battle-field. I could have picked up any number of guns, swords, knapsacks, cartridge-boxes, etc., but had no way to carry them. I found several rebel letters and brought them away, but have lost them. . . . I have not been on the battle-field since we left it several weeks since. I was sick and not able to go with the boys, who have been there frequently.

One of the boys, who was on the field a few days after the battle, told me that in the part he visited he saw eight or ten heaps of dead rebels that our men had gathered together to bury; and he counted the bodies in one heap, and there were 130. Our men were engaged between four and five days in burying the dead of both armies and carrying off the wounded. When the rebels retreated from the Antietam battle-field they took all their wounded that they could carry, or that could hobble along on foot, and then left more than 4,000 for our army to take care of.

You ask if anyone was shot near me? Yes, my file-leader, the man who stood directly in front, was shot in the head and fell heavily upon me. I supposed at first that he was killed, but he is living now. Samuel S. Gould stood within five feet of me when he was mortally wounded; he had been in the company but four or five days. He was fresh from Harvard College, and I got quite well acquainted with him. He was a wide-awake, noble fellow, about as tall as I am. He has relatives in West Cambridge. . . . One of the color bearers was shot in three places; he was a Belmont [Massachusetts] boy, named David Chenery. We had forty-one men in our company, twenty-one of whom were killed or wounded. My rifle was so hot that I could hardly touch the barrel with my hand, but it worked well. . . . Of course I had many narrow escapes from death during the day: a ball grazed me just below the temple, taking off the skin, drawing blood, and stunning me for some moments; and I was struck on the shoulder by some hard substance, which whirled me around and lamed me for some day, but I never thought these casualties worth mentioning in my previous letter. . . .

I felt quite cool and collected, and had no personal fear during the battle. The scenes of blood and strife that I have been called to pass through during the months that are passed, and my "baptism in blood," have nearly destroyed all the finer feelings of my nature. . . .

Warren

On the Potomac, June 25, 1864
Dear Father and Mother,— . . .

It makes me shudder to think of the terrible sights that I have seen this summer. I'm sure I see enough of the horrors of war without being obliged to participate. I think more of it, perhaps, because Warren is there. I hope I am correct in saying *there*—I dread to think of the poor boy, what he must have suffered; I do hope and pray he may be spared. We were glad to leave the White House: the stench was awful; thousands of dead men, and horses, mules, etc., lay there rotting under a burning sun, some of them half buried, some entirely exposed. If the "stay-at-homes" could only see these sights, it would sicken them, I reckon; but one soon becomes hardened to it. The first lot of wounded men that I ever saw, I was horror-struck; but now after seeing thousands upon thousands, I do not feel any horror, and after my face is turned, forget what I have seen anything so dreadful. I have scrutinized every face of a wounded man that I have seen, but as yet have not seen the one I looked for; yes, and I have looked at many a dead face too—lifting the coarse blanket from their discolored faces, with a sickening dread lest my fears should be realized. All soldiers agree (those that have been in hospitals, I mean) that it is by far a more horrible sight to see a lot of wounded men than it is to see the battle itself; for some of these wounds are of the worst descriptions. I have often seen wounds full of crawling worms, the horrible creatures having taken possession before their appointed time. . . .

Eugene

CARNAGE IN THE BATTLE OF ATLANTA

> The men halted, had opportunity to see some of their comrades dropping with moans and shrieks. A few lay under foot, still or wailing. (101)

George W. Bailey was a first lieutenant in the 6th Missouri Infantry of the Union army. Bailey writes of the Battle of Atlanta in July 1864, near the end of the war. In the preface to his memoirs, he speaks mysteriously of those who saw combat but were "*stricken dumb* at the time, and ever after remained silent." He asks them to come forward, as he is doing, to tell the truth about the war from actual experience. He writes of the tension under fire, of the incredible noise and confusion as well as the dead and wounded who litter the landscape.

FROM GEORGE W. BAILEY, *A PRIVATE CHAPTER OF THE WAR*
(St. Louis: G. I. Jones and Co., 1880, pp. 1–9)

July 22, 1864; before Atlanta, Ga.— . . . The day advanced and so did the enemy! Our lines were being extended on the extreme left; and the Seventeenth Corps had hardly arrived at its place in the extension, when away southward, and rather to the rear of the line of the Fifteenth Corps, began suspicious sounds of desultory skirmishing. The sounds grew heavier and heavier, until it was apparent that our lines were either seriously opposed or else being attacked. The sputtering of skirmish-rifles now became a continuous rattle of musketry. Huge volumes of powder-smoke arose above the tree-tops, and the thunder of artillery was added to the conflict. Then we readily understood what we might soon expect in our front. "We are going to have a fight here," said Gen. Smith, as he sat on his horse in rear of our lines, surrounded by his staff. "They are raising the devil on our left, and we'll catch it here soon!" Already the Confederate shells burst in uncomfortable proximity over our heads, causing our horses to prance to such an extent that they were sent to the rear. A shell burst less than fifteen feet overhead. "Spherical case," said the General, as the bullet missiles hissed and whistled among the foliage. "Oh me! oh me!" cried one of our boys, as he held one arm with the other and limped toward the rear. "Dry up! dry up!" ordered the General. "You're not hurt much, or you couldn't bellow like that." The roar of the conflict seems to increase and approach. An ambulance passes. An orderly says, "Gen. McPherson's killed! He's in that ambulance." Every face was sad; but no time now for inquiries. Every thing is excitement, and every eye is strained toward the woods skirting our front. An orderly sent to order in our outposts returned wounded. . . . Other pickets are coming in rapidly, and the general report is, "They are coming on us heavy!" While some are comparatively cool, others wear panic-stricken countenances, point wildly toward the woods, and huskily exclaim, "They are right on us!" and hastily climb over the works, and seek shelter behind them. Now there follows a death-like stillness. The sounds of battle have suddenly ceased, and there is a calm before the coming tempest. Ominous silence! Every rifle is cocked, every eye gazing across the space intervening between us and the timber. . . . Here and there among the brave boys in the works were faces pale as death. They could not have been more ghastly had they been reflections of the countenance of the writer. At last there is observable a great commotion in the distant foliage, and emerging from it, three lines deep, in extraordinary order, come the advancing enemy. . . . Their prowess is unquestioned, but their glory is short! Our lines open! Fire leaps from the crest of our works; the deadly roll of musketry is heard continuously amidst the crashes of double-shotted cannon. Angry-hissing rifle-balls rival grape and canister in spreading dismay and death among our gallant enemies. The continuous roar of the battle drowns all other sounds, and mother earth trembles as if convulsed with an earthquake. Through the smoke and battle, the writer could discern confusion and disorder among the Confederates, while the ground was thickly strewn with dead and wounded. . . . Shells tear off the limbs of trees, and scream fearfully through the air; while solid shot tear up the earth, sending great clouds of dust skyward. . . . Bullets madly hissing from the front, bullets spitefully whizzing from the rear; obscuring smoke of battle; . . . "confusion worse confounded." But the officers still encourage: "Once more, boys!" "Give it to 'em again!" "Aim low, boys!" . . .

[He is captured and taken into Atlanta.]

The cries and moans of the wounded arose through the thick smoke. Some Federal dead lay stretched in and near our works, but in front of them was an awful scene. The ground for over one hundred yards was thickly strewn with the rebel dead and wounded. Many cries arose for "water;" some were struggling to extricate themselves from tangled heaps of dead, and calling for aid; some were vainly striving to stop the flow of crimson tide gushing from ghastly wounds; many were fitfully gasping their last breath. But the great majority were grim and cold in the strong embrace of death, lying in almost every conceivable position; some were riddled with rifle-balls; some were torn with grape or canister shot, and at not infrequent intervals the bodies were literally heaped together. There were young and old; some distorted, other calm. Stony eyes gazed meaninglessly at us as we picked our way; other stared wildly into space. . . . History records the result: Total Union loss, 3,521; total Confederate loss, about 8,000 men, 5,000 stand of arms. . . .

WILLIAM BIRCHER

> Under foot there were a few ghastly forms motionless. They lay twisted in fantastic contortions. Arms were bent and heads were turned in incredible ways. (36)

William Bircher, only fifteen when he joined the Union army as a drummer boy, had the shattering experience of surveying the battlefield after the Battle of Shiloh. Here he sees mountains of dead soldiers, including some who had burned alive when shells set fire to trees that had fallen onto them in the heavy shelling. He feels changed by the experience, the battlefield being more horrible than he had ever imagined.

FROM WILLIAM BIRCHER, *A DRUMMER-BOY'S DIARY: COMPRISING FOUR YEARS OF SERVICE WITH THE SECOND REGIMENT MINNESOTA VETERAN VOLUNTEERS*
(St. Paul, Minn.: St. Paul Book and Stationery Co., 1889, pp. 32–36)

About noon we arrived at Pittsburgh Landing, and what a horrible sight met our gaze. Dead men were lying in the mud, mixed up with sacks of grain and government stores, some lying in the water and others trampled entirely out of sight in the deep mud. This was where the great stampede occurred, and no pen can picture the horrors of this part of the field. . . . The battle-field was strewn with the wreck and carnage of war; caissons, dismounted cannon, and dead artillery-horses and their dead riders were piled up in heaps, and the warm sun caused a stench that was almost unbearable. Here and there we could see where a wounded soldier had been pinned to the ground by a fallen limb of a tree, and the shells setting fire to the dry leaves, the poor fellows had been burned alive to a crisp. No historian can ever depict the horrors of a battle-field. The dead lying in every direction and in every stage of decomposition. Squads of men scattered all over the field digging trenches, rolling the dead in, and covering them up with three or four inches of dirt, only to be washed off by the first rain, leaving the bones to be picked by the buzzards and crows. Such is the terror of war.

I had frequently seen pictures of battle-fields and had often read about them; but the most terrible scenes of carnage my boyish imagination had ever figured fell far short of the dreadful reality, as I beheld it after the great battle of Shiloh. . . . Before we passed beyond our front line, evidences of the terrible carnage of the battle environed us on all sides; fresh, hastily-dug graves were there with rude head-boards telling the poor fellow's name and regiment. . . . The trees around about were chipped by the bullets and stripped almost bare by the leaden hail; while a log house near by in the clearing had been so riddled with shot and shell that scarcely a whole shingle was left to its roof.

But sights more fearful awaited us as we stepped out beyond the front line. We picked our way carefully among the fallen timber and down the slope to the scene of the fearful charge. The ground was soaked with recent rains, and the heavy mist which hung like a pall over the field, together with the growing darkness, rendered objects but distinctly visible and all the more ghastly. As the eye ranged over so much of the field as the shrouding mist would allow us to see, we beheld a scene of destruction, terrible, indeed, if there ever was one in this wide world. Dismounted gun-carriages, shattered caissons, knapsacks, haversacks, muskets, bayonets, and accoutrements scattered over the field in wildest confusion. Horses—poor creature—dead and dying, and, worse and most awful of all, dead men by the hundreds. Most of the Union soldiers had been buried already, and the pioneers yonder in the mist were busily digging trenches for the poor fellows in gray. As we passed along we stopped to observe how thickly they were lying, here and there, like grass before a scythe in summer time. How firmly some had grasped their guns, with high, defiant look, and how calm were the countenances of others in their last solemn sleep. I sickened of the dreadful sight and begged my comrades to come away, come away. It was too awful to look at any more. Even the rudest and roughest of us were forced to think of the terrible suffering endured in this place and of the sorrow and tears that would be shed among the mountains of the North and the rice-fields of the far-off South.

THE BATTLEFIELD HOSPITAL: WALT WHITMAN

In December 1862, at the age of forty-three, Walt Whitman, already an experienced journalist and famous poet, visited his brother who had been wounded at Fredericksburg, Virginia. This experience seemed to have inspired him to serve in the Civil War as a medical assistant. His poems are rich in images of the hospital drawn from firsthand experience. "The Wound-Dresser" is a graphic description of what one would find in a battlefield hospital. Note also the view of death—not as a romantic, adolescent escape but as an agent of mercy. Like in the stories of World War II veterans that follow, Whitman the poet revisits the hospital in dreams long afterward.

FROM WALT WHITMAN, "THE WOUND-DRESSER," IN
LEAVES OF GRASS
(New York: W. E. Chapin and Co., 1867)

2

. . . Bearing the bandages, water and sponge,
Straight and swift to my wounded I go,
Where they lie on the ground after the battle brought in,
Where their priceless blood reddens the grass the ground,
Or to the rows of the hospital tend, or under the roof'd hospital,
To the long rows of cots up and down each side I return,
To each and all one after another I draw near, not one do I miss,
An attendant follows holding a tray, he carries a refuse pail,
Soon to be fill'd with clotted rags and blood, emptied, and fill'd
    again.

I onward go, I stop,
With hinged knees and steady hand to dress wounds,
I am firm with each, the pangs are sharp yet unavoidable,
One turns to me his appealing eyes—poor boy! I never knew you,
Yet I think I could not refuse this moment to die for you, if that
    would save you.

3

On, on I go, (open doors of time! open hospital doors!)
The crush'd head I dress, (poor crazed hand tear not the bandage
    away,)
The neck of the cavalry-man with the bullet through and through
    I examine,

Hard the breathing rattles, quite glazed already the eye, yet life
  struggles hard,
(Come sweet death! Be persuaded O beautiful death! In mercy
  come quickly.)

From the stump of the arm, the amputated hand,
I undo the clotted lint, remove the slough, wash off the matter
  and blood,
Back on his pillow the soldier bends with curv'd neck and side-
  falling head,
His eyes are closed, his face is pale, he dares not look on the
  bloody stump,
And has not yet look'd on it.

I dress a wound in the side, deep, deep,
But a day or two more, for see the frame all wasted and sinking,
And the yellow-blue countenance see.

I dress the perforated shoulder, the foot with the bullet-wound,
Cleanse the one with a gnawing and putrid gangrene, so
  sickening, so offensive,
While the attendant stands behind aside me holding the tray and
  pail.

I am faithful, I do not give out,
The fractur'd thigh, the knee, the wound in the abdomen,
These and more I dress with impassive hand, (yet deep in my
  breast a fire, a burning flame.)

4

Thus in silence in dreams' projections,
Returning, resuming, I thread my way through the hospitals. . . .

THE HORRORS OF WAR IN THE TWENTIETH CENTURY: JOHN BOUDREAU

In November 1996, reporter John Boudreau investigated the incidence of posttraumatic stress syndrome among a group of veterans with whom this term had rarely been associated: those of
World War II. The lifelong effect of the horrors of twentieth-
century warfare has usually been associated with Vietnam veterans
but rarely with veterans of World War II. Boudreau not only did

statistical research on the lasting effects of war on all living veterans; he followed one group of World War II veterans who sought help with their war-related emotional problems in a group therapy session designed for them.

FROM JOHN BOUDREAU, "WOUNDS THAT NEVER HEAL"
(*West County Times* [Pinole, Calif.],
[November 10, 1996], pp. 1A, 4A–6A)

The dead rise at night.

It's fall 1943 again. In memory's mist, Sgt. Shaffe Courey duckwalks in a crouch across a forest clearing. His heart pounds fiercely this frosty Italian autumn day.

The German steps out from behind a tree. Before the young Wehrmacht soldier can lift his rifle to eye level, Courey's Tommy gun shakes, kicks, spits—yakatayakatayakata. The German jolts backward, dead before he hits the dirt.

The GIs drop to the ground, firing blindly into the forest. Courey takes cover, quickly notes the dead among his own, and with a gesture commands his platoon to creep into the woods. Then he steps over the first man he ever killed. The soldier's helmet is pushed back; his eyes are vacant. Steam rises from his paste-gray face.

Courey wakes in a knot of seat-sodden bed sheets and breathless cries. "It used to be, in the beginning, I dreaded going to bed at night."

For the better part of five decades—some 18,000 nights—Courey carried the weight of his torment alone. He and his comrades had returned to a nation flush with victory and in no mood to hear about their suffering. Vietnam veterans came home to a country that had witnessed the carnage of combat on TV. World War II vets survived equally ferocious battles that sometimes didn't even make it into the papers back home.

"It's harder for our generation," says Everett Stanley, who fought in France as an infantryman. "We're all John Waynes. Damn the torpedoes! Full speed ahead! But there is a limit to what a man can take."

He and Courey are among perhaps 200,000 World War II veterans who suffer from post-traumatic stress disorder. For them, the war rolls on and on and on.

Old soldiers are coming to Veterans Affairs clinics across the country in search of psychological help. In some cities, World War II veterans are filling therapy groups faster than veterans from any other war.

The deluge began in 1995 as America celebrated the 50th anniversary of the end of World War II—a commemoration that stirred painful memories.

In the winter of their lives, these veterans struggle to leave the battle-field behind.

The men proudly answered duty's call. They fondly recall military life, bonds developed during extraordinary experiences. But many feel shame about unseen scars.

Society tells them to forget the war, says Brian Engdahl, a VA psychologist in Minneapolis and authority on post-traumatic stress. "But the body keeps the score. The pain will always be there."

"When I got my discharge in 1945 in Santa Ana, an officer stood up in front of us all," recalls airman Bob Tharratt. " 'You have gone through traumatic experiences, done things and seen things that are unbelievable. Now go home and forget the whole thing because what you've been through, what you've seen—nobody will believe you.' "

Their bodies have grown soft around the edges, hair receded with the years. They walk with canes, walkers and stiff gaits. But they still run for cover when a car backfires. Many are hearing impaired. Yet they still hear the thunder of artillery and the screams of the dying. Some have failing eyesight. But they see the eyes of buddies—handsome young bodies mangled and chewed up—peering back at them.

"I see those faces," says Al Costella of Walnut Creek, a former Marine corporal who led a mortar squad. His first battle was the 1944 invasion of the Pacific island Peleiu. Minutes after hitting the beach, a buddy next to him took a bullet in the forehead as Costella warned the private to hit the sand. Later that day Costella stacked the dead in a bomb crater. The pile of fresh corpses rose 16 feet brushing against a tree branch. "You can't forget those faces."

Courey, Tharratt and Costella didn't know each other during their tours of duty. Now they and nine others meet weekly for group therapy at the Martinez VA Mental Health Clinic.

It is their final mission: Find healing.

But time—and talk—does not heal all wounds.

"You can't imagine looking at somebody and there's no arm, just a bloody stump, just massive blood and guts—just meat," says Tharratt, who manned a bomber turret. "You're flying in a B-17, and you see just 130 feet on the side of you is an airplane with 10 men in it. There is flak all around and all of a sudden you see a red ball of flame and pieces of that plane going down. Nobody, nobody, nobody, unless they've witnessed it, will understand what it really feels like to see that happen. I can close my eyes and see all these things."

War can obliterate a soldier's sense of order.

"It destroys your God," says a veteran who served in an Army reconnaissance unit in Europe and asked to be identified only as "Joe."

"It's such a sad, sad thing to do to people. You come home and nobody understands what you've been through and what you've done and you're *not* going to tell them. You're a little bit ashamed.

"I had a tough time when my son would say, 'What did you do?' It's like what Rush Limbaugh says: You break things and you kill people."

Joe's voice trails off.

"You're walking around like it doesn't look like anything is wrong with a guy and something will happen and all of a sudden you're in a rage. You're beyond anger." . . .

In war this twisted state of mind is a lifesaver, says Dr. Lawrence Brass, a Yale Medical School professor who studies the relationship between stress and strokes. "Rage is good to have if someone is trying to kill you."

Then the fighting stops.

It was called shell shock in World War I, combat fatigue during World War II. Vietnam veterans were likely to be diagnosed schizophrenic. Not until 1980 did the American psychiatric community recognize post-traumatic stress disorder. In fact, traumatic stress has always been a human condition. Literature dating back to ancient Greece describes the emotional impact of war on soldiers.

Traumatic stress is not always related to combat. A natural disaster or a violent attack can cause it. Symptoms include insomnia, nightmares, flashbacks, anger, withdrawal, crying spells.

Even Vietnam veterans, whose generation is more accustomed to therapy, wait a few years before seeking help. According to the National Vietnam Veterans Readjustment Study in the 1980s, 35.8 percent of male Vietnam combat veterans met the full American Psychiatric Association diagnostic criteria for post-traumatic stress disorder—nearly 20 years after the war. That's 480,000 men. People who weren't on the front lines—men and women—also have the disorder.

No one knows how many World War II veterans suffered from post-traumatic stress because no survey was done and many of the combatants are dead.

We know it affected the best of men.

Audie Murphy, America's most-decorated World War II veteran and boyish leading man during the 1950s, was tortured by nightmares, insomnia, flashbacks, rage and depression for more than 25 years. He died a month before his 47th birthday in 1971.

The unconscious, Freud noted, is timeless. Memories of combat—its odd elation and its terror—last a lifetime.

They greet each other with crisp salutes—"highballs," they call them—and tender hugs. "Permission to come aboard, sir!" says one. All military branches are represented: Army, Navy, Air Force, Marines. . . .

"The general public, and I was one of them, thought anyone who had to see a psychiatrist wasn't functioning on all cylinders. I hate to go in there because I run into former students of mine working as clerks and such. I think, 'Oh God, I hope it doesn't get around: Courey has lost his marbles.' "

Clinical nurse Nancy Wolfe and clinical social worker Joan Zabih started the group four years ago after they noticed an increasing stream of older veterans complaining of sleep problems and depression.

About half of the 12 men in the group have taken antidepressant medication. Psychologists use "desensitization" therapy, a method of confronting traumatic memories, to ease anxiety and diminish symptoms. Group therapy offers emotional support.

Dan Meier, a retired Navy commander who lives in Vallejo, says his mental health has improved as he has told and retold his story. He lost an arm and an eye when his battleship, the *USS Colorado*, absorbed two dozen artillery hits during the invasion of Tinian in the Mariana Islands. In the chaotic aftermath, Meier, wounded and covered with a sheet, was mistaken for dead. He was carried feet first through narrow passageways, up ladders, onto the deck. He astounded the stretcher bearers when he uttered, "What do you guys think you're doing?"

Meier has taken on the role of prodding taciturn members. "Forget about it? Not only did they not forget about it, they also didn't have anybody to talk to. We understand each other. We've become important to each other."

Collectively, the 12 men have earned 12 Purple Hearts. They exhibit a quiet patriotism: The American flag and military relics adorn their homes, but the vets shy away from parades. Talk turns quickly to combat: What's it like to heap frozen corpses? Does salt water hurt the bodies of wounded soldiers ripped open by shrapnel?

They hid pain behind barracks humor. They call each other military nick-names—"flyboy," "dogface," "bellhop." One day a member sneaks a women's lingerie catalog, stuffed in a military magazine, into a session. The men, handing it around the room, snicker and tease like schoolboys. It briefly lightens the mood.

Sometimes the humor is dark. Early on, Wolfe asked how many of them had nightmares. She was greeted with silence. Then one quipped, "Do you want to go on night patrol with me?"

Mostly, though, they provide each other with emotional cover.

On a spring morning, one talks of a TV program about the National Rifle Association. "I hear those big rifles, the clip going *katunk*. The sounds of those rifles brought back memories. It reminded me of being back *there*."

"It opened up an area you hadn't been for a while," Wolfe interjects.

Another veteran joins in. "I'll be walking down the sidewalk and see a shadow. I'll walk around it. A shadow is like a person standing by the side of a building, ready to pounce on you."

The first continues, "I was scared that I was completely out of my wits."

The second becomes agitated, voice cracking, tears forming. "I'm off my rocker! I've been like this for 50 years. . . . They treat you like you're crazy. How can a person not feel any other way?"

He scurries out of the room. The meeting breaks up as others follow, comforting him in a reception area.

The troubled veteran won't have this support much longer. The 4-year-old therapy group is disbanding in January. It is time to start a new group, Wolfe and Zabih tell the men.

Some weep at the news. Zabih cries too.

They've been taught how to ease their symptoms. But here is no cure.

Airman Tharratt came home trained to kill and trained to drink. "As we walked in for the debriefing, the first thing they handed us was a straight shot of whiskey. You took one or two. Here we were, 19, 20, 21—without anything to eat for six, 10 hours or longer. The first thing that goes into your stomach was a straight shot of whiskey."

He returned at age 22, a lifetime of terrors and depression ahead of him.

"My father would come rushing in and throw himself on top of me, yell at me that I was dreaming, 'Get a hold of yourself, lad!' Then he'd usually give me a shot of whiskey and tell me to go to sleep.

"I went back to school, got married, started raising a family. But I was still having nightmares. I was still confused."

He drank heavily for three decades after the war.

Tharratt, 73, gave up booze 16 years ago. Now the retired sales representative passes around nonfat cookies during group therapy. He is youthful, slender and easygoing, with a face full of smile lines.

Tharratt lives with his second wife, Jeane, in a tidy Walnut Creek town house. His den is devoted to memorabilia—photos of his father and other family in uniform, a German officer's pistol, a portrait of his bomber. He has methodically filed all of his papers, telegrams notifying family of his disappearance behind enemy lines, newspaper clippings.

Tharratt was assigned the cramped belly turret of a B-17 because he was the smallest in the crew. He watched bombs blot cities like giant ink spots. On his 18th mission, after a bombing run over Nuremberg on Sept. 10, 1944, his plane began shuddering as artillery shells hit it. He assisted an injured crewmate, then slipped on his parachute and jumped.

Tharratt cups his hands. "I looked out and there was nothing, just sky.

I felt as calm as can be. I was in God's hands."

He landed near a Hitler Youth Camp and was captured. He ended up in Stalag Luft IV, near Berlin.

On Feb. 6, 1945, with the Russians advancing from the east, the prisoners were herded by SS guards for an 86-day, 500-mile march across the country. POWs were beaten, starved, humiliated. They suffered from dysentery and were forced to relieve themselves of bloody feces in the middle of streets as residents jeered.

Tharratt was liberated outside Bittefield, southwest of Berlin, by General Patton's Third Army. He weighed 109 pounds, down from 150.

Fifty years later, it is still dangerous to wake him.

"I was asleep on the couch one Saturday afternoon. My oldest daughter came running in 'Daddy, Daddy, Daddy.' She threw herself on top of me. I picked her up and threw her across the room. She hit the wall."

Today, he is at peace with his past. "One stepson called to wish me a happy Father's Day. I said once again, 'I'm sorry the early times weren't as happy as they could have been.' He said, 'Dad, I love you. I understand.' They forgive me."

Tharratt returned to Germany for the first time in 1990 with a church group. On a bus ride, he spotted a sign announcing the town of Bittefield, which he had passed 50 years ago during the death march. Tears welled in his eyes. He was given a microphone and asked to retell his story as the bus rumbled along.

"There was stunned silence. Then I sat down and immediately fell asleep. That night I slept the sleep of the dead for the first time since the war."

• • •

Shaffe Courey was a changed man when he returned from war. "Night and day" is how his wife, Pat, describes the difference. "He would lie there and shake all night. I said, 'I swear to God, if we ever get a big enough place, we would get two beds.' "

Even when he naps, Courey flails about. "I nearly broke her nose one night," he says. His gentle gaze falls on his wife, sitting across the living room.

Since 1961, when they were able to buy a bigger place, they've been sleeping in separate beds.

"The only thing that has kept us together is our religion," he says ruefully. "There are times when I know she'd like to be elsewhere. She stuck with me when times were tough. I thank the good Lord for her."

Here, the cost of sacrifice hits you full on.

Married in late 1942, the couple decided to wait until he returned from war to start their family. But Courey's severe combat injuries prevented him from having children. The couple's affections turned to Mac, an Irish setter-Labrador mix, who died in 1965. "He filled a large gap in our lives," says Courey, his words swelling with feelings. "I still miss that dog. When he passed away, I sat in that chair and cried like a baby for three days."

Courey is a deeply moral man, imbued with a sense of responsibility for country, community and the men in his unit. He volunteered for front-line duty because he wanted to settle the score for the death of his older brother.

Courey guided a 75-soldier platoon. He has spent a lifetime remembering the men he shepherded to death.

In the pre-dawn dark of Sept. 9, 1943, the 25-year-old sergeant slipped over the ship's gunwale and down the cargo netting to the landing craft. The invasion of Italy had begun. Artillery lit the sky. The air was violent with metal.

"We circled around and around and around. You lose all time and perspective. Shells from shore batteries are hitting all around. They hit some landing craft, which carried a whole platoon."

Colored flares signaled which regiment was to hit the beach. "It was kind of rough, guys getting sick from fear."

Finally, Courey's craft headed in. The men waded ashore, dodging dead bodies. The Allies won the battle of Salerno, but suffered twice the casualties of the Germans.

The sergeant killed his first man in Italy. He eventually led a platoon across France—spraying the enemy line, watching gray figures collapse, meditating on how to square his actions with his faith.

He wore his rosary around his neck, carried his prayer book in his shirt pocket. Before going in to battle, his men wanted to touch his symbols of God.

"I tried to stay aloof from them because you'd be three days to a week with them and then they were gone. They'd get you off to one side and beg you, 'Please, I'm scared. I don't know if I can handle it. Don't send me out there!' "

Courey pulled family men back. "One life is just as important as another. But I kind of cheated a little bit. I would assign them duties in the rear; keep them out of firefights and patrols.

"If I had to do it all over again, I wouldn't assume command. It's pretty rough to send out a party and only one or two—maybe none—come back."

In the chaos of combat, battle lines shift, and shift again. The platoon is spread across 100 yards, soldiers scuttling into harm's way, leap-frogging, crawling.

Advance and pursue. Retreat. Advance. Retreat. Advance, Hold.
Make contact.

"You're in the woods," Courey says. "It's pitch black. You can't even see your watch. You're trying not to make any sound. Then everything opens up—all you can see are the flashes of automatic and rifle fire. Everybody hits the ground. Bullets tug at you. You feel shells bouncing off your helmet. Man, I tell you, it's terrifying. I used to stop breathing for minutes."

In late fall of 1944, Courey was engaged in a firefight in the Vosges Mountains in northeastern France. Through the trees he could see Strasbourg. The ground was frozen. The whistle of shells filled the forest. Shrapnel and branches—which impaled soldiers—whipped through the brittle air.

"You tried to melt into the ground."

From the sound of one shell's trajectory, Courey knew it was coming his way. He never heard the explosion. He suffered severe concussion, whiplash, a partially collapsed left lung, and wounds to his chest, legs and lower abdomen. He was unconscious for a month.

When he awoke, Courey learned that much of his company was gone.

After all these years, he can't forget.

Courey sits in his darkened den, cluttered with mementoes collected over a lifetime. He fingers a small piece of jagged shrapnel capable of shredding a man.

"Taking a human life," he says slowly, staring into the middle distance as though gazing into eternity, "there aren't words to describe it."

Sgt. Shaffe Courey wakes from another haunting. Heart racing, body drenched, he changes his bed sheets. Then he shuffles off to the den and settles into his recliner.

He lights a cigar and smokes into the night.

FROM JOHN BOUDREAU, "FIFTY YEARS OF TERROR AND LOSS"
(*West County Times* [Pinole, Calif.], [November 11, 1996], pp. 1A, 4A)

Sixty young Americans marched in deep silence over the hard November ground. They listened to the rhythmic crunching of new boots sinking into ice, and the distant roll of the big guns.

Everything had unfolded methodically: the journey across the Atlantic, bivouacking outside Marseille, the four-day train ride. They piled out of 10-wheel troop trucks to leg the last miles to the front. The soldiers moved single file on either side of the road.

Twenty-six-year-old Pfc Everett Stanley, a Browning M-1 rifle slung over his shoulder, anxiously fixed on what awaited him at the end of the three-hour march. He was advancing to "the line."

No one talked. The icy crunching echoed in their minds. It wouldn't be long.

Against the cold metal-gray sky, the men in their clean bright-green fatigues passed those they had come to replace.

"They looked like dark shadows, really," Stanley recalls. "They'd been out on the line a long time. You wondered why you replaced them. They looked dead. Their eyes were hollow, glassy. You don't say anything to them. It was all strictly business. We'd be in the same position within a week."

It's impossible to measure the cost of combat on soldiers of Stanley's World War II generation. But the arithmetic is easy in one man's life.

Everett Stanley came back from war a broken man. He drank excessively. He picked fights with strangers and argued with bosses. He scared his wife and children and couldn't hold a job.

For five decades he has been on and off anti-anxiety medication. When he was in his 40s he developed a fear of crossing bridges—a terror tied to one obscure but barbaric battle near the French-German border.

He has not had a solid night's sleep in 50 years.

Stanley, 77, is of middle height with a half-dome forehead. The plain-spoken veteran wears a hearing aid, has a neighborly voice and calls his wife, "Mom." He takes pains not to offend members of a combat veterans therapy group he attends every week at the Martinez [California] VA Mental Health Clinic. He is always the first to show up. He arranges the chairs in a circle, then waits patiently for the others.

In a black-and-white photograph taken just after the war, Stanley has an unwavering gaze, brooding eyes.

"They make you into a killer. But they don't debrief you to ease you back into society. I was dangerous, dangerous to myself and to other people because you're so used to killing people who don't bend to your way."

Stanley is diagnosed with post-traumatic stress disorder.

Before the war, he was carefree. He worked in construction and didn't pay attention to news from Europe or the Pacific.

He'd met the woman who would become his wife, Mary "Angie" Arriaga, at a Vallejo dance hall where young people would swing, waltz and love late into the night to the velvety sounds of Glenn Miller, Benny Goodman, Tommy Dorsey.

"I was a lousy dancer," he says with a playful smile. "I just held on."

Then came his draft notice.

Boot camp began at Fort McClellan, Ala., on June 22, 1944—about two weeks after D-Day, the Allied invasion of France. Stanley trained for 12 weeks and took a 10-day furlough.

Then he was delivered to the front.

The noise was nerve-jangling—the whine of German shells called "screaming meemies," the crackle of bullets, the shouts of desperate men. They advanced, crouching 10 yards apart, into chaos.

"We swept down through a valley and up a hillside. The cussing, swearing—things you'd never heard in your life—screaming. We were in full battle. Even the language is violent."

The GIs zigzagged up a hill, taking fire from Germans perched in trees. "There was a tank on fire off to my right. I was the last guy going up this hill. People dead, people dying. A sniper fell out of a tree in front of me. I took a prisoner. My friend who came overseas with me had been on the line 10 minutes and his leg was off.

"You're looking at a guy and suddenly he has no face. You're looking at a guy and all of a sudden his head is hanging by a thread."

Stanley learned to sleep in rain and snow. He subsisted on K rations: packaged eggs, ham or Spam, fig or vanilla cookies, four Chesterfield cigarettes. The dead were everywhere—German corpses twisted and frozen in death throes, splayed out in ditches, on the side of the road. Surreal sentries in a surreal landscape. Men groped corpses for souvenirs, cutting off fingers to get rings.

The French countryside reminded him of the Ozarks. Cold clear nights were strangely quiet. Fear, like winter frost, seeped into soldiers' bones.

"The biggest guy we had in the company, probably the regiment, was about 6 feet 8 inches. He was 18. Whenever we were going to go into combat, his whole body would shake. I felt sorry for him. The young kids were just going to pieces, trembling, whimpering. I had guys run away from the front line."

Stanley, the son of an Assembly of God faith healer, didn't flee. But his faith evaporated on the fields of France.

"The prayer you said was, 'Yea, though I walk through the valley of death.' Period. That's all you can say. You can't say 'I fear no evil,' because you did fear evil. I felt, if there is a God, how come you're letting this happen? I thought that almost every day. 'How can this be happening?' "

Sometimes 26-year-old Pfc. Everett Stanley prayed for death.

The rain thrummed hard on his helmet that black night in early February 1945. The Russians were 46 miles from Berlin. Allied bombers were crippling the German railway system. American troops were surging through the Siegried line. Victory was near. But for soldiers like Stanley, the war was drudgery and death.

He had been on the line three months—five lifetimes for an infantryman is how he sums it up.

He didn't know the day of the week. His platoon was in combat or on alert every day, every night. "If one of us slept, the other one in the foxhole stayed up."

He lived a "wild life"—unshaven, dirty, wrapped in five pairs of long underwear, five wool shirts, dark-green fatigue pants. Hand grenades were hitched to his bandoleer. A bayonet dangled from his belt. He carried 50 pounds of ammunition.

He dozed, icy rain pelting his face.

Company K—Stanley's outfit in the 36th Infantry Division's 141st Regiment—was to join Company I in the assault. Men from Company I had yet to reach the staging area.

At 3 A.M. Stanley's company was on the move. The objective was the French village of Herrlisheim, north of Strasbourg on the German border, across a frightfully open plain.

Infantry School Quarterly describes the beginning of the operation: "Artificial moonlight supporting the division operations from high ground far to the rear cast a dull glow on the low, overhanging clouds. The quiet of the night was broken only by the occasional bark of an artillery piece and the muffled tread of feet on the wet, muddy ground."

The soldiers crossed a hastily built bridge over a raging tributary of the Rhine River—the bridge that would haunt Stanley for a lifetime. "We were supposed to have tanks. But they couldn't get tanks across. So we went in with bodies."

They forded a waist-deep lake created by the flooding river and heavy rain. "We had to hold hands four abreast to stand up because there was ice on the bottom."

Headquarters relayed good news. A reconnaissance squad had reported that there were few Germans in Herrlisheim.

"We were all happy about that. All we did was march."

Headquarters didn't tell the infantry that the 12th Armored Division had been decimated several weeks earlier trying to take the town of 700 citizens. Hulls of American tanks, still in formation, littered nearby fields, but the soldiers couldn't see them.

The German high command, after failing to divide Allied defenses during the Battle of the Bulge, had hoped to recapture Strasbourg—something of a birthday present for Adolph Hitler—and drive the Allies from the Alsace-Lorraine region.

Waiting for Stanley and his comrades were an SS troop division and a Panzer tank division.

As the Americans emerged from the muck a quarter- to half-mile out of town, soaked and exhausted, the air exploded. Streaking red tracer bullets from machine guns flew at Stanley's head.

He lurched into this spray of death—mortar shells pocking the earth,

Tiger tank artillery blasts flashing in the dark, bullets lashing the air. The wall of fire was blinding. He'd scramble a few yards, dive face down in muddy tank tracks, scramble again. At daylight the soldiers made a dash for cover in buildings. Units intermingled. Communication became confused.

They fought house to house, room to room, hurling grenades into basements, not knowing whether they'd kill Germans or a French family. A tall, husky lieutenant standing six feet from Stanley jumped up to fire a volley through a window. "Those dirty sons of bitches!" the officer bellowed, his carbine rattling. A burst from a German burp gun ripped his guy open. He fell back, dead.

German tanks fired on buildings, which crumbled on the Americans. The attack stalled, guns jammed with mud, ammunition ran low. Officers darted building to building, futilely trying to organize the assault.

They were being annihilated.

By late morning, having advanced only a few houses, Stanley was alone. A retreat was ordered, though no troops were in position to provide cover.

The private fled pell-mell across the field. His gun was gone. All he had was his life.

Chunks of grass flopped around him as bullets spattered the air. Stanley sprinted past the dead and dying. One soldier, crippled by shots to his legs, sat arms outstretched, bleating for help. "He was one of those big guys. You couldn't ever have moved him. If you had stopped, they'd blow you to pieces.

"I still see him in my visions. Facing north. No helmet."

The last body he hurdled was a dark-haired poker buddy. He was lying on his left side, arms frozen in a running position. "His neck was blown out and a fountain of blood was squirting straight out over his hands like a waterfall. He'd made it clear to the bank," Stanley says softly, tears rimming his tired brown eyes. "This young fellow from New York was a little short guy. He had a lot of spunk. He was a very nice kid. I really liked him."

The dead boy's face was calm, etched with a thoughtful expression. He could have been playing cards.

Only 80 of the 200 attacking Americans made it back across the river. Most of the survivors were injured. The campaign received only a terse mention in the *New York Times* on Feb. 5, 1945: "Stiff resistance and flooded terrain resulted in our withdrawal in the vicinity of Herrlisheim."

A few days later, the Germans repositioned. They pulled out of Herrlisheim and the Americans walked in.

After 18 months in Europe, Stanley returned home, a corporal wearing an Army-issue, olive drab Eisenhower jacket. Angie, though, didn't like him in his soldier's dress. And it wasn't just the uniform. He was not the same man.

At a dance, when a jitterbugging man bumped into him a couple of times, hurting his injured hip, Stanley kicked the man's feet out from under him and threatened to fight him outside.

"I got pretty wild. I was quite passive before I went into the service."

"I'd get to drinking, and she'd leave the house," says Stanley, nodding at his wife in their Benicia townhouse. "It got me away from it. You become nice and happy—and belligerent, too. I got very belligerent."

"It took a toll on me," Angie murmurs.

Stanley held and lost maybe 100 different jobs. "I could not get along with what I called stupid foremen. . . . They were probably a lot smarter than I was.

"Nothing ever satisfied me. I'd say, 'What the hell am I doing here?'"

His wife found steady work, first as a beautician, then as a buyer at Mare Island Naval Shipyard.

Daughter Joanne Taylor recalls bill collectors pounding on the door. "I'd have to tell them, 'No, you can't come in and take the couch!' It was very painful. I remember one day coming home from school and seeing a 'For Sale' sign on our lawn. It was traumatic. It was shameful."

Taylor, a Benicia attorney, recently helped her parents with the down payment on their home.

She remembers her father as warm and giving. But he had a mean streak. "My brother and I spent the early part of our childhood on the floor of the car. He would tailgate, yelling, 'Get out of the way!' "

David Stanley knew two fathers. The first experienced panic attacks. At one time he told his 12-year-old son good-bye. He thought he was dying.

The second was a dream dad. "He coached me in Little League, took me fishing, built my kayak with me. We were never homeless and unfed. I got only one spanking from him."

David, who was in the Army reserves, was called up for Vietnam but did not follow his father into combat. He deserted and turned himself in. The Army court-martialed David, then discharged him.

The elder Stanley doesn't resent his son's actions. "I would never begrudge anyone who got out of combat. It was such a horrible experience."

Stanley returned to Herrlisheim to collect the dead. The helmetless man crying for help had been stabbed to death. The lieutenant lay by the window of the bombed house. The poker buddy was frozen in his running position near the water.

Bodies were cold and bloated. Soldiers jammed one dog tag in each mouth, then piled corpses in one of four trucks—the same 10-wheelers that had brought them into combat. Stanley loaded 30 bodies onto the truck he was assigned.

That night, after going without sleep for three days, Stanley was ordered back to the line. He pleaded for rest, but his lieutenant—whose life would end a few days later—refused. Casualties had left the regiment thin.

A mist clung to the land. Stanley and four others stumbled out to foxholes along a river. He was on the verge of cracking.

As the soldiers crept toward battle, a loud explosion and fireball sliced through the still air. A mortar shell burst over them, lifting the private off the ground. A piece of shrapnel lodged five inches into his hip, missing an artery by a quarter-inch.

He never again saw the men who carried him off the battlefield. He was told they were killed.

Fifty years later Stanley's hip wound sends shivers of pain through his body. He walks slowly, unevenly, grimacing. One leg is shorter than the other. Stanley turned down a request to dance from the bride of his grandson during their recent wedding. His hip hurt too much.

"Everybody else was dancing. I felt bad. I still do."

Fifty years later the nightmares still come. Stanley and his wife sleep in separate beds. He keeps a glass of water on the night stand. In his sleep, arms waving, he sometimes knocks it over.

Stanley leans back on his recliner, looking dapper in suspenders and gray slacks. He quit drinking and became a vegetarian to reduce extraordinarily high blood pressure and heart irregularities.

He enjoys being fussed over by his daughter, sharing a meal with his son, playing pinochle every week with his grandson. Stanley has undergone something of an existential change: Through therapy he has gained understanding of his pain, its impact on his life.

Yet, he adds, "I can't shake it. I can't get rid of the thoughts and sights."

The old soldier resists going to church and avoids funerals at all costs. The recent death of his brother, who dropped dead near him, brought back the intensity of loss, the unspeakable sensation when someone so alive is suddenly so dead.

"You start thinking: You've got your family, your kids, grandchildren," says Stanley, his voice distant and frail. "All those young guys didn't have this. I saw them die—18, 19 years old, handsome men, wonderful people."

He is filled with deep grief. He watches television and suddenly starts crying for no reason. He wakes at night, tears rolling down his cheeks.

Once Stanley started attending the therapy group, his stories began spilling out at home. One evening, he pulled out a map of France and started talking.

"It's hard to see him in a new light," his daughter says. "My father always seemed so stoic. Mother worried. I wish he wouldn't bring this up now. It will kill him."

"She doesn't know how to stop the pain."

FROM JOHN BOUDREAU, "NIGHT PATROL NEVER ENDS"
(*West County Times* [Pinole, Calif.], [November 11, 1996], p. 5A)

Dusk was closing in. The Korean militiamen, dressed in Russian fatigues, slipped up from behind like shadows.

Bill and another soldier, a good buddy, sat in a jeep in a southern Korea alley. There were detached from the 6th Army Infantry Division on a mission to spot guerrilla groups and call for an attack.

It was fall 1945. Americans were celebrating the end of World War II. But Bill was in an undeclared war zone. U.S. forces had landed in Korea to dismantle Japanese colonialism. Chaos filled the country. Bands of militia massacred each other and civilians in skirmishes that would erupt into the Korean War five years later. Bill's assignments included gathering mutilated bodies and patrolling the dangerous region around the city of Taegu in southern Korea.

It was hand-to-hand combat. Killing with guns, bayonets, his hands.

The two were expecting the enemy to come from the mouth of the alley, not the back. The attack was swift.

His friend, a fun-loving, 19-year-old from Kansas nicknamed "Cotton," never saw the bayonet as it plunged into his belly. He collapsed in Bill's arms—blood soaking Bill's uniform, seeping into his soul.

Bill grabbed his .45 and shot the attacker dead. The others escaped.

"Nobody knows—nobody knows—the feeling when you have your very best friend, the guy who went over with you—whenever you saw one of us, you saw the other—to see him, to feel him, to know he died right in your arms."

The 73-year-old former sergeant has been on patrol ever since. He thrashes violently in bed, never getting more than four hours' sleep. He is paranoid. He has tried to kill himself three times.

"Until eight, nine years ago, my wife knew absolutely nothing," said Bill, who asked that his last name not be used. "I never talked to my kids about it. I never talked to my brothers and sisters about it."

• • •

Bill's post-combat experience added to his torment. After Bill suffered flashbacks and depression, he was escorted onto a ship bound for home.

"I think they thought I was crazy and I'd go berserk, either kill some-one, kill myself or jump overboard. They put me in the bottom of the ship, in the brig. I stayed in there for 21 days. I was in a wire cage. There was a steel door, and they would scoot a food tray under the door."

• • •

"I cannot get over it. I try and try and try."

Bill says he has made peace with God. But as he looks over life's trou-bled landscape, his heart is tortured: "It's been miserable. I see heart-ache, sadness, disappointment, sorrow, fear."

IN BATTLE IN THE PACIFIC: SAM TURNER

The universal horror of the battlefield can be seen not only in the personal records of soldiers from classical Greece up to the Civil War, but in the memories of veterans who fought in World Wars I and II, the Korean War, and the Vietnam War.

Sam Turner is such a veteran. But Turner was no ordinary sol-dier. We see from his memoir that he is a man of extraordinary courage and humility who ventured in under heavy fire to rescue a comrade when no one else would go. Only some forty years later did Sam and others in his outfit disclose to his friend that it was Sam who had saved his life. And this was just one of his many heroic actions.

In many ways Sam at the time was very unlike Henry Fleming: he was some six or eight years older than Henry when he joined the army; he was already married; he knew something of what true battle was like from his uncle who had fought in some of the bloodiest battles in human history in France in World War I; and he was well trained before he ever saw action.

However, the battlefields he fought on had many similarities with Henry's experience. Like Henry, he entered the army as a private. He observed cowardice in action and admits to his own shaking fear on one occasion; tried to counsel a man who was especially frightened of going into his first battle; saw many younger guys who "had no idea" what the horrors of the battle-field would be like; like Henry's friend Jim who looks like his side has been chewed by wolves, Sam's friend has an unspeakable wound, which leaves his brain exposed. He also observes the heavy psychological toll taken on many men when their friends are killed and is suggestively reticent about speaking about his own friends who were killed or maimed.

"IN BATTLE IN THE PACIFIC: AN INTERVIEW WITH
SAM TURNER"
(March 20, 1997)

CJ: Let's start out with some particulars about you before you joined the armed forces.

Sam: I was born in Non, Oklahoma. That's the eastern part of Oklahoma.

CJ: Was that where you grew up?

Sam: When I was one year old, my dad moved to western Oklahoma. And that's where I grew up—in the town of Minco.

CJ: And what interested you when you were a young man?

Sam: I was always playing with tools, or something, you know. But anyway, my sports—I loved baseball. I used to think I was a great pitcher. But they used to get too many home runs on me.

CJ: What line of work did your parents follow?

Sam: My dad was a rancher—a farmer and a rancher.

CJ: And did you go to school in Minco?

Sam: Yes. But I missed too much school when I was growing up. I was always having to stay out of school to help out on my dad's farm. But then working on the farm was what I was really interested in. As far as schooling goes, the job that I ended up in out here in California called for a college degree.

CJ: What was your line of work?

Sam: Well, I came to California when I was eighteen years old, and I put in an application to work in a fiber board factory. They made roofing and several different things. I went in as a young guy to do a clean-up job and ended up working up through the ranks to the job of department manager. I was working there when I went in the service, and my job was waiting for me when I came back.

CJ: How old were you then when you enlisted?

Sam: I was twenty-four, I think. I was twenty-six when I came out.

CJ: So you were working at that job when the war broke out.

Sam: Yes, when I left that job for the army, we were doing 45 percent government work.

CJ: What was your attitude about joining? Were you eager, gung-ho, reluctant, worried, what?

Sam: Well, I was all gung-ho to volunteer until I found out my wife was pregnant. With my brother, I was getting everything in order to join

Sam Turner, World War II hero, in a photograph made in the Philippines. Reprinted by permission.

the Air Corps. He thought I had chickened out. You see, I didn't tell him that my wife was pregnant. The company got me three deferments because of the government work I was doing. The baby was born the first of May, and June 6 I went into the service.

CJ: Did you volunteer?

Sam: I was drafted. I let them draft me. I was hoping to be sent to the Pacific. My uncle was in World War I, and he always said, "If ever there is going to be another war, do everything you can to stay out of the cold countries. I almost froze to death over there."

CJ: So you probably learned from him about what the battlefield was all about?

Sam: Oh yeah. He told me to remember to keep my mouth shut. And I went along with that. I saw too many guys get into trouble for no reason at all, and then they wondered why they were getting into trouble.

CJ: Do you feel like you had a romantic view of battle?

Sam: Well, I don't know what would be romantic about it.

CJ: You had a realistic view going in?

Sam: Yeah, my uncle used to tell me a lot of stuff about World War I. And I thought he was the greatest guy. Yes, I listened to him. He told me, "Don't volunteer for anything." Somebody will ask you if you can drive a truck, and if you say yes, the first thing you know you're going to be pushing a wheel barrow.

CJ: What about the guys you signed up with? Did they seem to know as much about what it was like to be in the front lines as you did from your uncle?

Sam: They had no idea. But they were nice guys. We had good training in the army. I was actually made an acting sergeant the first week I was in the army.

CJ: Working up to your first experiences with battle: had you ever had any experiences with death before you began to encounter such massive deaths on the battlefield?

Sam: When I was fourteen years old, I was staying all night with a friend of my mother, and he died on me. The worst thing I remember was me having to go to find the neighbors to try to get help.

CJ: Had you ever had any fights when you were a boy or young man?

Sam: Oh, a few. My father taught me not to fight. So when these boys would pick on me, I'd run from them. One night I decided I wasn't going to run anymore. There were about seven of them. So I told the older ones if they would keep the others off me, I would take them on one at a time. So I told the biggest, "You'll be the first," and I made a believer out of him. Then I said, "Who's next?" and they all came up to shake my hand. They didn't want anymore of me. And I used to fight guys who would make fun of poor kids who could only bring biscuits and gravy for their lunch. I just didn't think it was right.

CJ: What kind of training did you receive before you saw your first action?

Sam: Well, I had thirteen weeks at Camp Roberts, California, and that's normal for guys in the infantry. I went to the Hawaiian Islands and spent five and a half months there in training.

CJ: And then you shipped out.

Sam: Then I went to New Guinea.

CJ: That was a culture shock for you?

Sam: Oh, that was the prettiest sight you ever saw as you were going in to land. Beautiful timber all around, you know. We had to build our own campsite and everything. The mud was deep, so we had to haul sand in.

CJ: Were you in the jungle for part of your duty?

Sam: Oh, yes, I was eleven months in the jungle. See what—they'd capture a site in New Guinea and were trying to just hold ground. We'd go in and push the Japanese back into the jungle. So we had to go out on patrol all the time. The longest one I went on was eight days. Some lasted as long as eighteen days. Anyway, this first time I went in for a special reason. The Japanese had an airfield there and were planning an attack, but they didn't have enough fuel to take off right away. Anyway, we thought they were planning to bust some heads pretty soon.

CJ: And you wanted to know when and how.

Sam: That's right. The first action I got into, we had this Alamo Scout bunch [a special force dispatched to secure military positions] going out and setting a trap to catch a couple of Japanese, see, and bring them in for questioning. So we went out and set this deal up, but they caught on to what we were doing so they didn't fall into our trap, and we got into it. And the leader of the Alamo Scouts got killed there. They hit us pretty hard. So what we did—we called for some backup because we had to get across the river, and they were picking us off like flies there on the edge of the river. That's the first time I saw action.

CJ: Was your first action the first time you had actually seen men shot?

Sam: Yes, there were about twenty of them. About four of us came back in good shape. Oh yeah. We had to make stretchers to carry them out of there. This river we had to cross—we had to float them down that. And the Japanese left them alone because they were more interested in catching us alive and able. They weren't interested in the wounded.

CJ: How many of those wounded actually made it?

Sam: Well, two of them died. The next time we walked into a similar situation, we had about fifty men knocked down. The Japanese had good camouflage, and we didn't think any of the enemy were there. The Japanese let the scout pass, and then when we advanced, they opened fire on us.

CJ: I guess in situations like that, it is impossible to bring the dead back.

Sam: That's one thing all of us guys agreed on: we'd never leave a man there. If we had to, we'd go back and get them. And the Japanese were good about that too. We'd knock them over and knock them over, and when daylight came, you couldn't find a one that somebody had hit the night before.

Their attacks were called *banzai*. They'd come at you and come at you and get cut down themselves as if their lives didn't mean anything to them. Suicide—that's what it is.

CJ: Did you have a greater disadvantage than the enemy?

Sam: Oh, yeah. They had lived in those hills for years. And that's where they did their training—up there. We were at a big disadvantage in not knowing near as much about the place. For instance, I was out in the field one day, having my food brought to me and stuff, and there was this new guy, and he was going to show our men how to drop mortars. And I'm down below, and he dropped them all on me! He dropped twenty-eight mortars on me. Had holes in my clothes, my mess kit, had holes in all my equipment, and I never got scratched.

That old New Guinea climate is something else, I tell you. Snakes. You'd come across a little clearing where the sun could shine in, and it would be loaded with snakes.

CJ: What about action in the Philippines?

Sam: My company—regiment—was picked to go through part of the mountains. It's where we had to go. We got into lots of these scraps in there.

CJ: So it was just all along the way?

Sam: Yeah, yeah. I have seen guys just get blown up. You'd be sitting there as pretty as you please, and somebody would come up and say, "Son, your buddy just got killed." It would just blow their minds—some of those guys. You know I think, more than anything, what caused men to go crazy was when their best friends got killed.

CJ: What was done in the case of those men who lost it over the death of a friend?

Sam: They were just put on stretchers and carried back to the camp. What they'd do was take them to hospitals, and then they just shipped them out because they were just no good in action anymore.

CJ: Were any of those killed your own close friends?

Sam: Oh, yeah, yeah.

CJ: And you managed to hang onto your sanity through all that?

Sam: Well, you got to—figure that. Those that didn't got into mental trouble.

CJ: What about the pressure of getting shot at?

Sam: Some of them would just go crazy under the pressure. I remember one guy that always took his shaving stuff with him—because he had to be shaved all the time, a first-class shave. He was putting this stuff on and running around telling us that he's shot, he's shot, he was bleeding to death. And all he had on there was just his shaving soap. They'd just go crazy. Then we had this old guy—he was too old to be in the army, but he wanted to go, and they let him go. And he took care of the kitchen stove—the gas and everything—he did the same thing, just went crazy.

CJ: Just being frightened under fire?

Sam: Yeah, yeah. It was bad under fire. Yeah, I've laid down, going in to knock out a machine-gun nest and—you can't see five or ten feet ahead of you so heavy with shrubbery and stuff, see—and the Japanese were cutting limbs only a few feet from my back. There was one guy— the radio man—came over to tell me the captain got shot—and I said, "Well, what do you want me to do about it?" "Well, I thought you'd better know," he says. So we knew we were pinned down, and we knew how they handled their guns and stuff—so I said, "Don't move." Telling him, "Don't move," you know, and he kept raising up, and I said, "You know you can't move here because they've got you spotted and they're just waiting for a place to see where you're going to move and then they're going to get you." And at that point he had his head down and a bullet hit his helmet. If his head had been just a hair higher, it would have hit him right between the eyes. You could lay your hand right in the crease in the helmet. And he's still got the helmet too! That old steel hat.

But going up the mountains, some of them over three thousand feet high, the enemy would spy on us through holes drilled in some of the trees and then radio back to their camps and say we were coming through. And then that's when they would try to cut us down, see.

But you know I was lucky. I never got a scratch. I did get one across the back of the neck that was pretty hot one time.

CJ: Did you think when you first landed that you would never get fired at?

Sam: No, no, no. You expected that. You really didn't know whether you were coming back or not.

Another thing I was in the army was a flame-thrower, and that's dangerous. All they have to do is hit that one little cylinder, and you're finished.

CJ: Before you saw your first action, did you and the other men worry about how you were going to behave under fire, how you'd hold up?

Sam: I don't know about the others, but I know I was going to try to protect myself. I told my wife before I left—and I had a hunch I was going to the Pacific—"They will never take me alive." I was not going to be a prisoner of war. I'd fight there until I dropped over.

CJ: But, Sam, I know some of your actions in the war show that your main concern was *not* always trying to protect yourself. You put your life on the line when others would not in order to save other people.

Sam: Well, yeah, you were helping people, but at the same time if you didn't help somebody, the Japanese might get me next.

Shoot, one time in San Tomas, some of the Japanese were fighting us and they had a bunch of their crew stored in some houses there and they were turning them out so fast we didn't have a chance. As one of our men got killed, they would send one of theirs through the gap in our lines. And there was a guy with me who was a machine-gunner, too. And he said, "Are you thinking what I'm thinking?" We decided we had to stop that thing, stop them from sending them in there and there's only one way—just shoot right through them. So that's what we did. We went so far together and then split into a Y. And we got back where we wanted to go, and we stopped that stuff. And the others were hollering, "Hey! You dumb guys!" But they were all happy when they saw that we got through there.

CJ: Tell me that story about your rescue of one of your men.

Sam: Well it happened in the Philippines—actually right over a gold mine. And so we were going to take this mountain which was Santa Mais—and this one guy I knew had been in the hospital, for what reason, I don't know. Still, he shouldn't have been with us. But he just had to go, and so he went. Well, a bullet hit him in the head and just flipped a big piece of skull off the top of his head. His brain was sticking out. Nobody ever told him for years and years who brought him out.

CJ: How did you decide to get him and bring him out?

Sam: Well, I got word that this guy was down—and was pretty bad. So I just took—got some volunteers to go with me to get him out. But the other guys all chickened out on me. But I went ahead, see. So I went in and got him so he could breathe and told him what his problems were so he'd know that I was trying to get him to an ambulance. So some of the guys saw me in there, and they came on in to help, and we got him to an ambulance.

And he lived. I ran into him several years ago at a reunion.

CJ: Were there other incidents when you put your life on the line, Sam?

Sam: Well, there were several times when I had to run out under fire a pretty long way carrying a machine gun to help somebody, protect somebody. Bullets passing me. I said I didn't know whether those bullets were passing me or I was passing them! And they tried to get me, too.

There was an Italian guy, and I said, "Come on, Glennie, got to have the rest of that ammo in here!"

CJ: Sam, talking about the opposite behavior, did you ever see guys just run?

Sam: Oh, yeah. I ran one time, but I was running toward them. You just can't stand still.

This old cowboy, named Porter, from Wyoming, he'd had three brothers who were killed by the Japanese, and he was there to get revenge. He and I got into a fight with the Japanese, and all night long they tried to kill us—even threw a hand grenade into our trench, and I grabbed it and threw it back at them. My legs were just shaking like that—uncontrollable. And I said, "Hey, hey, Porter, you scared?" And he said, "Well, that ain't my teeth rattlin'." And I said, "Well you're listening to *my* legs hitting together. That's not your legs." Well, anyway, we had it all night. And early in the morning, when it was just getting daylight, the captain, he sent somebody because it was quiet then, and he figured we were both dead. So he sent somebody down there to find out about us, and we about shot them.

See, these Japanese, at nighttime, they'd find out your name, and they'd run around calling you: "Hey, Sam, I'm hit over here. Come help me!" Try to make you think your buddies were out there. But we got onto that and just started shooting toward them.

One day somebody told me that a new recruit had come in who was scared to death and that I needed to talk to him. So I went down and talked to him. He was just sitting on his bunk, you know. Been in New Guinea maybe an hour and a half. So I said in an extra cheerful voice, "What's the matter, old buddy?" He said, "Man, I don't like this country." I said, "Ah, you'll love it when you get used to it. Let's go get something to eat and meet the guys."

CJ: So what kind of things did you tell him to ease his mind?

Sam: Oh, I just kidded with him, told him that we had these Japanese on the run. What his job—was carrying ammunition, carrying bazookas.

Speaking of being scared: That guy that dropped all the mortars on me, we got rid of him. To show you what kind of an officer he was, we'd go out and get into a fight with the enemy, he'd get down in a ditch behind a log or something trying to holler orders and didn't even know what he was hollering about. But our captain, who trained us—I would have followed him anywhere.

CJ: One of my questions, Sam, has to do with courage and how you define it. Ernest Hemingway, an American writer who was in several wars in his time and had seen a lot of both the battlefield and the wartime hospital, said that if there is no fear, there can't be any courage.

Sam: I'll buy that.

CJ: You were talking about your friend that wanted revenge. I guess if you were driven by revenge, you wouldn't call that real courage either.

Sam: No, I wouldn't call that real courage either. But he got his wish that night. All the fighting he wanted.

CJ: What about the people actually *living* in the areas where you were fighting?

Sam: Oh, we hired them. We worked with them. On our patrols, we always had a couple of natives with us. They often carried our ammunition, our machine guns. Many of them were very, very old. But for the most part, they weren't involved in fighting.

One time we came on this cave, sort of a cellar, and we heard some noises, so we shouted down there. Then we saw a lock on it, so we shot the lock off. Hey, there were five nuns in there. And the Japanese were using them for their sex life and their cooks and everything and kept them locked up in there. So we freed them and got an airplane the next morning and got them out of there. Boy, you talk about somebody being grateful to get out. Can you imagine being like that? Being locked up and bringing them out so they could cook for them and have sex?

We had a young Filipino woman who had been taken to what the Japanese called a rest camp, and they had stabbed her with bayonets over and over in forcing her to have sex. When we rescued her, she took off all her clothes to show us where they had stabbed her over and over, all over her body. Can you imagine that? People being that cruel?

And another time, we were taking this hill, and we found an old Filipino woman and a man in a cave and the Japanese had put their eyes out. We got so shook up about that thing. Never seen a worse thing in that war.

CJ: Do you believe your experiences in battle changed you in any way?

Sam: No. I don't think it changed me. Just—I have nightmares sometimes.

TOPICS FOR ORAL AND WRITTEN PRESENTATION

1. Write an essay comparing the Civil War battlefield, as portrayed in the fiction of Stephen Crane, with the firsthand accounts of the Civil War in this chapter. Would you argue that Crane's account is realistic? Overly dramatized? Romanticized?

2. From what you have read here, how would you classify Whitman's poem: as realistic or romanticized? Explain your answer.

3. Do the firsthand accounts in this chapter provide any clues as to an interpretation of the end of *The Red Badge of Courage*?

4. The *Red Badge of Courage*, the Whitman poem, and the feature stories on World War II all present particular and somewhat different views of death. Write an essay on the subject.

5. Using *The Red Badge of Courage* and the firsthand accounts of the Civil War and World War II, write an essay comparing the battlefield in the Civil War to that of World War II.

6. Write an essay on the impact of the loss of friends in battle.

7. Interview a veteran of World War II, the Korean War, or the Vietnam War who served in the front lines under fire or in a battlefield hospital. Does your interview change your view of the person or the event? Explain. You may want to videotape and edit the interview.

SUGGESTED READINGS

Benfey, Christopher. *The Double Life of Stephen Crane*. New York: A. A. Knopf, 1992.

Guterson, David. *Snow Falling on Cedars*. New York: Vintage, 1994.

Keegan, John. *The Face of Battle*. New York: Viking, 1976.

Labor, Earle. "Crane and Hemingway: Anatomy of Trauma." *Renascence* XI (Summer 1959), 189–196.

Linderman, Gerald. *Embattled Courage: The Experience of Combat in the American Civil War*. New York: Free Press, 1987.

Reid, Mitchell. *Civil War Soldiers*. New York: Viking, 1988.

Shay, Jonathan. *Achilles in Vietnam: Combat Trauma and the Undoing of Character*. New York: Simon & Schuster, 1994.

Simpson, Harold B. *Audie Murphy: American Soldier*. Hillsboro, Tex.: Alcor Publishing, 1975.

Weiss, Daniel. "*The Red Badge of Courage*": *Psychoanalytic Review* LII (Summer 1965), 176–196; (Fall 1965), 460–484.

The Soldier's Life in Camp

Two scenes in *The Red Badge of Courage* are set not on the march or on the battlefield but in camp—where soldiers spent much of their time. A camp scene opens the novel, and another is placed between the two days of battle.

For Henry Fleming, the camp is naturally the place of greatest reflection. Crane provides a brief glimpse of this mundane part of military life during the Civil War. The first camp, which opens the novel, is a fairly long-standing one. The men are housed in what are described as "rows of squat brown huts" (1), likely made of light boards and canvas over dirt floors. The young recruits share these quarters with one another, likely two to a hut. Henry's hut is described as having an "intricate hole [that] served it as a door" (2), perhaps made of overlapping canvas. Inside is a wide bunk stretching across one entire end, which he shares with his friend Jim Conklin. At the other end is a homemade, makeshift fireplace and furniture made of cracker boxes:

A picture from an illustrated weekly was upon the log walls, and three rifles were paralleled on pegs. Equipments hung on handy projections, and some tin dishes lay upon a small pile of firewood. A folded tent was serving as a roof. The sunlight, without beating upon it, made it glow a light yellow shade. A small window shot an

oblique square of whiter light upon the cluttered floor. The smoke
from the fire at times neglected the clay chimney and wreathed into
the room, and this flimsy chimney of clay and sticks made endless
threats to ablaze the whole establishment. (3)

The length of time they have spent in camp has led one corporal
to lay a wood floor in his hut.

Later, in the second camp scene, when the regiment is on the
move between battles, the men sleep not in huts but on rubber
blankets laid on the ground around an open fire.

Crane makes only one mention of their rations: on the morning
after Henry returns to camp, Wilson serves him coffee and fresh
meat, almost certainly from some animal he has hunted while
Henry was still asleep.

While Henry's regiment seems sufficiently clothed and fed, he
does see evidence on a dead soldier of one of those curses of the
Civil War armies, both North and South: the inadequate supply of
shoes. On one soldier he sees shoes "worn to the thinness of writing paper" with "a bare foot protruding through the end" (22).

Crane also gives a glimpse of the possessions of the men: a knapsack in which they carried personal articles and clothing, canteens,
haversacks for food, blankets, and arms and ammunition. Many
soldiers provided these articles for themselves—the only arms of
some of the Southern soldiers, in particular, being their personal
hunting rifles brought from home. On the march made by Henry
Fleming's regiment, the men having to give up some of the weight
they are carrying to the battlefield either throw away their knapsacks or hide or bury them in the impossible hope that they can
return to retrieve them.

In camp before the battle, life is tedious, and the men constantly
struggle with excruciating boredom and anticipation. They spend
their days, as Henry describes it, being "drilled and drilled and
reviewed, and drilled and drilled and reviewed" (2). When they
are not being drilled, they entertain themselves with dance per-
formances, card playing, talking with the Confederate pickets, listening to the scary stories told them by veteran soldiers, letter
writing, fighting each other, and, most of all, arguing over rumors
and battle strategy.

Although Crane shows that Henry suffers no deprivations of
food, clothing, and shelter, in the early years of the war, the Union

Guard Mount Headquarters, Army of the Potomac. Reprinted by permission of the Houghton Library, Harvard University.

army did lack food and clothing especially, but conditions improved in the final war years, when those for Confederate soldiers had become abominable.

As Crane suggests in his description of the first dead soldier Henry sees, the item of clothing most in demand was shoes. The following information comes from the 1928 research done by Ella Lonn on desertion in the Civil War (*Desertion During the Civil War*. N.Y.: The Century Co., 1928):

> The clamor for clothing, particularly for shoes, was incessant at first. General Schofield reported many of his men as barefoot in July, 1861; General Patterson declared that his men were barefoot and indecently clad and had just cause of complaint. Generals sometimes felt that their commands were discriminated against and sent wails such as the following when their men were traveling with frozen feet. "If you can, for God's sake, send me all the shoes to spare and at once." Lack of shoes was a general cry through 1861 and 1862 and undoubtedly operated as a cause of the failure of the three-months' men to reenlist. As late as October, 1862, General Meade was unable to secure shoes, blankets, or overcoats for his men and received marching orders although he had declared that he could not move without those necessities. Even in December, 1863, the quartermaster's department was not yet able to meet the demands for clothing, as the report of a medical director from Tennessee attests: "Having just returned from a personal inspection of the men in this command, I have the honor to report that I find them exceedingly destitute of clothing. The entire outfit of many soldiers consists of a blouse, worn as a shirt, a pair of pants, well worn, a pair of shoes, and in some instances not even those, an oil or woolen blanket, and a hat or cap." Some complaints of barefoot men occured [*sic*] as late as December, 1864. (128, 129)

In 1864 General Meade wrote in a letter that it was distressing to find horses being shod when men had to go barefoot, and many letters home carried pleas for families to send shoes. Many soldiers fought the whole war with no more clothing than they had brought with them on the day they enlisted.

Not only were the men frequently without shoes and other articles of clothing, but they were without shelter. Regiments were either unwilling or unable to furnish the men with tents when they needed them. In 1862, one outfit slept for thirty-eight days out in the open, exposed to cold and rain, without any shelter. Soldiers who were forced to sleep in the bitter cold and soaking wet inevitably filled the hospitals.

Rations were often just as scarce as shoes, many men going without food for over twenty-four hours at a time. Others stayed alive by foraging and stealing food. Union troops in West Virginia under General John Frémont were issued only beef and a little salt for weeks. Others were on the edge of starvation. One Union general reported that in twenty days, he had been provided with only three days' worth of rations. Just before the Battle of Chancellorsville in Washington, D.C., the troops in December were living on salt pork and hardtack, much of the food allotted to the regiments being held up by paperwork or bought by civilians or sold by crooked commissary officials.

The bad weather coupled with inadequate food and shelter made the men particularly subject to diseases: fevers, infections, diarrhea, measles, and mumps.

The Union army, including Henry Fleming presumably, was quartered in Washington, D.C., before the Battle of Chancellorsville. The pastimes of the troops there were much like Crane describes in his novel. Ernest B. Furgurson, in *Chancellorship 1863* (New York: Alfred A. Knopf, 1992), describes the army as waiting and waiting for action:

> Except when their number came up for picket duty, they huddled against the cold and thought of home. Sometimes men off duty were like cattle, herded together, passive, awaiting someone to prod them to move again. Now and then they flared into wild games, or violence against a bunkmate or the squad next door, and then settled back into time-killing card games, letter-writing, reading the religious tracts that poured into their camps, waiting. (11)

The following selections describe a variety of aspects of life in camp. The first is an overview of what it took the nation to service an entire army. The rest describe diet, foraging, shelter, possessions, and arms.

ASPECTS OF LIFE IN CAMP

CHARLES CARLETON COFFIN'S ACCOUNT

Coffin's account is an overview of the massive headquarters of the Army of the Potomac in Washington, D.C., where Henry Fleming was initially quartered before moving on. He describes the food and the shelter, imagines what the whole area would look like from the perspective of a balloon, describes the various groups into which an army is organized, and goes on to speculate, from an administrative point of view, what massive supplies are needed to keep an entire army going.

FROM CHARLES CARLETON COFFIN, *MY DAYS AND NIGHTS ON THE BATTLEFIELD*
(Boston: Dana Estes and Company, 1865, pp. 24–30)

• • •

But there is activity everywhere. Drums are beating, men assembling, soldiers marching, and hastening on in regiments. They go into camp and sleep on the ground, wrapped in their blankets. It is a new life. They have no napkins, no table-cloths at breakfast, dinner, or supper, no china plates or silver forks. Each soldier has his tin plate and cup, and makes a hearty meal of beef and bread. It is hard-baked bread. They call it *hardtack*, because it might be tacked upon the roof of a house instead of shingles. They also have Cincinnati *chicken*. At home they called it pork; fowls are scarce and pork is plenty in camp, so they make believe it is chicken!

There is drilling by squads, companies, battalions, and by regiments. Some stand guard around the camp by day, and others go out on picket at night, to watch for the enemy. It is military life. Everything is done by orders. When you become a soldier, you cannot go and come as you please. Privates, lieutenants, captains, colonels, generals, all are subject to the orders of their superior officers. All must obey the general in command. You march, drill, eat, sleep, go to bed, and get up by order. At sunrise you hear the reveille, and at nine o'clock in the evening the tattoo. Then the candle, which has been burning in your tent with a bayonet for a candlestick, must be put out. In the dead of night, while sleeping soundly and dreaming of home, you hear the drum-beat. It is the long roll. There is a rattle of musketry. The pickets are at it. Every man springs to his feet.

"Turn out! turn out!" shouts the colonel.

"Fall in! fall in!" cries the captain.

There is confusion throughout the camp,—a trampling of feet and loud, hurried talking. In your haste you get your boots on wrong, and buckle your cartridge-box on bottom up. You rush out in the darkness, not minding your steps, and are caught by the tent-ropes. You tumble headlong, upsetting to-morrow's breakfast and beans. You take your place in the ranks, nervous, excited, and trembling at you know not what. The regiment rushes toward the firing, which suddenly ceases. An officer rides up in the darkness and says it is a false alarm! You march back to camp, cool and collected now, grumbling at the stupidity of the picket, who saw a bush, thought it was a Rebel, fired his gun, and alarmed the whole camp.

In the autumn of 1861 the army of the Potomac, encamped around Washington, numbered about two hundred thousand men. Before it marches to the battle-field, let us see how it is organized, how it looks, how it is fed; let us get an insight into its machinery.

Go up in the balloon which you see hanging in the air across the Potomac from Georgetown, and look down upon this great army. All the country round is dotted with white tents,—some in the open fields, and some half hid by the forest-trees. Looking away to the northwest you see the right wing. Arlington [Virginia] is the centre, and at Alexandria [Virginia] is the left wing. You see men in ranks, in files, in long lines, in masses, moving to and fro, marching and countermarching, learning how to fight a battle. There are thousands of wagons and horses; there are from two to three hundred pieces of artillery. How long the line, if all were on the march! Men marching in files are about three feet apart. A wagon with four horses occupies fifty feet. If this army was moving on a narrow country road, four cavalrymen riding abreast, and men in files of four, and all the artillery, ammunition-wagon, supply-trains, ambulances, and equipment, it would reach from Boston to Hartford, or from New York City to Albany, a hundred and fifty miles.

To move such a multitude, to bring order out of confusion, there must be a system, a plan, and an organization. Regiments are therefore formed into brigades, with usually about four regiments to a brigade. Three or four brigades compose a division, and three or four divisions make an army corps. A corps when full numbers from twenty-five to thirty thousand men.

· · ·

The army must have its food regularly. Think how much food it takes to supply the city of Boston, or Cincinnati every day. Yet here are as many men as there are people in those cities. There are a great many more horses in the army than in the stables of both of those cities. All must be fed. There must be a constant supply of beef, pork, bread, beans, vinegar, sugar, and coffee, oats, corn, and hay.

The army must also have its supplies of clothing, its boots, shoes, and coats. It must have its ammunition, its millions of cartridges of different kinds; for there are a great many kinds of guns in the regiments,—Springfield and Enfield muskets, French, Belgian, Prussian, and Austrian guns, requiring a great many different kinds of ammunition. There are a great many different kinds of cannon. There must be no lack of ammunition, no mistake in its distribution.

• • •

Look at what was wanted to build this mighty machine and to keep it going.

First, the hundreds of thousands of men; the thousands of horses; the thousands of barrels of beef, pork, and flour; thousands of barrels of hogsheads of sugar, vinegar, rice, salt, bags of coffee, and immense stores of other things. Thousands of tons of hay, bags of oats and corn. What numbers of men and women have been at work to get each soldier ready for the field. He has boots, clothes, and equipments. The tanner, currier, shoemaker, the manufacturer, with his swift-flying shuttles, the operator tending his looms and spinning-jennies, the tailor with his sewing machines, the gunsmith, the harness-maker, the blacksmith, all trades and occupations have been employed. There are saddles, bridles, knapsacks, canteens, dippers, plates, knives, stoves, kettles, tents, blankets, medicines, drums, swords, pistols, guns, cannon, powder, percussion-caps, bullets, shot, shells, wagons,—everything.

WILLIAM BIRCHER: *A DRUMMER-BOY'S DIARY*

The hardships of marching long miles each day with no shoes and inadequate rations and water are detailed by drummer boy William Bircher, whose Union outfit is moving through parts of Tennessee and sailing by boat to Kentucky.

FROM WILLIAM BIRCHER, *A DRUMMER-BOY'S DIARY: FOUR*
YEARS OF SERVICE WITH THE SECOND REGIMENT MINNESOTA
VETERAN VOLUNTEERS, 1861 TO 1865
(St. Paul, Minn.: St. Paul Book and Stationery Co., 1889, pp. 33, 37–45)

• • •

Having no shelter of any kind, we peeled the bark off the gum-trees, and took half of it and laid it on the ground and crawled under it; a small place, but it sheltered us from the elements.

• • •

Orders were issued to carry two days' rations in our haversacks and to unload all extra ammunition; but this order was unnecessary, as the boys had unloaded without orders the day before. At 9 A.M. we continued our march and did not halt until 1 A.M., June 1 [1862], at a deserted rebel camp. We found a large quantity of flour, which we soon appropriated, and cooked it in every way known to the soldiers' culinary art. . . . On the 9th we marched twenty-five miles toward Boonville, passing through two deserted towns called Rienzi and Danville, and went into camp. We remained here three days without tents, but the weather was splendid and tents were useless.

Here we had more rations issued, and received orders to return to Corinth on the 13th, where we arrived after a few days' march, with nothing to mar the monotony of the trip. We remained at Corinth a few days, cleaning up, washing our clothes, and doing all necessary repairing. From there we moved east six miles and went into camp. The men had to dig wells to obtain water, and each company built bake-ovens from the clay dug from the wells, and they proved to be a perfect success in every particular. The young apples and peaches were now about large enough to gather for sauce, and the boys took advantage of it. It was laughable to see the different dishes they tried to make, and a few of them became very ill in consequence of overeating. A man named Wesley, of my company, died from the effects of eating too much green fruit.

• • •

September 9: There [on the Lebanon Pike] we received orders to leave all surplus baggage and tents, and prepare ourselves for marching orders. September 14 flour was issued to us, but no salt. The boys were in a very ragged condition, as all of the quartermaster's stores were shipped from here before our arrival, they expecting that Bragg would take Nashville before we should reach it. . . . We had no coffee or tea,—using sassafras and pennyroyal as a drink,—and no meat, but plenty of flour, of which we made what the boys called "dough-gods." This was done by mixing flour and water into a dough, wrapping it around their ramrods, and baking it before the fire. This was not very palatable without salt, but as it was all we had, we were of course compelled to eat it. The supply of water was short, the streams along the roads being all dry, also the wells at most of the houses. September 16 we marched twenty-two miles. I had no shoes, so I tore up my shirt and wrapped it around my bleeding feet, they being so sore that I could not march without great pain.

• • •

September 25: Marched to the mouth of Salt River, where it empties into the Ohio. Here we found the boys all barefooted, and no shoes to be had. My rags were worn out, and I had taken the pocket from my blouse and wrapped it around my feet; but as it was very thin stuff, I did not expect it would last over an hour or so. Here we found a boat-load of provisions, but the captain of the boat, being afraid to land, had anchored out in the river. The boys lined the bank of the river, and begged him to throw off some pork and hard-tack. Colonel Uline then appeared and told the boys to go back to camp, that rations would soon be issued if they would let the boat land. His orders had the desired effect, and shortly after the boys had dispersed the boat landed, and soon afterwards we were furnished with a bountiful supply of bacon, hard-tack, and coffee, and we ate as only half-famished men can. Only he who has marched in the hot sun ten days, with dough and sassafras-tea as a diet, can realize our condition.

• • •

October 1: We marched from Louisville and encamped eight miles from Shepherdsville. The country was destitute of water. None was to be had except in pools and puddles along the road, which was very warm and putrid. Weather very hot and the roads dusty. . . .

October 3: More clothing issued. Remained in camp all day, and on October 4 we resumed our march over the dusty roads; the weather very hot. Crossed the dry bed of Salt River, and encamped with an abundance of straw and wood, but the usual scarcity of water. Found a puddle where we dipped it up with a spoon and strained it through our dirty, sweaty handkerchiefs. . . .

October 7: Marched eight miles. Squads were detailed to hunt water, but all came back discouraged and tired out, having found no water except in one well, and there were a hundred there waiting for a chance to get at it.

JAMES KENDALL HOSMER: "CAMP LIFE"

James Kendall Hosmer, a soldier in the Union infantry, kept a detailed diary throughout the Civil War and wrote several books and articles about the life of soldiers. This selection provides details about soldiers' shelter, sometimes a makeshift affair that only the inventive could put together. Hosmer also stresses the discomfort from rain and cold and the impossibly cramped quarters, whether they were put together from blankets or government-issued tents.

FROM JAMES KENDALL HOSMER, "CAMP LIFE (1862)," IN *THE ROMANCE OF THE CIVIL WAR*, ED. ALBERT BUSHNELL HART
(New York: Macmillan, 1903, pp. 119–124)

Nov. 23, 1862. I proposed to keep a diary of my soldiering, and am now making my first entry. . . . It is the Fifty-second Regiment of Massachusetts Volunteers. I am in our little tent at Camp N.P. Banks, not far from Jamaica, in Long Island. The tent is perhaps eight feet square, and meant for seven soldiers. A leg of ham partly devoured, with gnawed loaves of bread and some tin cups, lie just at my right foot. Corporal Buffum, six feet and two or three inches tall, is writing home, just at the other foot. Joseph McGill is sleeping, wrapped up in his rubber blanket. The floor of the tent, at the sides, is covered with knapsacks, blankets, and soldiers' furniture. . . .

We left Camp Miller, where the Fifty-second organized, two or three days ago. For the first time, the knapsacks, full-loaded, were packed on, the canteens were filled, the haversacks were crammed with two days' rations. It was a heavy load as we set off in a cold November rain, nearly a thousand of us. It rained harder and harder. . . .

• • •

It is dreary, dismal, miserable. There are no overcoats; we are all perspiration with our march under the burden and there's no chance for tea or coffee, or anything warm: it is a sorry prospect, boys, for comfort tonight. But never mind. Behold how the yankee will vindicate himself in the face of the worst fortune! Fences are stripped of rails; and we have blazing fires in no time, which make the inhospitable, leaden sky speedily blush for itself. Rubber blankets are tacked together, and tents extemporized. . . . We find two sticks and a long rail. We drive the sticks into the ground for uprights, then lay the rail on top. Buffum and I tack our blankets together with strings through the eyelet-holes. We place the join-ing along the cross-timber, let the blankets slope away, roof-fashion, on each side toward the ground, fastening them at the edges with pegs, and strings straining them tight. Then we spread Ed's rubber blanket on the ground underneath, put our luggage at one end, and crowd in to try the effect. . . . The north-wind blows, and the air threatens snow. We survey our wigwam with great admiration. I lie down for the night with revolver and dirk strapped one on each side, unwashed, bedraggled, and armed like Jack Sheppard himself. We freeze along through the hours. We get into one another's arms to keep warm as we can, and shiver through till daylight.

When morning comes, all is confusion. The regiment looks as if it had rained down. It is clear, but raw. There is no chance to wash now, nor all day long. Our tents come. We pitch them in long rows, well ordered; floor them from fences near by; and carpet them with straw and marsh hay. Six or seven of us pack in here like sardines in a box, lying on our sides, "spoon-fashion."

JAMES KENDALL HOSMER: "ON THE WAY TO WAR"

Hosmer, now a corporal and writing of his voyage on a ship called the *Illinois*, intended for the transport of troops to a desti-nation unknown to the enlisted men, focuses on the dark, stifling quarters of the privates who must stow away in the hold. He de-scribes not only his own cramped quarters but his investigation of the privates' quarters and his experiences bedding down with the privates for one awful night.

FROM JAMES KENDALL HOSMER, "ON THE WAY TO WAR," IN
THE ROMANCE OF THE CIVIL WAR
(New York: Macmillan, 1903, pp. 125–130)

Each man now has his place for the voyage assigned him: so, if you can climb well, let us go down and see the men below. It is right through the damp, crowded passage at the side of the paddle-wheel first. Here is a fence and a gate, impervious to the private, but in his badge the cor-poral possesses the potent golden bough which gains him ingress into Hades [hell]. Just amidships, we go in through a door from the upper deck. The first large space is the hospital; already with thirty or forty in its rough, unplaned bunks. From this, what is half-stairway and half-ladder leads down the hatch. A lantern is burning here; and we see that the whole space between decks, not very great, is filled with bunks,—three rows of them between floor and ceiling,—stretching away into darkness on every hand, with two-feet passages winding among them.

. . . Presently I go through the narrow passage, with populous bunks, humming with men, on each side,—three layers between deck and deck. I can only hear them, and once in a while dimly see a face. At length we come to a railing, over which we climb, and descend another ladder, into regions still darker,—submarine, I believe, or, at any rate, on a level with the sea. Here swings another lantern. Up overhead, through deck after deck, is a skylight, which admits light, and wet too, from above. it is like looking from the bottom of a well.

As above, so here again, there are three tiers of bunks, with the narrow passages among them. The men lie side by side, with but two feet or so of space; but are in good spirits, though sepulchred after this fashion. The air seems not bad. It is dark in the day-time, except right under the skylight. A fortnight or so from now, a poor emaciated crowd, I fear, it will be proceeding from these lower deeps of the *Illinois*. I go back with an uneasy conscience to our six feet by eight up above, so infinitely preferable to these quarters of the privates, though five big sergeants with their luggage share it with me, and two waiters have no other home; so that we overflow through door and window, on to the deck and floor outside.

Ed and I turn in at half-past eight, lying on our sides, and interrupting one another's sleep with, "Look out for your elbow!" "I am going over the edge!" "You will press me through into the Company C bunks!" This morning I took breakfast in the berth,—dining room, study, and parlor, as well. There is room enough, sitting Turk-fashion, and bending over.

• • •

I resolve I will try a night with the men in the hold. Elnathan Gunn, the old soldier, invites me to share his bed and board. Life on a transport becomes so simplified, that bed and board become one; the soldier softening his plank with his haversack of beef and biscuit for a mattress and pillow. . . .

I stoop low, it is the lowest tier of bunks,—climb over two prostrate men, then lie down sandwiched helplessly between two slices of timber above and below, where I go to sleep among the raw-head and bloody-bone stories of Elnathan Gunn. I wake up at midnight hot and stifled, as if I were in a mine caved in. "Gunn, give me my boots!" Gunn fishes them out of some hole in the dark. I tug at the straps, half stifled, bump my head as I rise, grovel on my stomach out over two or three snorers, and hurry through the dark for the upper deck, thankful that, being corporal, I can have quarters where I can see and breathe.

WILLIAM HENRY BISBEE: *THROUGH FOUR AMERICAN WARS*

William Henry Bisbee was a brigadier general who had experience in four wars, starting with his service as a Union soldier in the American Civil War and ending with World War I. What Bisbee, a green recruit in the Civil War from 1863 remembers most vividly about his experiences is the filth with which soldiers had to contend: lack of sanitary conditions of any kind, only muddy water to bathe in occasionally, and vermin.

FROM WILLIAM HENRY BISBEE, *THROUGH FOUR AMERICAN WARS*
(Boston: Meador Publishing Co., 1931, pp. 109, 114, 115)

Poor, patriotic "rookies," how little we knew of the small space allotted to a private soldier in the company wagon after the rations, ammunition and cooking utensils are loaded, much better described as zero, as we soon found. Inspections were frequent with every inspector growing severer in eliminating useless articles. Everything not carried on the person and much of this, soon found a better resting place by the roadside. Bibles and housewives' or needle books in fancy covers that are said to save so many lives by stopping bullets, grew scarce, and shocking as it may sound, I remember no tooth brushes.

• • •

We were learning, each day improving our mobility, but not for a year or two did we get down to true principles under [General] Sherman, of the blanket roll to a man and one wagon to a battalion.

• • •

The work was all hard, tramp, tramp, tramp, and at night a tent and the ground, wet or dry, for a mattress, with two blankets for cover unless on picket duty, when it would be no tent and one blanket. . . .

Take it all in all, these days were among the filthiest of the War. Baggage trains were all behind, leaving us without change of clothing, and April showers soaking us daily, had in conjunction with natural exudations of the body and all absence of anything but mud holes to bathe in, left us in bad shape. We were alive with vermin, known as army "graybacks," not to be altogether overcome until fresh clothing could be obtained. The best we could do was to wash at the muddy pools, pick off the heads of families from our undergarments while we stood in the sun to dry and permit the little ones to multiply, ignorant of their fate, should they dare to grow up.

GEORGE F. NOYES: "OFF FOR THE FRONT"

Noyes, a Union soldier, describes the march from Washington, D.C., to join General McClellan who is moving on Richmond. He describes the soldiers as being very jubilant that they are to get into action rather than endure another period of intense boredom. Many reports of the Army of the Potomac encamped in Washington mention the heavy drinking this boredom in part has led to. One of the rare mentions of alcohol in *The Red Badge of Courage* comes from Henry's mother, who warns him that soldiers swear and drink heavily and that he must resist all such behavior himself.

Noyes also records the individual possessions with which a soldier marches. It becomes obvious that the knapsack is often the first thing to be relinquished when the burden gets too cumbersome, because it contains things the least necessary for his survival, keepsakes and clothes.

FROM GEORGE F. NOYES, "OFF FOR THE FRONT (1862)," IN
THE ROMANCE OF THE CIVIL WAR, ED. ALBERT BUSHNELL HART
(New York: Macmillan, 1903, pp. 136–139)

To get the horses safely on board the steamer is no easy task, for wharf and deck are lumbered up with all the paraphernalia of a campaign, and squads of heavy-knapsacked men are still hurrying on board, all jubilant and some quite intoxicated with patriotism and poor whiskey.

• • •

As we stand a while on the upper deck, cast your eye at the stalwart private near us, that you may know how a soldier looks in full war rig. The square knapsack on his back is crowned with a great roll of blankets, and contains his entire wardrobe—a change of clothes, a few toilet articles, probably a little Bible, and certainly a keepsake or two from the loved ones at home; his cartridge box, strapped beneath, holds only a few rounds of ball cartridge: as no battle is impending, his shoulders are festooned with his shelter tent, an oblong piece of thick cotton cloth, compressed into a roll; his haversack is stuffed with three days' marching rations; his water canteen dangles at the other side, while his musket is stacked with the rest in the centre of the deck.

Thus he carries his food, and drink, and clothing, and canvas house, and weapon with him; he may be said, indeed, to be quite independent of society. Musket and all, his equipment weighs sixty pounds, and with it he can safely march from fifteen to twenty miles a day.

JOHN D. BILLINGS: "HARDTACK AND COFFEE"

The testimony of John D. Billings, who wrote extensively on living conditions in the Civil War, would seem at first to contradict the evidence of many soldiers that they were inadequately fed and of many generals that their units were short of rations for months on end. However, his description of hardtack, the chief staple of the men in the Union army, appears to be a self-contradiction in that a day's ration of nine biscuits as the primary diet, too hard to be eaten without soaking and often maggot ridden, could hardly be considered adequate for a hard-marching, hard-fighting army.

FROM JOHN D. BILLINGS, "HARDTACK AND COFFEE (1861)," IN *THE ROMANCE OF THE CIVIL WAR*, ED. ALBERT BUSHNELL HART (New York: Macmillan, 1903, pp. 226–230)

A false impression has obtained more or less currency both with regard to the quantity and quality of the goods furnished the soldiers. I have been asked a great many times whether I always got enough to eat in the army, and have surprised inquirers by answering in the affirmative. Now, some old soldier may say who sees my reply, "Well, you were lucky. I didn't." But I should at once ask him to tell me for how long a time his regiment was ever without food of some kind. Of course, I am not now referring to our prisoners of war, who starved by the thousands. And I should be very much surprised if he should say more than twenty-four or thirty hours, at the outside. I would grant that he himself might, perhaps have been so situated as to be deprived of food a longer time, possibly when he was on an exposed picket post, or serving as rear-guard to the army, or doing something which separated him temporarily from his company; but his case would be the exception and not the rule.

• • •

I will now give a complete list of the rations served out to the rank and file, as I remember them. They were salt pork, fresh beef, salt beef,

rarely ham or bacon, hard bread, soft bread, potatoes, an occasional on-
ion, flour, beans, split pease, rice, dried apples, dried peaches, desiccated
vegetables, coffee, tea, sugar, molasses, vinegar, candles, soap, pepper,
and salt. (Note: Canned goods were unknown in wartime.)

. . .

I will speak of the rations more in detail, beginning with the hard
bread, or, to use the name by which it was known in the Army of the
Potomac, Hardtack. What was hardtack? It was a plain flour-and-water
biscuit. Two which I have in my possession as mementos measure three
and one-eighth by two and seven-eighths inches, and are nearly half an
inch thick. Although these biscuits were furnished to organizations by
weight, they were dealt out to the men by number, nine constituting a
ration in some regiments, and ten in others; but there were usually
enough for those who wanted more, as some men would not draw them.
While hardtack was nutritious, yet a hungry man could eat his ten in a
short time and still be hungry. When they were poor and fit objects for
the soldiers' wrath, it was due to one of three conditions: first, they may
have been so hard that they could not be bitten; it then required a very
strong blow of the fist to break them; the second condition was when
they were mouldy or wet, as sometimes happened, and should not have
been given to the soldiers; the third condition was when from storage
they had become infested with maggots.

When the bread was mouldy or moist, it was thrown away and made
good at the next drawing, so that the men were not the losers; and in
the case of its being infested with the weevils, they had to stand it as a
rule; but hardtack was not so bad an article of food, even when traversed
by insects, as may be supposed. Eaten in the dark, no one could tell the
difference between it and hardtack that was untenanted. It was no un-
common occurrence for a man to find the surface of his pot of coffee
swimming with weevils, after breaking up hardtack in it, which had come
out of the fragments only to drown; but they were easily skimmed off,
and left no distinctive flavor behind.

Having gone so far, I know the reader will be interested to learn of the
styles in which this particular article was served up by the soldiers. Of
course, many of them were eaten just as they were received—hardtack
plain; then I have already spoken of their being crumbled in coffee, giving
them "hardtack and coffee." Probably more were eaten in this way than
in any other, for they thus frequently furnished the soldier his breakfast
and supper. But there were other and more appetizing ways of preparing
them. Many of the soldiers, partly through a slight taste for the business
but more from force of circumstances, became in their way and opinion

experts in the art of cooking the greatest variety of dishes with the smallest amount of capital.

Some of these crumbled them in soups for want of other thickening. For this purpose they served very well. Some crumbled them in cold water, then fried the crumbs in the juice and fat of meat. A dish akin to this one which was said to make the hair curl, and certainly was indigestible enough to satisfy the cravings of the most ambitious dyspeptic, was prepared by soaking hardtack in cold water, then frying them brown in pork fat, salting to taste. Another name for this dish was skillygallee. Some liked them toasted, either to crumb in coffee, or if a sutler [merchant who follows and sells supplies to the army] was at hand whom they could patronize, to butter. The toasting generally took place from the end of a split stick.

Then they worked into milk-toast made of condensed milk at seventy-five cents a can; but only a recruit with a big bounty, or an old vet, the child of wealthy parents, or a reenlisted man did much in that way. A few who succeeded by hook or by crook in saving up a portion of their sugar ration spread it upon hardtack. And so in various ways the ingenuity of the men was taxed to make this plainest and commonest yet most serviceable of army food to do duty in every conceivable combination.

CARLTON MCCARTHY: "ON THE MARCH"

Carlton McCarthy writes of the need to leave behind what most would consider necessary supplies when the order was given to march in the Union army. He also writes of the miseries of the march caused by dust and rain.

FROM CARLTON MCCARTHY, "ON THE MARCH (1861)," IN *THE ROMANCE OF THE CIVIL WAR*, ED. ALBERT BUSHNELL HART
(New York: Macmillan, 1903, pp. 230–234)

Orders to move! Where? when? what for?—are the eager questions of the men as they begin their preparations to march. Generally nobody can answer and the journey is commenced in utter ignorance of where it is to end. But shrewd guesses are made, and scraps of information will be picked up on the way. The main thought must be to get ready to move. The orderly sergeant is shouting "Fall in!" and there is no time to lose. The probability is that before you get your blanket rolled up, find your frying-pan, haversack, axe, etc., and fall in, the roll-call will be over, and some extra duty provided.

No wonder there is bustle in the camp. Rapid decisions are to be made between the various conveniences which have accumulated, for some must be left. One fellow picks up the skillet, holds it awhile, mentally determining how much it weighs, and what will be the weight of it after carrying it five miles, and reluctantly, with a half-ashamed, sly look drops it and takes his place in the ranks. Another having added to his store of blankets too freely, now has to decide which of the two or three he will leave. The old water-bucket looks large and heavy, but one stout-hearted, strong-armed man has taken it affectionately in his care.

This is the time to say farewell to the bread tray, farewell to the little piles of clean straw laid between two logs, where it was so easy to sleep; farewell to the girls in the neighborhood; farewell to the spring, farewell to our tree and our fire, good-by to the fellows who are not going, and a general good-by to the hills and valleys.

Soldiers commonly threw away the most valuable articles they possessed. Blankets, overcoats, shoes, bread and meat,—all gave way to the necessities of the march; and what one man threw away would frequently be the very article that another wanted and would immediately pick up; so there was not much lost after all.

• • •

Troops on the march were generally so cheerful and gay that an outsider, looking on them as they marched, would hardly imagine how they suffered. In summer time, the dust, combined with the heat, caused great suffering. The nostrils of the men, filled with dust, became dry and feverish, and even the throat did not escape. The grit was felt between the teeth, and the eyes were rendered almost useless. There was dust in eyes, mouth, ears and hair. The shoes were full of sand, and the dust penetrated the clothes. The heat was at times terrific, but the men became greatly accustomed to it, and endured it with wonderful ease. Their heavy woolen clothes were a great annoyance; tough linen or cotton clothes would have been a great relief; indeed, there are many objections to woolen clothing for soldiers, even in winter.

If the dust and heat were not on hand to annoy, their very able substitutes were: mud, cold, rain, snow, hail and wind took their places. Rain was the greatest discomfort a soldier could have; it was more uncomfortable than the severest cold with clear weather. Wet clothes, shoes and blankets; wet meat and bread; wet feet and wet ground; wet wood to burn, or rather not to burn; wet arms and ammunition; wet ground to sleep on, mud to wade through, swollen creeks to ford, muddy springs, and a thousand other discomforts attended the rain. There was no comfort on a rainy day or night except in bed,—that is, under your blanket and oil-cloth. Cold winds, blowing the rain in the faces of the men, increased the discomfort. Mud was often so deep as to submerge the horses and mules, and at times it was necessary for one man or more to extricate another from the mud holes in the road.

JAMES KENDALL HOSMER: "A TURKEY FOR A BEDFELLOW"

Corporal James Kendall Hosmer writes of the hardships of the camp. By 1863 his clothes were ragged and dirty. Rations had grown slim. But he is blessed with the gift of a turkey that a friend foraged (read stolen) from a nearby farm likely and given to Hosmer, who must first sleep with the bird before killing and cooking him.

FROM JAMES KENDALL HOSMER, "A TURKEY FOR A
BEDFELLOW (1863)," IN *THE ROMANCE OF THE CIVIL WAR*, ED.
ALBERT BUSHNELL HART
(New York: Macmillan, 1903, pp. 259–261)

So we live and listen and wait. I am reduced now to about the last stage. My poor blouse grows raggeder. My boots, as boys say, are hungry in many places. I have only one shirt; and that has shrunk about the neck, until buttons and button-holes are irretrievably divorced, and cannot be forced to meet. Washing-days, if I were anywhere else, I should have to lie abed until the washer-woman brought home the shirt. Now I cannot lie abed, for two reasons: first, I am washer-woman myself; second, the bed is only bed at night. By daytime, it is parlor-floor, divan, dining-table, and library, and therefore taken up. I button up in my blouse, therefore; and can so fix myself, and so brass matters through, that you would hardly suspect, unless you looked sharp, what a whited sepulchre it was that stood before you. I have long been without a cup. Somebody stole mine long ago; and I, unfortunate for me, am deterred, by the relic of a moral scruple which still lingers in my breast, from stealing somebody else's in return. My plate is the original Camp-Miller tin plate, worn down now to the iron. I have leaned and lain and stood on it, until it looks as if it were in the habit of being used in the exhibitions of some strong man, who rolled it up and unrolled it to show the strength of his fingers. There is a big crack down the side; and, soup-days, there is a great rivalry between that crack and my mouth,—the point of strife being, which shall swallow most of the soup; the crack generally getting the best of it.

Rations pall now-a-days. The thought of soft bread is an oasis in the memory. Instead of that, our wearied molars know only hardtack, and hard salt beef and pork. We pine for simple fruits and vegetables. The other day, however, I received a gift. An easy-conscienced friend of mine brought in a vast amount of provender from a foraging expedition, and bestowed upon me a superb turkey,—the biggest turkey I ever saw; probably the grandfather of his whole race. His neck and breast were decorated with a vast number of red and purple tassels and trimmings. He was very fat, moreover; so that he looked like an apoplectic sultan. I carried him home with toil and sweat; but what to do with him for the night! If he had been left outside, he would certainly have been stolen: so the only way was to make a bedfellow of him. Occasionally he woke up and "gobbled;" and I feared all night long the peck of his bill and the impact of his spurs. In the morning, we immolated him with appropriate ceremonies. The chaplain's coal-hod, the next thing in camp to make a soup in, was in use; but I found a kettle, and presided over the preparation of an immense and savory stew, the memory whereof will ever steam up to me from the past with grateful sweetness.

JENKIN LLOYD JONES: *AN ARTILLERYMAN'S DIARY*

Jones, a Union foot soldier, traveled down the Mississippi River, stopping along the way in Tennessee and Mississippi in areas where the mosquitoes, breeding in the muggy swamps along the river, posed a constant threat of disease. Jones's diary documents the necessity of the common soldier's having to forage in order to get enough to eat in camp and the struggles with monotony and ill health.

FROM JENKIN LLOYD JONES, *AN ARTILLERYMAN'S DIARY*
(Madison: Wisconsin History Commission, February 1914, pp. 5, 38, 39)

Rienzi, Saturday, Sept. 13 [1863]. The 3rd Section, Lieutenant Hood, went out to front and the first fell back to its old grounds. Foraging party brought in two loads of corn, three neat of cattle, one sheep, twelve geese, seven hens, two or three bushels of sweet potatoes.

• • •

Near Helena, Saturday, March 12. Fine weather. Washed my clothes in the forenoon. In the afternoon joined in the funeral procession of a member of Co. G., 72nd Illinois. Laid him in the swamp and left him in the cheerless spot, a soldier's grave. Many of the boys in spite of high water, went out foraging and brought in fresh pork and beef in plenty.

. . .

Near Helena, Saturday, March 14. Health not very good. Seven months ago I enlisted in the service of the U.S. Then I hoped that by this time a different phase of the matter could be seen. But alas, it is very dark ahead, yet I do not despond, neither have I regretted my enlistment. I can only do the best I can, and be satisfied. A hard tug is before me. May God grant me health and courage to do my duty.

. . .

Near Helena, Monday, March 16. A fine spring day. Still troubled with diarrhea. All monotonous in camp. Spent most of the day patching. Vaccinated by George Fisher, hospital steward.

. . .

Near Helena, Thursday, March 19. Exercised and washed my horses. Health in camp poor. Eighteen on the sick list.

. . .

Near Helena, Sunday, March 22. Cloudy and indications of rain. Infantry embarked. Ordered to be ready to go on at 12 P.M. but the boats did not come. Drizzled rain nearly all day. Health none the best. Diarrhea very bad. Water rising very fast.

ALBERT O. MARSHALL: *ARMY LIFE*

Marshall's account of army life contains a description of the standard issue of supplies, including the necessity of the soldiers' ridding themselves of some of these important pieces of equipment when they were on the march. Marshall also describes the arms issued to his particular regiment. Disappointing to all the soldiers, it was a difficult-to-operate, inaccurate musket instead of the rifles they had been led to expect.

FROM ALBERT O. MARSHALL, *ARMY LIFE: FROM A SOLDIER'S*
JOURNAL
(Joliet, Ill.: Printed for the Author, 1883, pp. 16, 17, 25, 27–28)

Learning to Use the Knapsack, Etc.

Our knapsacks, haversacks and canteens were issued to us at once. Many funny scenes occurred as the young soldier boys were trying to understand the new, and to them, curious soldier trappings. Each commenced trying to solve the unknown mystery at once. Most of the soldiers could, at first sight, understand the use for which the different articles were designed, but the more awkward ones made some laughable blunders. The canteens being simply a round tin water flask with flat sides and a strap attached to carry it by, so plainly showed for what it was intended that all could understand its use at once, except a few of those odd fellows who never understand anything, and who were laughed at for the way in which they explained their supposed powder-horns. This was the only mistake made with the canteens, unless the enthusiastic endorsement of one soldier could be called a mistake, who, when he received his canteen, earnestly embraced it and spontaneously exclaimed, "What a neat and convenient thing to carry a drop of whiskey in to have in case of an accident."

The knapsacks with their different parts, pockets, and straps, puzzled them more. The haversacks being simply a canvas bag with a strap attached long enough to go over the shoulders, were so plain and as simple that they could, as they erroneously supposed, understand its use at once. By the time a single blanket was crowded into it, the haversack, never intended for such purpose, was full and running over, and the perplexed and bewildered soldier would look with blank astonishment and comical dismay at the large pile of necessary blankets and clothing for which he had no room. By this time the more dexterous ones had solved the mystery of their knapsacks and with them fully packed were trying them in position on their backs. Upon looking at the more ingenious ones, the unhappy and confused soldiers began to see where they were wrong, and soon understood that the haversacks they had been trying to use as a bag for their blankets and clothing was only designed for a dinner bag. With the help of their more efficient comrades the awkward soldiers learned how to pack their knapsacks. In this way even the dullest volunteer was set right as to the different and proper uses of the knapsack, haversack and canteen, and we were soon pronounced to be all in marching order.

• • •

First March.

After lying upon the roadside all night we got up at an early hour and returned to our old camp, where we took an early breakfast and then marched to Jimtown, the nearest railroad station.

Our first march, although a short one, only two and a half miles, was to us a hard one. Lying as we did by the roadside all night, expecting every moment to be called into line to go to the supposed waiting railroad train, with little chance to sleep or keep warm during all the long hours of a chilly September night, did not have a tendency to put us in an extra good marching trim. Besides this, we were all heavily overloaded. Each was carrying about as heavy a load as he could lift. And then our knapsacks, the awkward things, would not set right; or rather perhaps we did not know how to make them do so; something was wrong. Going in this condition, by the time our little march was ended, many of the young and unseasoned soldiers were completely exhausted. This, it must be confessed, was rather a poor beginning for soldiers who had such high expectations of the great wonders they were to accomplish when opportunity offered.

• • •

Camp Hovey. . . .

It would surprise any one not acquainted with the inexhaustible resources and utility of Yankee ingenuity, to see how soon apparently useless pieces of boards and planks and even the broken remains of deserted secesh buildings were transformed into articles of convenience and utility. Tent floors, bunks, tables, writing desks, seats, etc., were made with surprising rapidity and skill. Three hours after our tents were pitched our camp presented the appearance and contained all of the conveniences of an old and well arranged camp.

• • •

The guns we drew were muskets of a European make, said to be some of those purchased for our Government by General Fremont. The boys were very much disappointed. They had expected to get some of the best rifles in use. They had enlisted with the understanding that this regiment was to be armed with the Enfield rifles, or better, if better were to be had. It was to be the crack regiment of the State [Illinois], you know. Every regiment organized was formed upon the idea that *it* was without fail to be number one, the especially favorite and pride of the Union army.

Expecting to get the best rifles and then to get a musket—and such a musket! Phew! A musket that needed the services of a skilful engineer to run it successfully. To load one of them: commence by taking a cartridge out of the cartridge-box, tear off the end of it and pour the powder down in the gun, then place the ball in after the powder; now go for the long iron ramrod, which must be pulled out of its pocket, inserted in the mouth of the gun, and with it drive the ball down upon the powder; then take out the ramrod and return it to its own pocket. At this stage of the proceeding, with a decent gun, a percussion cap would be taken from its box, the hammer of the gun raised, and the cap placed upon the gun tube, but these guns do not go off with a simple little percussion cap, such as we are acquainted with. No, indeed. First, the hammer has to be raised and then a little trap door must be opened, then a funny little primer about two thirds of an inch in length with a pretty little wire string attached, must be taken from its box and inserted "just so" in a cunning little pocket, and then the amusing little trap door must be carefully closed down over it, and thus go through all of this elaborate ceremony before the gun can be loaded. These guns must be intended for soldiers who go out and fire one shot and then return leisurely to camp and go back the next day to fire the second volley. But they are so cunning. Yes, just as cunning as a little red wagon and probably about as dangerous. They are a smooth bore gun and the charge contains one ball and three buck shot. They are good for nothing except at short range, and even at that but little better than a common shot gun and much more complicated and unhandy. In every respect except for use as a club, where their weight would be available, a double barrelled shot gun would be far more desirable. These guns were a poor apology for those the members of our regiment had expected; the promised rifles with which they could pick off a rebel with perfect ease at a distance of nine hundred yards.

TOPICS FOR WRITTEN AND ORAL EXPLORATION

1. Discuss why Stephen Crane spent so little time describing the camp life of the Union soldier in *The Red Badge of Courage*.

2. Why is it reasonable to suppose that Henry would not have had the problem that the drummer boy has with inadequate shoes and other articles of clothing?

3. Make some hardtack, let it harden, and then see what you can do to make it edible, using no more than a Civil War soldier would have in the way of supplies and cooking conveniences.

4. Approximate as nearly as you can the full complement of supplies generally carried by the soldier. Go on a five-mile march carrying them as far as you can. (Remember that the drummer boy and his comrades walked as many as twenty-five miles a day!)

5. Detail the personal items (as opposed to necessary supplies) you would have wanted with you in your stay in the army during the Civil War and why.

6. Assume that you are in Washington, D.C., and are in charge of army rations. Given the prospect of spoilage and the absence of any effective way to can food, what could you issue to soldiers in Mississippi? What would be an effective way of doing that?

7. Do some research on the history of army rations in the field in World Wars I and II, the Vietnam War, and the Gulf War. How are these different from what was available in the Civil War?

8. Estimate how long it would take you to reload and fire an Enfield musket.

9. Do some research on the history of small arms weaponry in the past hundred years. What technical advances have been the most dramatic in the development of small arms?

10. Do some research on the advances made in food taken on space trips.

11. Consider how you might have spent your time in camp when you were not being drilled and reviewed.

SUGGESTED READINGS

Hagerman, Edward. *The American Civil War and the Origins of Modern Warfare*. Bloomington: Indiana University Press, 1988.

Katcher, Philip. *Civil War Uniforms: A Photo Guide*. London: Arms and Armour, 1996.

Meyer, Steve. *Iowa Valor*. Garrison, Iowa: Meyer, 1994.

Morton, John Watson. *The Artillery of Nathan Bedford Forrest's Cavalry*. Nashville: M.E. Church, 1909.

Stern, Philip Van Doren, ed. *Soldier Life in the Union and Confederate Armies*. Greenwich, Conn.: Fawcett, 1961.

Wiley, Bell Irwin. *The Life of Billy Yank: The Common Soldier of the Union*. Garden City, N.Y.: Doubleday, 1971.

6

The Red Badge of Courage as an Antiwar Novel

The Red Badge of Courage has often been called America's first antiwar novel. Coming almost thirty years after the Civil War, from the pen of a man who had heard stories about war from the veterans in his home town and who had grown up in the backwash of a war that had left a nation full of maimed men and widowed women, the novel is a clear expression of antiwar sentiment in a number of ways.

Most obvious is the unflinching realism of the battlefield, with its graphic pictures of the dead and dying. One is led to ask: Is any cause worth this suffering? And nowhere in the novel do we have a soldier even thinking of "the cause."

Second is the novel's theme that war emphasizes the lowest faculties of the human character rather than the highest. Whether Henry is running from the front line in sheer terror or charging ahead toward the enemy with fervor, it is the lowest—the animalistic side of him—that is in charge. Even his so-called bravery is generated not by some noble cause but by his hatred of the enemy because they have not let him rest and his hatred of his superior officers, who have humiliated him and his comrades.

Third, the reader sees that the experience with war does not clarify Henry's vision or refine his character. There is a real question as to whether this battle has "made a man of him." Even at the end, a convincing argument can be made that Henry continues to rationalize his actions by persuading himself that he is just a helpless pawn in the universe.

Fourth, the military machine has produced leaders who think of the men they lead as less than fully human. The lower ranks are called "men," ironically, but are really regarded as animals. To the officers, they are not individuals; they are part of a storehouse of cannon fodder—"mule drivers." A diversion is needed? Send a company of men in on a suicide mission. These military officers are portrayed not as noble and honorable but as petulant five-year-olds with trivial concerns, temper tantrums, and callous views of other people.

Finally, the novel shows that war reinforces an unjust and rigid class system based on social privilege, not ability. Only the officers are dressed like dandies; only the officers ride on horses. An even greater peril than the enemy's bullets is being mowed down by one's own officers, riding recklessly in horse-driven carts.

In the Civil War, antiwar sentiment arose primarily from particular interpretations of Christianity and biblical teaching. While many Christians, especially during the religious Crusades of the eleventh and twelfth centuries, attempted to justify war from Old Testament scripture, it was countered by pacifists that even the Old Testament, with its many warriors and vengeful, warlike God, who frequently sent his people on military missions, taught, "Thou shalt not kill." In the New Testament, martial valor was replaced by meekness, submissiveness, and forgiveness. Jesus, known as the Peacemaker, taught that one should turn away from an insult, resist fighting back, love one's enemies.

Pacifists took as their chief text the Sermon on the Mount (Matthew 5), especially the following:

> Blessed are the meek, for they shall inherit the earth. . . .
>
> Blessed are the peacemakers, for they shall be called sons of God.

Another key passage from the New Testament quoted by pacifists came from the Book of Luke, Chapters 27 through 35:

> But I say to you that hear, Love your enemies, do good to those who hate you, bless those who curse you, pray for those who abuse you.

To him who strikes you on the cheek, offer the other also; and from him who takes away your cloak do not withhold your coat as well. . . .

But love your enemies, and do good, and lend, expecting nothing in return.

So, while the pacifist might acknowledge that the Old Testament condoned, often even encouraged, war, the spirit of the New Testament was an argument against war.

As Christianity developed from its earliest days, theologians who were not committed to pacifism developed the notion of the just war. They could turn to Deuteronomy 7 for example:

And when the Lord your God gives them over to you, and you defeat them; then you must utterly destroy them; you shall make no covenant with them, and show no mercy to them.

St. Paul, for example, used many military metaphors that provided fuel for war between believers and nonbelievers. And St. Ambrose turned to the Old Testament figures of Moses, Abraham, and David to support the idea of a war waged for a just cause. When the barbarians invaded Rome, Christians argued that when the Christian state is attacked, war is justified if the final object is to restore peace. War can be righteously waged in order to end war. (A contemporary extension of this argument is that the dropping of the atomic bomb was necessary to end the war with Japan in World War II.) Violence was excusable not only to defend one's life, but the life of the nation as well.

The fifteenth century, in which so many Christians went as warriors to the Crusades, ironically saw the rise in many pacifist religious sects. Most prominent of these were the Quakers, or Society of Friends, which had a very high profile in the United States. Others of like mind included the Anabaptists or Mennonites. The Quakers argued that others could fight for justice if they insisted, but they, the Quakers, would work for peace through politics. In principle, going to war was to be a matter of individual conscience for them, even though history tells us that occasionally Quakers who did go to war were thrown out of their congregations.

The Quakers also had strong objections to the military itself, even above and beyond its purpose of waging war, for the Quakers were egalitarian. They refused to establish a hierarchy of pastors, deacons, priests, and bishops, even in their own congregations. Why, they argued, should they condone a highly hierarchical military that was structured into ranks, including officers and foot soldiers?

No more trying time came for the Quakers and other pacifists than the American Civil War, for the chief crusade of the Quakers in the nineteenth century was the abolition of slavery. The owning of slaves by a Quaker was absolutely prohibited by the Society. And Quakers had been among the most active in spiriting slaves into Canada on the Underground Railroad. When a war to end slavery erupted, pacifists were in an agonizing situation. How could they refuse to fight for an end to slavery, the cause to which many had already risked their lives? Other Northern churches, especially the Congregationalists, Unitarians, Presbyterians, Baptists, and Methodists, had encouraged their members to join the fight against the slaveholding South.

Finally, drawing on the idea that Quakers should decide as a matter of individual conscience, some did join the Union army, but most continued in their belief that they should take an active stand against both slavery and war and refused service.

Stronger protests were raised against two other wars in which Americans became involved in the nineteenth century: the Mexican War, fueled by America's belief that it was its "destiny" to democratize all of the Americas, and the Spanish-American War, also fought in the name of imperialism, of gaining more territory and control on the American continent. Those who lived farthest from these battles, in New England, were the most vociferous in their antiwar sentiments. In England, wars of imperialism, including the Crimean War and the Boer War, were also being waged. Many opposed to war, on the purely secular grounds that England had no business fighting wars outside the bounds of the British Isles, joined ranks with religious pacifists. The strongest voices in the latter camp continued to be the Quakers, who were represented most eloquently by Quaker statesman John Bright. Bright's opposition to England's involvement in war was especially effective because he argued from a pragmatic public policy perspective rather than from his own Christian principles. Bright, from either a religious or secular perspective, was able to argue that "war is probably the greatest of all human calamities."[1] His view was underscored by British parliamentarians such as Lord John Morley, who in speaking to his constituency on the matter of the Boer War concluded his appeal with the following words:

> You may carry fire and sword into the midst of peace and industry: it will be wrong. A war of the strongest government in the world with untold wealth and inexhaustible reserves against this little republic will bring you no glory: it will be wrong. You may make thousands of women widows, and thousands of children fatherless: it will be wrong. It may add a new province to your empire: it will be wrong.[2]

Russia's greatest novelist, Leo Tolstoy, who may have had considerable influence on Stephen Crane, was one of the voices raised most strongly against the war between Russia and Turkey in the Crimea. Tolstoy's criticism of his own country's involvement in war, especially the misuse of Russian peasants by the country's leaders, considered by the British press to be reckless and dangerous, was a forewarning of the Russian revolution:

> That ceaseless stream of unfortunate deluded Russian peasants now being transported by thousands to the Far East—these are those same—not more than 50,000 live Russian men whom Nicholas Romanoff and Alexis Kuropatkin have decided they may get killed and who will be killed in support of those stupidities, robberies, and every kind of abomination which were accomplished in China and Korea by immoral, ambitious men now sitting peacefully in their palaces and expecting new glory and new advantage and profit from the slaughter of those 50,000 unfortunate defrauded Russian workingmen guilty of nothing and gaining nothing by their sufferings and death.[3]

General discontent with war reached a new high during and after World War I when there was no clear reason for fighting, and it was difficult, if not impossible, to make an argument it was a just war or that it was a matter of national self-defense. The horrible carnage of World War I only increased the intensity of pacifism in England and the United States. The magnitude of loss of English soldiers was such that some towns in Britain lost their entire male population. It was not until World War II that the nation's pacifists faced a situation comparable to the one their fathers had to grapple with in the Civil War: the uncomfortable conviction that they were being asked to fight for a just cause. With the attack by the Japanese on Pearl Harbor and the invasion of Poland by the Germans who had already shown signs of massive persecution of Jews and others, there was a general feeling that this was "a good war," making an antiwar position more difficult to maintain. The lifelong pacifist asked himself, "Should I continue to refuse to join the military and fight if war is the only way to end atrocities?" There was no easy answer for many pacifists. The truth seemed to be that the war resulted in almost inconceivable suffering of civilians on both sides: in concentration camps across Europe, millions of men, women, and children were tortured and incinerated by the Germans. And in Dresden, Hamburg, and Hiroshima and Nagasaki, civilians were, it was reported, incinerated more completely than in the process of cremation by the Allies. Yet it also appeared to many that atrocities against children could be stopped only with further atrocities against other children.

With the escalation of the Vietnam War in the 1960s and early 1970s, however, it became much simpler to make the decision to resist military service, to espouse pacifism and work actively against the waging of war. This was true because most citizens were not convinced that this was a just or a justifiable war. No national defense seemed to be involved, no invasion of U.S. territories, no clear notion that *any* territory was being invaded against the will of the majority. As a consequence, the whole notion of pacifism reignited, and pacifist arguments from the pre–Civil War days found their way into the public forum. Interest grew in *The Red Badge of Courage* as an argument against the waging of war. And other antiwar novels appeared on the scene, notably Kurt Vonnegut's *Slaughterhouse Five*, which was set in World War II and made references to historic wars like the Children's Crusade, but was actually about the Vietnam War raging at the time. Another famous antiwar novel was Joseph Heller's *Catch-22*, again a picture of World War II commenting on all war, which showed that the root of war is greed and its effects are not only death but insanity.

The following documents throw light on the resistance to war and *The Red Badge of Courage* as an antiwar novel: three poems by Stephen Crane, Mark Twain's *The War Prayer*, the pledge of War Resisters International, and an interview with Dick Brown of

Berkeley, California, who has been a devoted pacifist for sixty-eight years.

NOTES

1. Margaret E. Hirst, *The Quakers in War and Peace* (London: George Allen and Unwin, 1923), p. 275.
2. John Morley, *Recollections* (London: Macmillan, 1917), 2: 86.
3. *Literary Digest* XXIX nos. 4, 5 (January 1904), 115–16, 141.

STEPHEN CRANE, "XIV" ("THERE WAS A CRIMSON CLASH OF WAR") AND "XXVII" ("A YOUTH IN APPAREL THAT GLITTERED")

The following poems by Crane appeared untitled in *The Black Riders and Other Lines*, first printed in 1895, the same year that he published *The Red Badge of Courage*. In the first poem, note the use of color in both the volume title and first line, the use of irony, and the lack of traditional form, which seems to mirror the chaos and failure of order. Note also that the victims are identified as people, whereas those who attempt to explain are nonhuman "tongues."

The second poem makes use of the romantic deception, found in so much literature on the Middle Ages, that war is noble and ennobling. What is the grim forest?

STEPHEN CRANE, "XIV," IN *THE BLACK RIDERS AND OTHER LINES*
(London: William Heinemann, 1896)

There was crimson clash of war.
Lands turned black and bare;
Women wept;
Babes ran, wondering.
There came one who understood not these things.
He said, "Why is this?"
Whereupon a million strove to answer him.
There was such intricate clamor of tongues,
That still the reason was not.

STEPHEN CRANE, "XXVII," IN *THE BLACK RIDERS AND OTHER LINES*
(London: William Heinemann, 1896)

A youth in apparel that glittered
Went to walk in a grim forest.

There he met an assassin
Attired all in garb of old days;
He, scowling through the thickets,
And dagger poised quivering,
Rushed upon the youth.
"Sir," said this latter,
"I am enchanted, believe me,
"To die, thus,
"In this medieval fashion,
"According to the best legends;
"Wh, what joy!"
Then took he the wound, smiling,
And died, content.

STEPHEN CRANE, "69" ("DO NOT WEEP, MAIDEN, FOR WAR IS KIND")

Shortly after his experience in covering the Spanish-American War in Cuba in 1898, Crane published his volume of poetry *War Is Kind* (1899). As in the earlier volume, none of the poems have titles. The first line of poem "69," which was actually written in 1895, contains the ironic phrase from which the collection takes its title. Each of the refrains is addressed to a different member of the soldier's family, who must be told the reason for his death.

STEPHEN CRANE, "69," IN *WAR IS KIND*
(New York: F. A. Stokes, 1899)

Do not weep, maiden, for war is kind.
Because your lover threw wild hands toward the sky
And the affrighted steed ran on alone,
Do not weep.
War is kind.
　　Hoarse, booming drums of the regiment
　　Little souls who thirst for fight,
　　These men were born to drill and die
　　The unexplained glory flies above them
　　Great is the battle-god, great, and his kingdom—
　　A field where a thousand corpses lie.
Do not weep, babe, for war is kind.
Because your father tumbled in the yellow trenches,

Raged at his breast, gulped and died,
Do not weep.
War is kind.
    Swift, blazing flag of the regiment
    Eagle with crest of red and gold,
    These men were born to drill and die
    Point for them the virtue of slaughter
    Make plain to them the excellence of killing
    And a field where a thousand corpses lie.
Mother whose heart hung humble as a button
On the bright splendid shroud of your son,
Do not weep.
War is kind.

SAMUEL CLEMENS, *THE WAR PRAYER*

Clemens (Mark Twain), who had deserted and headed for the western territories after his brief service in the Civil War, wrote *The War Prayer* around March 10, 1905, but it was not published until 1923, some thirteen years after his death. Along with other works written toward the end of his life, *The War Prayer* is a bitter comment on what he called the "cursed human race." In the brief narrative, a community hungry for war sends off its sons, who are hungry for the glory of martial success. In the church meeting that follows the parade, after the minister prays for victory, a stranger enters the church and ascends the pulpit, announcing that he is sent from God to tell them of the other, inevitable meaning of the prayer for victory.

Like Crane in his poems, Clemens uses an ironic punch at the end to secure his antiwar message.

SAMUEL CLEMENS, *THE WAR PRAYER*
(New York: Harper and Row, 1923)

It was a time of great and exalting excitement. The country was up in arms, the war was on, in every breast burned the holy fire of patriotism; the drums were beating, the bands playing, the toy pistols popping, the bunched firecrackers hissing and spluttering; on every hand and far down the receding and fading spread of roofs and balconies a fluttering wilderness of flags flashed in the sun; daily the young volunteers marched down the wide avenue gay and fine in their new uniforms, the proud fathers and mothers and sisters and sweethearts cheering them with voices choked with happy emotion as they swung by; nightly the packed mass-meetings listened, panting, to patriot oratory which stirred the deepest deeps of their hearts, and which they interrupted at briefest intervals with cyclones of applause, the tears running down their cheeks the while; in the churches the pastors preached devotion to flag and country, and invoked the God of Battles, beseeching His aid in our good cause in outpourings of fervid eloquence which moved every listener. It was indeed a glad and gracious time, and the half dozen rash spirits that ventured to disapprove of the war and cast a doubt upon its righteousness straightway got such a stern and angry warning that for their personal safety's sake they quickly shrank out of sight and offended no more in that way.

Sunday morning came—next day the battalions would leave for the front; the church was filled; the volunteers were there, their young faces alight with martial dreams—visions of the stern advance, the gathering momentum, the rushing charge, the flashing sabres, the flight of the foe, the tumult, the enveloping smoke, the fierce pursuit, the surrender!—then home from the war, bronzed heroes, welcoming, adored, submerged in golden seas of glory! With the volunteers sat their dear ones, proud, happy, and envied by the neighbors and friends who had no sons and brothers to send forth to the field of honor, there to win for the flag, or, failing, die the noblest of noble deaths. The service proceeded; a war-chapter from the Old Testament was read; the first prayer was said; it was followed by an organ-burst that shook the building, and with one impulse the house rose, with glowing eyes and beating hearts and poured out that tremendous invocation—

> God the all terrible! Thou who ordainest,
> Thunder thy clarion and lightning thy sword!

Then came the "long" prayer. None could remember the like of it for passionate pleading and moving and beautiful language. The burden of its supplication was, that the ever-merciful and benignant Father of us all would watch over our noble young soldiers, and aid, comfort, and encourage them in their patriotic work; bless them, shield them in the day of battle and the hour of peril, bear them in His mighty hand, make them strong and confident, invincible in the bloody onset, help them to crush the foe, grant to them and to their flag and country imperishable honor and glory—

An aged stranger entered, and moved with slow and noiseless step up the main aisle, his eyes fixed upon the minister, his long body clothed in a robe that reached to his feet, his head bare, his white hair descending in a frothy cataract to his shoulders, his seamy face unnaturally pale, pale even to ghastliness. With all eyes following him and wondering, he made his silent way; without pausing, he ascended to the preacher's side and stood there, waiting. With shut lids the preacher, unconscious of his presence, continued his moving prayer, and at last finished it with the words, uttered in fervent appeal, "Bless our arms, grant us the victory, O Lord our God, Father and Protector of our land and flag!"

The stranger touched his arm, motioned him to step aside—which the startled minister did—and took his place. During some moments he surveyed the spell-bound audience with solemn eyes, in which burned an uncanny light; then in a deep voice he said—

"I come from the Throne—bearing a message from Almighty God!" The words smote the house with a shock; if the stranger perceived it he gave it no attention. "He has heard the prayer of His servant your shepherd, and will grant it if such shall be your desire after I, His messenger, shall have explained to you its import—that is to say, its full import. For it is like unto many of the prayers of men, in that it asks for more than he utters it is aware of—except he pause and think.

"God's servant and yours has prayed his prayer. Has he paused, and taken thought? Is it one prayer? No, it is two—one uttered, the other not. Both have reached the ear of Him who heareth all supplications, the spoken and unspoken. Ponder this—keep it in mind. If you would beseech a blessing upon yourself, beware! lest without intent you invoke a curse upon a neighbor at the same time. If you pray for the blessing of rain upon your crop which needs it, by that act you are possibly praying for a curse upon some neighbor's crop which may not need rain and can be injured by it.

"You have heard your servant's prayer—the uttered part of it. I am commissioned of God to put into words the other part of it—that part which the pastor—and also you in your hearts—fervently prayed silently. And ignorantly and unthinkingly? God grant that it was so! You heard these words: 'Grant us the victory, O Lord our God!' That is sufficient. The *whole* of the uttered prayer is compacted into those pregnant words. Elaborations were not necessary. When you have prayed for victory you have prayed for many unmentioned results which follow victory—*must* follow it, cannot help but follow it. Upon the listening spirit of God the Father fell also the unspoken part of the prayer. He commandeth me to put it into words. Listen!

"O Lord, our Father, our young patriots, idols of our hearts, go forth to battle—be Thou near them! With them—in spirit—we also go forth from the sweet peace of our beloved firesides to smite the foe. O Lord, our God, help us to tear their soldiers to bloody shreds with our shells; help us to cover their smiling fields with the pale forms of their patriot dead; help us to drown the thunder of the guns with the shrieks of their wounded, writhing in pain; help us to waste their humble homes with a hurricane of fire; help us to wring the hearts of their unoffending widows with unavailing grief; help us to turn them out roofless with their little children to wander unfriended the wastes of their desolated land in rags and hunger and thirst, sport of the sun-flames of summer and the icy winds of winter, broken in spirit, worn with travail, imploring Thee for the refuge of the grave and denied it—for our sakes who adore Thee, Lord, blast their hopes, blight their lives, protract their bitter pilgrimage, make heavy their steps, water their way with their tears, stain the white snow with the blood of their wounded feet! We ask it, in the spirit of love, of Him Who is the Source of Love, and Who is the ever-faithful refuge and friend of all that are sore beset and seek His aid with humble and contrite hearts. Amen."

[After a pause.] "Ye have prayed it; if ye still desire it, speak!—The messenger of the Most High waits."

It was believed afterwards, that the man was a lunatic, because there was no sense in what he said.

PLEDGE OF THE WAR RESISTERS INTERNATIONAL

The English pacifist organization that issued the following pledge after World War I has gone by different names: the Peace Pledge Union and the British Section of the War Resisters International, one national wing of a group that included sections in over a hundred countries. Adopted in 1921 by the organization, it was ratified at the First International Conference in 1925 and reaffirmed in each subsequent conference. Countering the long-standing defense of war for a "just cause," the International has argued that a war is damaging to any good cause.

PLEDGE OF THE WAR RESISTERS INTERNATIONAL, 1921

Statement of Principles

WAR IS A CRIME AGAINST HUMANITY.
It is a crime against life, and uses human personalities for political and economic ends.

WE, THEREFORE,
actuated by an intense love of mankind,

ARE DETERMINED NOT TO SUPPORT
either directly by service of any kind in the army, navy, or air forces, or indirectly by making or consciously handing munitions or other war material, subscribing to war loans or using our labour for the purpose of setting others free for war service.

ANY KIND OF WAR,
aggressive or defensive, remembering that modern wars are invariably alleged by Governments to be defensive.
Wars would seem to fall under three heads:

(a) *Wars to defend the State* to which we nominally belong and wherein our home is situated. To refuse to take up arms for this end is difficult:
 1. Because the State will use all its coercive powers to make us do so.
 2. Because our inborn love for home has been deliberately identified with love of the State in which it is situated.

(b) *Wars to preserve the existing order of society* with its security for the privileged few. That we would never take up arms for this purpose goes without saying.

(c) *Wars on behalf of the oppressed proletariat,* whether for its liberation or defence. To refuse to take up arms for this purpose is most difficult:

1. Because the proletarian regime, and, even more, the enraged masses, in time of revolution would regard as a traitor any one who refused to support the New Order by force.
2. Because our instinctive love for the suffering and the oppressed would tempt us to use violence on their behalf.

However, we are convinced that violence cannot *preserve order, defend* our home, or *liberate* the proletariat. In fact experience has shown that in all wars, order, security, and liberty disappear, and that, so far from benefiting by them, the proletariat always suffer most.

We hold, however, that consistent pacifists have no right to take up a merely negative position, but *must recognize*

AND STRIVE FOR THE REMOVAL OF ALL THE CAUSES OF WAR.

We recognize as causes of war not only the instinct of egoism and greed, which is found in every human heart, but also all agencies which create hatred and antagonism between groups of people. Among such, we would regard the following as the more important today:

1. Differences between *races*, leading by artificial aggravation to envy and hatred.

2. Differences between *religions*, leading to mutual intolerance and contempt.

3. Differences between *classes*, the possessing and the no-possessing, leading to civil war, which will continue so long as the present system of production exists, and private profit rather than social need is the outstanding motive of society.

4. Differences between *nations*, due largely to the present system of production, leading to world wars and such economic chaos as we see today, which eventualities, we are convinced, could be prevented by the adoption of a system of world economy which had for its end the well-being of the entire human race.

5. Finally, we see an important cause of war in the prevalent misconception of the State. The State exists for man, not man for the State. The recognition of the sanctity of human personality must become the basic principle of human society. Furthermore, the State is not a sovereign self-contained entity, as every nation

is a part of the great family of mankind. We feel, therefore, that consistent pacifists have no right to take up a merely negative position, but must devote themselves to abolishing classes, barriers between the peoples, and to creating a world-wide brotherhood founded on mutual service.

War Resistance is not an end in itself, it is a way of life to achieve an end. The goal, in the expression of the Socialist is, Liberty, Equality, Fraternity; in that of the Christian it is, Truth, Beauty, Love, a world where all men can and will desire to co-operate for the common good.

AGAINST WAR: AN INTERVIEW WITH DICK BROWN

Dick Brown, a semiretired building contractor living in Berkeley, California, has been a devoted pacifist since before the outbreak of World War II, joining the Society of Friends in 1940. As a conscientious objector, he was incarcerated in a work camp and then a federal penitentiary during World War II. Since that time, he has consistently devoted himself to the cause of peace.

Brown's account is especially interesting not only because of his reasons for deciding not to go to war and his acknowledgment of the difficulty involved in making that decision, but because he remembers vividly his great-grandfather's stories of being wounded in Virginia during the Civil War.

"AGAINST WAR: AN INTERVIEW WITH DICK BROWN"
(April 9, 1997)

CJ: Tell me something about your life now. I understand that you're retired but still working part time as a building contractor.

Dick: Yes, I'm seventy-eight years old now. I've been a building contractor for a long time. My father was a building contractor. My father didn't want me to become a carpenter. But by some strange quirk of fate, I ended up in his trade. I don't need to work any longer, but I tried complete retirement and found that doing carpentry work is more fun than anything else.

CJ: So you worked with your father—

Dick: I worked with him intermittently whenever jobs were available. And then the war was coming on; that was about 1936—I graduated from high school in 1936—and I wanted to travel. And I had read about people sailing around the world. And I thought that's great. But they had all had boats, which is quite necessary! And I knew that getting together enough money to buy a boat would be so far in the distant future that it was impossible so I built a canoe and sailed it about halfway to Alaska. That worked out pretty well. And I probably got in a lot more sailing actually and it was quite a bit more dangerous than it would have been if I'd sailed around the world, because they are rather dangerous waters.

CJ: So you were drawn toward adventure and danger, even though you are a man of peace. Was your father or grandfather in any wars?

Dick: I'll show you a picture of my grandfather—great grandfather, who was in the Civil War. He was born in Vermont and volunteered as soon as the Civil War came along—hiked all the way to the First Battle of Bull Run at Manassa. Fired one shot. And was badly wounded himself. Hit in the face. You don't see it in this picture, but the bullet—a Minié ball—went through one side of his face, knocked out all of his teeth, knocked out one eye—he had a glass eye—and wounded him so badly that, although he was taken prisoner, they thought he was going to die, and they decided to trade him. So they did. He was traded back to the Northern side, and he went into a hospital because he had lost a lot of blood and also caught pneumonia. The hospital was an open field with crisscrossed fence posts and they'd take the fence posts and lay them to keep the men up out of the mud. Everything was soaking wet, he said, so that the doctor paid a visit to him every day and said, "Son, the only way you are going to get well is to hike down the road about a mile where there's a waterfall down there and if you take a bath in that every day, you're going to get better." And he did. And when he got better, he was discharged and hiked all the way back to Vermont again. He'd hike a few miles a day. He was pretty weak.

But too many people were moving westward. So he became part of the westward migration. He was all his life kind of a creature of the frontier. He went to Alaska during the gold rush. And my grandfather grew up as a professional hunter in Wisconsin. My father turned into the generation that said, "The frontier's over. We're going to settle down in one place and stay there."

CJ: Did you have any indication from him about his feelings in the Civil War?

Dick: He just told the story and laughed. He just felt that it was one of those things that happened, you know. He didn't have any great regrets or anything like that. As a matter of fact, he was rather proud of his service. There was no question. And when World War II came along, that's what they expected me to do too.

CJ: What do you remember being your first exposure to pacifism?

Dick: In about 1936 there was still a great feeling that the First World War had been a terrible mistake. And, of course, in a place like England the suffering had been tremendous. In our local Methodist church, the pastor was host to a group called the Oxford Group. And they sent around speakers getting people to sign petitions saying they would never go to war again under any circumstance. And I was suspicious of signing that, so I didn't, but I thought—they made a pretty good case.

CJ: Did your father sign it?

Dick: No, my father wasn't a religious man. My mother sent me to Sunday school for the time that I was a small kid. So I was interested in the Christian aspect of pacifism, and at that time the Methodist church was emphasizing the positive aspects of Christianity rather than the hell-fire and damnation aspects of it. So pacifism sounded like a pretty good idea. But as the war began to get near—the Second World War—the pastor who was an Englishman began to creep away from the idea of pacifism, which he had earlier espoused quite strongly.

There weren't many pacifists in town. In fact, I can't think of a single person who eventually stuck with the idea of pacifism that had been so popular four or five years earlier. But I was pretty stubborn. And I thought, "A good idea is a good idea, no matter who may think otherwise."

When the war came along, I was number twelve out of my town to be drafted. And I filled out a conscientious objector form.

CJ: What year was this?

Dick: This was in 1940. I think it was the draft act of 1940. And then in 1941 came Pearl Harbor. My brother had been taken very early. He was interested in radio, and they came even before the war started—they came in a jeep and took him away because he was a radio expert. Then they put him into a secret school, which we learned later was radar. And he spent all the war in the bowels of a battleship. And he was in Pearl Harbor. And I can remember the day *that* happened.

CJ: You were in the CO [conscientious objector] camp by that time?

Dick: No, I was several months away from camp at that time. That was in 1941. December 1941. I was at my relatives' house. We were having a family dinner in Seattle. And suddenly in the middle of the afternoon, there was a sudden break in the radio program, and the man came on and said, "I'm sorry to inform you that the Japanese have bombed Pearl Harbor." We knew that my brother was there. He was on the battleship *Nevada* at that time. Soon as we heard that, my mother was just devastated. She almost fainted. So, good lord, this is it all right. The fat's really in the fire. Then the next day the news came out that Pearl Harbor had indeed been bombed and that there was damage, but they wouldn't say how much damage. We only learned later that my brother had been out in the bowels of the ship where they have the radar equipment; he suddenly felt the whole ship jolt sideways, and they knew that something bad had happened. Then the order came to close all doors. So there they were, locked in. Never knew whether they were below water or above water. They stayed there for quite a while. An hour or so later, they were given orders to abandon ship. And the ship had been run up on dry land at the entrance to Pearl Harbor. They all swarmed over the side in nets and walked all the way to Honolulu, where a big celebration was in progress. Liquor was being passed out in the streets. People were drunk and wildly singing. And in the middle of the harbor was the smoking remains of the *Arizona*. Airplanes were buzzing around. So the same time the war was going on, this drunken celebration was going on. I thought it was a bizarre scene.

CJ: Why *was* it going on? Did it have nothing to do with it?

Dick: It had to do with men being psychologically relieved after a big emotional event. They knew that the bombing was over for the time being and that their whole lives were changed from now on. And they were—I suppose they felt they were glad they were alive. I was surprised when he told that story.

CJ: I take it, looking back, the bombing of Pearl Harbor was not only a national but a personal crisis.

Dick: Yes, all the young men were discussing it, and I remember standing by the public library in the summer nights and talking about it with the other young men. They had ideas about what they were going to do. They all ended up one way or another in the service. Some of them had wild adventures. My roommate from college had been in the naval reserve in college. He decided he was going to become a PT boat skipper, and he did. He was badly wounded when his PT boat was shot out from under him in the Mediterranean. He still carries a lot of shrapnel in his head. Another young man was on the *Ticonderoga*, an aircraft carrier that was sunk in the Pacific. And he was in the water for twelve hours until he was finally picked up—hundreds of miles from the nearest shore. Other wild stories like that happened to my friends. Another friend stepped on a land mine in Normandy. That was the end of him.

CJ: But you took a different course.

Dick: I had taken a completely different course. It took about a year for all the paperwork to get done, but eventually I was sent to a work camp—a labor camp—in Oregon on the banks of the Columbia River. And we did forestry work—tree planting and that kind of thing. Then eventually I was sent out to another camp on the coast of Oregon, and we did the same kind of work there. The experience in the camp was very mixed. No one knew what to expect. But they had people from all sorts of religious organizations. And some of them without any religious organization whatsoever. I listened to all of them. Living there was very boring, of course, because none of us had any money. We worked, of course, but the government didn't pay us anything. We were fed, but it was like being in jail. You couldn't leave without permission. It wasn't much different from the penitentiary. Then after two years in that camp, I walked out. A lot of others did the same thing as a further protest. When I walked out of camp, I did what other people did who wanted to make a protest in that way.

I told the FBI where they could find me. And I moved into a little co-op house—young men and women—north of the university in Seattle. I realized they'd get around to me eventually. One day I was in the public library reading and one of the people came up all out of breath and said, "The FBI is here. They said that they were coming back at four o'clock and you'd better be there." All the people around me had very sad faces. I got my toothbrush and put it in my pocket. The FBI men came and—when we got into the car, I was the last person that they were dealing with during the week. They were going home to their families and Saturday night. I remember they asked me for identification. When I reached for my pocket, the FBI man's hand automatically moved to his pistol. Just a reflex. Went to his pistol. They said, "Kid, we think you're making a big mistake." They said, "We think you ought to do what the government tells you. You may not like it; we're all in this situation. None of us like it. We've been out arresting communists today." I said, "I thought they were supposed to be our allies." They said, "You don't believe that, do you?" They said, "We think you're going to ruin your life. You're going to jail, and lord knows what will happen to you. There're a lot of violent people there. If you get out eventually and you're still alive, you won't be able to find employment. Nobody'll hire you." And I thought, "Maybe they're right, I don't know. But it's too late now, and I'm not going to quit."

A situation comes up like that, and you've had a chance to think about it for a while and your back gets up and you say, I'm not going to quit, no matter what. And they took me down to the jail, and I spent several weeks to be transferred to Portland, to another county jail there.

The whole jail experience is an incredible one, but most people, of course, never get anywhere close to it. It's a separate reflection of the kind of situation we live in. I'll bet if we had a lot more university professors who went there, we'd have a profound change in the way we treat people there.

I got a three-year sentence and stayed there six months and was paroled to Berkeley. That's how I happened to come here. I worked in a hospital until the end of the war, and then I got a job with a building contractor and worked on houses on these hills around here.

CJ: What do you think led to your pacifism?

Dick: I thought about it quite a bit. A lot went into it. Of course, there was my great-grandfather's experience in the Civil War, and then I can remember as a little kid reading a book about the First World War. It was a history of the war with all the famous battles—Verdun, the Somme, the Argonne Forest. It showed black and white photographs of all those. Some of those photographs are clear in my head after all this time. One was of a horse and team that had been hit by a high-explosive shell, and the reins were kind of strewn about. And there was a picture of a bunch of bayonets sticking up out of the mud. And it happened in one of the great battles; the cannon fire had been very heavy, and the men who had been waiting with their bayonets in a trench were suddenly inundated with mud, and the side of the trench fell in on them, and only the bayonets were above ground. And I thought about that—what those men must have felt.

I thought and thought about that when the time came to make the decision not to go into the army. And I thought, you have to be able to think about it in a very realistic way. What happens in a war is that you kill people. And you don't just kill guilty people; you have to make up your mind that you're going to have to kill innocent people. And that may mean children, and women, and old people. Modern wars are that way. And you ought to be able to explain to a child, say, in some bombed city, that his or her life was taken because it was a necessary thing and that it had to be done and their life was forfeit. And I felt, that isn't good enough. I never did find a satisfactory answer as to why I didn't take part in the Second World War. But I was fairly sure that I wasn't going to kill anybody if I could get through my life without killing anybody. But that isn't a satisfactory explanation to most people.

CJ: I suppose most young men think that going to war is part of growing up. As Stephen Crane wrote, they want that red badge of courage.

Dick: Yes, one of the things that young men think of is, "Sure that's tough, but you have to prove yourself." But every young man has to find courage where he can. And nobody ever knows whether he'll have courage enough to face whatever that might be, and you want to find out. So you put yourself in a dangerous situation just to see how it feels. The difficulty, of course, is that the problem of courage is never solved. Because you may be able to drive down the street fast. Or you may be able to face bullets, but you may not be able to face a whiskey bottle. And you may not be able to sit with a steady job when your family needs support. So I decided after a long time that it is never solved and that you just do the best you can. And you hope that you'll have courage for what you need to do.

CJ: Basically your position was not a biblically based one.

Dick: Partly, it was biblically based, because I had grown up in the Methodist church—Christian position. But I had lots of questions about the Christian church. You know, people would say Jesus Christ would not have done a thing, and I thought nobody *knows* what Christ would have done. Anyway, I had a lot of questions about everything that had been taught me in the Christian church, in the Methodist church. They didn't really love me there in the Sunday school. I remember once I brought in what I thought was a wonderful book for the Sunday school class: a collection of essays by Bertrand Russell. I thought the preacher would love it because he was an Englishman, and the preacher was scandalized that I would bring a book like that into the Sunday school. So I was always doing things like that that were not very orthodox.

CJ: So the reasons for your pacifism were primarily rational rather than scriptural?

Dick: I think so, yeah. I think I was affected by the Christian argument, but not totally. I thought that killing people was a very serious thing. And if you're going to do it, you should know what you're doing and you should take full responsibility for it. I decided that that situation wasn't for me, and I wasn't going to kill anybody unless I absolutely had to. I think one of the great tragedies of war is that you're attempting to kill somebody on the other side who's very much like yourself that under other circumstances you might be friends with.

CJ: Did you have qualms about your position?

Dick: Yes. Mainly because everybody around you—all your friends— are going in. But I thought, on the other side, in Japan and Germany, they're going in for the same reason. And the whole situation is a madness because everybody's gathering together and fighting because the other side's gathering together. Of course, it was too late by then to stop anything. But joining in would be equally as mad as staying out. Now maybe if they had come along and put a pistol to my head, then I would have joined up. But I would have determined by that time to deceive in every possible way. My guess is that a lot of people who went into the European armies took that position. Some of them, I imagine, escaped in some way, and some of them didn't. I imagine in the Civil War, the same thing happened. Old Samuel Clemens spent two weeks in the army and decided to light out for the territories. Of course, there were territories to light out for in those days, but nowadays there aren't any.

Anyway, I have no regrets.

CJ: What about the military itself? What objection did you have toward the military, apart from its being a war machine?

Dick: Well, the objection that I had to the military was that you give obedience to a higher authority. And I had this feeling that that is something that nobody should ever do. I always hated just going along with the crowd. Before the war, I was a member of the Civilian Conservation Corps, which was a semi-military organization—about 1937—and I got my fill of the military then. We wore military uniforms that came from World War I. And we lived in camps, in barracks. I was graphically reminded of how the military mind works in looking at the arrangement of these barracks: they take open space, and they arrange these buildings like soldiers standing at attention in rows when they could have spaced them out and surrounded them with trees. Instead, the military mind makes the buildings and their arrangement as ugly as possible.

There's always conflict and always will be conflict between people. But the ordinary murders in the street of husbands killing wives and wives killing husbands and that sort of thing would probably account for a small number of deaths over a period of a century or several centuries. And as soon as a war comes along, it is a totally different story. And the reason for it is that people turn over their good judgment to the government as to where they're going to go and who they're going to kill. That's where the real problem lies.

CJ: Was there conflict in your family about your position?

Dick: There was. But my mother took a very commonsense position.

CJ: Do you believe your stance has taken any personal toll?

Dick: No, I was from a small town. My father didn't make much of it, of course, when I came home. He just said, "I don't want you to talk about this with people. Just keep it a little quiet." Once the war began, I was away from home and very seldom got back again.

CJ: Did you ever talk to soldiers who came back from the war who were changed by their experience, who had changed their attitude toward war?

Dick: Most of those I remember were young men who had come back from Vietnam who wanted out and were tired of shooting at people. In the Second World War, of course, people came back as heroes. Most of them like my brother wanted to settle down and forget about the war and never talk about it again. Just make a living and get married and have kids.

CJ: Were there any bad feelings between you and your heroic roommate from college?

Dick: No, none at all. I've visited him, and he's invited me out on his yacht. We used to go hunting together before the war. I was very keen on firearms in those days. As a matter of fact, I joined the National Rifle Association. I was in my teens. Then I started to think about it and thought I'd better decide what side I was on. So actually, I ended up on the other side, opposed to the NRA. But hunting was a long tradition of the West.

Actually, I even get along very well with people in the military. It's the people who have never fired a shot or have never had a shot fired at them that always gave me a hard time. I think perhaps that people who have actually *been* in battle have a sense of its being endless and that it doesn't really do anything.

CJ: Did you subsequently, after the war was over, become involved as an activist?

Dick: Pretty steadily all my life. I went to the South during those troubles and rebuilt churches that had been burned down by the Ku Klux Klan. I went to Nicaragua in 1986—I was sixty-eight by then—to build houses with a crew from the Bay Area. I felt that the president was carrying on a secret war against the Nicaraguans and that this was very unfair and somebody ought to do something about it. Let's see what else: I worked with the American Friends Service Committee for a while, employed to work with a group that was starting up, working with black and Latino and Asian contractors who wanted to get government contracts. During the Vietnam War, for almost ten years (it was a long, long war), the Quaker meetinghouse had an office for advising people about the draft. I spent one night a week there, advising them what their rights were. We had to be very careful, because I know that the government sent spies in from time to time. What we were doing was legal as long as we didn't pass over the border and advise somebody. Other people were doing much more dangerous work in those times. They were getting people into Canada. They'd take them by boat or by car into Canada.

CJ: Funny, the similarity with the preslavery days before the Civil War. Kind of like an underground railroad.

Dick: Yes, but I was scandalized by the way they went about it sometimes. I felt that Quakerism, where you're dealing pretty honestly with people most of the time, doesn't train you for underhanded ways. I think when the police and spies found Quakers bringing young men over the border into Canada, they thought, "If we arrest them, it is going to be a bunch of bad publicity. Better just let the whole thing drop. Make it as difficult for them as possible, but don't make public waves over it." By this time, the Vietnam War was so unpopular that the government had a critical situation on its hands, and knew it.

CJ: Were you ever involved in demonstrations?

Dick: Oh, yeah, we had demonstrations almost every week. I was a member of the Marin Peace Committee. We were working with various churches, year after year. It all started out with demonstrations in which fifty or a hundred people would turn out in San Francisco. We eventually ended up with thousands of people and extremely successful demonstrations. I always felt, of course, that we wouldn't be successful, that there was no way of beating the government, but I was wrong. The people who had confidence that they could do it and the public sentiment that they could make a difference, they actually won, and they made the government back down.

CJ: Those were turbulent times.

Dick: Indeed, they were.

CJ: Am I mistaken in believing that some Quakers *do* take up arms?

Dick: Quite a few of them did. I was surprised. I thought it would be an issue in the meetings. I'm a Quaker myself and have been for a long time, since 1940. I was surprised that they wouldn't be read out of meeting or something like that.

CJ: It is always then a matter of conscience?

Dick: Yeah, a matter of conscience. And those who did go to war were quite well treated by other Quakers. Nobody judged them.

During the Revolutionary War there was a renegade Quaker named Nathaniel Greene who was overly interested in military matters and was told he had to give up his interests or be read out of meeting, it was called. So they read him out of meeting, and he became a famous general. He was an ancestor of mine, so I have always taken an interest in that.

CJ: What would you say to convince a believer in the necessity of wars, a believer in military buildup, that he or she is taking the wrong course?

Dick: Well, for one thing, I don't think I'd try to convince anybody. I'd put it a little differently and say that this is the sort of thing that you have to think about. That when you make war, you're going to have to know that you're going to kill innocent people. And you have to be able to justify this in your own soul.

TOPICS FOR WRITTEN AND ORAL EXPLORATION

1. Suppose that as a class you are asked to ratify the pledge of the War Resisters International. You will have to debate each point and vote on the wording as it stands or on a modification.

2. Invite a supporter of and an objector to the war in Vietnam to class to debate or discuss their opinions.

3. Make a film of a class dramatization of Clemens's *The War Prayer*, making sure that you include the reaction of the congregation.

4. From some source such as the American Friends Society (the Quakers), seek out a conscientious objector and interview him about his convictions and the difficulties he may have encountered in upholding them.

5. Write a research paper on a religious sect (other than the Quakers) that does not believe its members should engage in war.

6. From Stephen Crane's book of poetry entitled *War Is Kind*, make a selection of poems for a reading.

7. Do some research on British antiwar poems of World War I. Either write a paper on them or present a reading with explanatory introductions to each.

8. Make a written report on Kurt Vonnegut's *Slaughterhouse Five*. Conclude with a comparison of this modern novel to *The Red Badge of Courage* which Vonnegut refers to in his novel.

9. After adequate research, write a paper on why resistance to fighting in World War I was generally considered less difficult than resistance to fighting in World War II.

10. Who is the assassin? Characteristically, Crane makes heavy use of irony. After reading both poems, connect them with Crane's novel, *The Red Badge of Courage*.

11. Regarding Stephen Crane's "69," ask yourself, who speaks the poem? Is this the same as the voice of the poet? What reasons are given for the death of the soldier? What words strengthen the irony?

SUGGESTED READINGS

Bainton, Roland H. *Christian Attitudes Toward War and Peace. A Historical Survey and Critical Re-evaluation*. New York: Abingdon Press, 1960.

Cady, Duane. *From Warism to Pacifism*. Philadelphia: Temple University Press, 1989.

Coakley, Robert W. *Antiwar and Antimilitary Activities in the United States*. Washington, D.C.: Histories Division, 1970.

Conscientious Objection. Rodenbosch: The Centre, 1984.

Eller, Cynthia. *Conscientious Objectors and the 2nd World War*. New York: Praeger, 1991.

McCarthy, Colman. *All of One Peace*. New Brunswick, N.J.: Rutgers University Press, 1994.

Rosenblatt, Roger. *Children of War*. Garden City, N.Y.: Anchor Press, 1983.

Index

Alcott, Louisa May, 113
The American War of Secession 1863: Chancellorsville and Gettysburg (Dalbiac), 47–48, 75–76
Animalism, 14–16
Anonymity, 43
Antietam, 69, 113–114
Antiwar sentiment, 175–201
Arms and equipment, 168–171
Army Life: From a Soldier's Diary (Marshall), 169–171
Army of the Potomac, headquarters of, 152–154
An Artilleryman's Diary (Jones), 104, 167–168
Atlanta, 115–117

Badges, 2
Bailey, George W., 115–117
Bates, Samuel P., 51–53, 76–78, 80
Battlefields: chaos of, 2–3, 102; effects of, 101–145; hospitals on, 109–110, 118–120; and

psychological problems, 105–107; stark cruelties of, 104–105, 175
"In Battle in the Pacific: An Interview with Sam Turner," 137–145
Battle of the Bulge, 72
Battles and Leaders of the Civil War, 42, 49–53, 55–57, 77–78, 83–86
The Battles of Chancellorsville and Gettysberg, 65
Beace, James, 79–82
Beer, Thomas, 43
Benfrey, Christopher, 102, 105
Biblical teaching, 176–177
Billings, John D., 162–164
Bircher, William, 117–118, 154–156
Bisbee, William Henry, 160–161
The Black Riders and Other Lines (Crane), 182–183
Boer War, 179
Boudreau, John, 120–136

Boyhood, 5
Bright, John, 178
Brown, Dick, 192–201
Brown, John, 23, 27
Bull Run (Manassas), 28
Burnside, Ambrose E., 29, 52, 64

Camp life, 37, 147–171; diseases,
    151; foraging, 166–167; rations,
    148, 151, 162–164; shelter, 147–
    151
"Cannon fodder," 58
Cavalry, 37–38; charge of, 30–32,
    40, 54–60
Chancellorsville, 24–25, 29–44;
    and desertion, 64–69; halt at,
    47–48; losses at, 46; rations be-
    fore, 151
Chancellorsville (Beace), 79–82
"The Chancellorsville Campaign"
    (Couch), 49–50
Chancellorsville 1863 (Furgur-
    son), 151
Chancellorsville and Gettysburg
    (Doubleday), 46
Chaos, 2–3, 102
Character, 175–176
"The Charge of the Eighth Penn-
    sylvania Cavalry" (Huey, Wells),
    55–57
Christianity, interpretations of,
    176–178
Civil War: causes of, 25–27; chro-
    nology of, 23–25; main fronts
    of, 28. *See also* Desertion
Class system, 176
Clothing, 148–150, 161, 165
Coburn, James, 65
Coffin, Charles Carleton, 152–154
Collins, John, 82–84
Combat fatigue, 107
Confederacy, capital of, 27

Confederate army, 37; conditions
    of, 150
Conklin, Jim, 2–3, 37, 91; camp
    life of, 147; death of, 7–8, 39,
    102, 104
Conscientious objectors, 194
Couch, Darius N., 49–50
Courage, 2
Cowardice, 63, 73
Crane, Stephen: artistic technique
    of, 43; brother of, 43; determin-
    ism of, 13–16; irony of, 17–19;
    poetry of, 182–184; and Tol-
    stoy, 179; as war correspon-
    dent, 104–105
Crusades, 177–178

Dalbiac, P. H., 47–48, 75–76
Davis, Jefferson, 27
Davis, Richard Harding, 105
Desertion, 7–8, 11, 63–98; and ex-
    ecution, 87–89; and individual
    relationships, 72–74; reasons
    for, 69–72
Desertion During the Civil War
    (Lonn), 150
Determinism, 13–16
Discovery of self, 5
Diseases, 151, 167–168
Doubleday, Abner, 46
A Drummer Boy's Diary (Bircher),
    117–118, 154–156
Drunkenness, 65, 161

Economy, 25–26
Elstob, Peter, 72
Episodic form, 3–4
Execution, 87–89

"Fifty Years of Terror and Loss"
    (Boudreau), 128–135
Fleming, Henry, 1, 28; attitudes
    and actions of, 13–16; boyhood

of, 5; camp life of, 147–151;
character of, 175–176; cowardice of, 73; desertions of, 7–8,
11, 39, 64, 73; elderly, 35–36,
44, 90–94; initiation of, 3–5,
102; mother of, 5–6; rebellion
of, 4, 6, 10–11; regiment of, 38–
42; revelation of, 17–19
Foraging, 166–168
Fort Sumter, 27
Fredericksburg, 29, 119; losses at,
64
Frémont, John, 151, 170
Freud, Sigmund, 123
Fugitive Slave Law, 26–27
Furgurson, Ernest B., 151

Germans, 40, 68, 84–86
Gettysburg, 36–37
Glazier, Willard, 30–32, 68
Gordon, George H., 87–89
"The Guilty Deserter" (Gordon),
87–89

Hart, John E., 4–5
Hawthorne, Nathaniel, 71
Hazel Grove, 30–32, 54–60
Hemingway, Ernest, 144
Hitler's Last Offensive (Elstob), 72
Hooker, Joseph, 29–34; arrival of,
37, 64–65, 79; charges of incompetence, 47–51; defense of,
51–53; and desertion, 65–68;
and Howard, 80; Schurz's letter
to, 86
"Hooker's Comments on Chancellorsville" (Bates), 52–53, 76–78
Hosmer, James Kendall, 157–159,
166–167
Hospitals, 109–110, 118–120, 158,
193; ambulance ship, 105
Howard, Oliver O., 29–31, 54–55,
66, 80; charges of incompet-

ence, 75–78; and desertion, 67,
79, 82; retreat of, 83–84;
Schurz's report to, 85–86
Huey, Pennock, 55–56
The human situation, 18
Hungerford, Harold R., 35–44

Impressionism, 17–19
Initiation, 1–19; parody of, 1
Irony, 2, 17–19

Jackson, Thomas Jonathan (Stonewall), 31–32, 52, 54, 66, 76;
death of, 40, 75; onslaught of,
81
Johnson, Rossiter, 55
Jones, Jenkin Lloyd, 104, 167–168

Keenan, Peter, 32, 54–60
"Keenan's Charge" (Lathrop), 58–
60
Knapsacks, 148, 169

LaFrance, Marston, 17–18
Lathrop, George Parsons, 58–60
Leaves of Grass (Whitman), 119–
120
Lee, Robert E., 29, 31; at Chancel-
lorsville, 49–50, 52; surrender
of, 36
Letters from the front, 113–115
Lincoln, Abraham: election of, 27;
and McClellan, 29
Lonn, Ella, 150

Manassas, 28
Manhood, initiation into, 1–19
Marching, 156
Marshall, Albert O., 168–171
McCarthy, Carlton, 164–166
McClellan, George B., 29, 36, 69
McClure's Magazine, 90–94
McDowell, Irvin, 28

Meade, George Gordon, 29, 71; and Union Army conditions, 150
Mentors, 8
Mexican War, 178
Military training, 28
Missouri Compromise, 26; nullification of, 27
Mortality, 104
Murphy, Audie, 123
Muskets, 154, 170–171
My Days and Nights on the Battlefield (Coffin), 152–154

Nana (Zola), 12
Naturalistic literature, 12–16
Nature, indifference of, 7–10
Nelson, A. H., 65
New York Journal, 104–105
New York World, 105
Nicaragua, 199–200
"Night Patrol Never Ends" (Boudreau), 135–136
Nott, Charles C., 108–112
Noyes, George F., 161–162

Officers, 7; character of, 176; competence of, 29–30, 71; disillusionment with, 9–11

Pacifists, 176–181, 189–201
Patriotism, 124
Pearl Harbor, 194–195
Plantations, 26
Pleasonton, Alfred, 29, 31, 50–51; and the sacrifice at Hazel Grove, 54–55
Pledge of the War Resisters International, 189–191
Posttraumatic stress disorder, 107, 120–145
A Private Chapter of the War (Bailey), 115–117

"The Private History of a Campaign that Failed" (Twain), 94–98
Psychological problems, 105–107

Quakers, 177–178, 200

Rappahannock River: crossing of, 30, 33, 36, 38, 66; encampment by, 37
Rations, 148, 151, 162–164; foraging for, 166–167
Rebellion, 4, 6, 10–11
The Red Badge of Courage (Crane): as an antiwar novel, 175–201; camp life in, 147–150; chaos in, 28; Civil War setting of, 23–60; desertion in, 7–8, 11, 63–98; factual framework of, 35–44; futility in, 44; literary analysis of, 1–19
Retreat, 7
Richmond, Virginia, 27–28, 36
Rifles, 148, 168, 170–171
Rogers, Jimmie, 8
The Romance of the Civil War (Hart), 87–89, 157–159, 161–167

Schurz, Carl, 77, 79; report of, 84–86
Sedgwick, John, 29, 32–33, 52
Self, discovery of, 5
Sermon on the Mount (Matthew 5), 176
Shell shock, 107
Shelter, 147–151
Shiloh, 108–112, 117–118
Shoes, 148–150, 156
Short-timers, 64–65
Sickles, Daniel E., 29, 31–32, 54, 80

Sketches of the War (Nott), 108–112

Slavery, 26–27; abolition of, 178

Slocum, Henry W., 29, 77

Soldiers: arms and equipment of, 168–171; as "cannon fodder," 58; diseases of, 151, 167–168; drunkenness of, 65, 161; foraging, 166–168; possessions of, 148; short-timers, 64–65. *See also* Desertion

Spanish American War, 105, 178, 183

Staff work, 48

The Story of a Great Conflict (Johnson), 55

Stowe, Harriet Beecher, 27

Stuart, James Ewell Brown (Jeb), 81

"The Successes and Failures of Chancellorsville" (Pleasonton), 50–51

Tariffs, 25–26

The tattered man, 8; as a saint, 73

Territories, 26–27

" 'That Was at Chancellorsville': The Factual Framework of *The Red Badge of Courage*" (Hungerford), 35–44

Through Four American Wars (Bisbee), 160–161

Tolstoy, Leo, 179

Turner, Sam, 136–145

Twain, Mark (Samuel L. Clemens), 94–98, 185–188

Uncle Tom's Cabin (Stowe), 27

Underground railroad, 178

Union army: food and clothing of, 148–150; headquarters, of, 152–154; winter camp of, 37

"The Veteran" (Crane), 35–37, 90–94

Vietnam War, 180

Von Gilsa, 66–67

Walcott, Charles C., 16

War: Boer, 179; Crimean, 179; between Greece and Turkey, 104; horror of, 6–7, 105, 175; and human character, 175; indictment of, 16–17, 175–176; Mexican, 178; romantic view of, 5–6; sentiment against, 175–201; Spanish American, 105, 178, 183; Vietnam, 180; waged for a just cause, 177; World War I, 179; World War II, 120–136, 179–180, 194–195. *See also* Civil War

War Is Kind (Crane), 183–185

"The War Prayer" (Clemens), 185–188

War Resisters International, 189–191

Washington, D.C., 28, 36; defense of, 29

Wells, Andrew B., 56–57

Western territories, 26–27

Whitman, Walt, 118–120

Wilson, 3–4, 148; pride of, 8

World War II, 120–136

"Wounds that Never Heal" (Boudreau), 121–128

Zola, Émile, 12

About the Author

CLAUDIA DURST JOHNSON is Professor Emeritus of English at the University of Alabama, where she chaired the Department of English for 12 years. She is series editor of the Greenwood Press "Literature in Context" series which includes her works *Understanding To Kill a Mockingbird* (1994), *Understanding The Scarlet Letter* (1995), *Understanding Adventures of Huckleberry Finn* (1996), and *Understanding Of Mice and Men, The Red Pony, and The Pearl* (1997). She is also author of several other works, including *To Kill a Mockingbird: Threatening Boundaries* (1994), and *The Productive Tension of Hawthorne's Art* (1981), as well as numerous articles on American literature and theatre.